VALERIE LOVE

Spellcrafting for the Christian Witch

A Compendium of Christian Witchcraft

First published by Butterfly Rising Publishing 2020

First edition

ISBN: 978-0-578-79426-6

This book was professionally typeset on Reedsy.
Find out more at reedsy.com

This tome is dedicated to the wild Christian Witches all over the globe who are bold and brazen enough to practice Christian Witchcraft in the face of those who say it cannot be done.

ROCK ON WITCHES... YOU INEXORABLE CREATURES OF THE DARK AND KEEPERS OF THE LIGHT FANTASTIC. I LOVE YOU!

"Magick is the Science of understanding oneself and one's conditions. It is the Art of applying that understanding in action."

ALEISTER CROWLEY

Contents

I CLARIFICATIONS, WARNINGS & DISCLAIMERS

III Holistic Magick

IV Spellcrafting in Christian Witchcraft

V Angel Magick

Acknowledgement

There are many people to thank for this project, and of course, the order presented here is no indication of whom I cherish and appreciate most. **ALL HERE ARE LOVED and APPRECIATED!**

First, a big shout out to my cover designer, TJM Cover Designs! Book cover design is such an integral and important aspect of the book creation process that I can say this book and the series it belongs to — including How to Be a Christian Witch, Christian Witches Manifesto, Magickal Prayers for the Christian Witch — would not have taken off and become what they are without your artistry. **THANK YOU**.

Next, a big hug of appreciation to Craig Hostetler, host of the Black Sheep Experience podcast for friendship and encouragement from a pastor turned Christian Witch. You're an inspiration. Your work is sublime. THANK YOU for your thoughtful, wise presence and all you bring to the movement that is Christian Witchcraft. You give us much to consider. Your courage in speaking up and sharing your walk has been a game-changer. I didn't know people like you existed until you showed up. **THANK YOU FOR SHOWING UP IN A POWERFUL WAY.**

A huge happy thanks goes to Divine Lady Ninhursag for all you do for the Christian Witches community behind the scenes, without ever asking to be celebrated. Your service to the Christian Witches Facebook community, the Christian Witches Mystery School and myself is beyond what I could have asked for. God is good! **THANK YOU**.

To Roberto Del Ray, the Musical Director for Christian Witches, THANK

YOU for showing up and BOOMING IN with that voice of yours! It's melody made in heaven! THANK YOU for being at the historic, first ever Christian Witches Convention, and for singing at every inspirational service we've ever had. **YOU ARE A GIFT**!

To my amazing Executive Assistant, Gaia Ethereal, THANK YOU for holding it together! Thank you for being a second me! Thank you for getting it done! THANK YOU for all you do so I stay focused on creation and vision. **HALLELUJAH**!

To the entire Christian Witches community around the globe, this is is a movement beyond any person. I'm blessed and awed to be a part of the whole and to add my energy to a movement that's been happening for thousands of years, since the original Christian Witch: **CHRIST**.

I love and appreciate you. **ROCK ON WITCHES**!

Who I Am

I am Valerie, daughter of Jacqueline, daughter of Frieda, daughter of Pinky, daughter of Dell. Great honor, homage and gratitude go to the souls and wombs that made my life possible.

I am from a long line of Witches who mastered and utilized natural healing for all manner of issues in the body temple. These skilled healers routinely turned to herbs, pot liquor, liniments, poultices, rubs, ointments, copper pennies, oils and more items from nature than could be recounted and described in one book. They worked with salts and oils and such to make lotions and potions that reeked and worked.

The healing remedies these Witches used was simple and did the job like nobody's business. When calamine lotion was NOT doing the trick to relieve my unbearable itchiness when I had chicken pox (yes, I still remember the episode), Grandma took things into her own hands. She looked at me and without saying a word went into the kitchen. She came back a couple of minutes later with her mixture of baking soda, vaseline and a few other choice 'secret ingredients' that only Grandma knew about (and took to her grave). She rubbed it all over me and the itchiness went away INSTANTLY.

My paternal grandmother used pot liquor (the juices left in the pot after she cooked her collard greens, mustard greens and/or greens in general) to heal all manner of issues from colds to constipation.

My mother kept a mixture of honey, lemon, onion, garlic and cod liver oil in the fridge. It was dreadful to taste and could knock out any issue immediately. She loved healing with aloe vera, one of her favorite plant allies.

I don't even remember seeing a doctor when I was growing up.

They had dreams about fish and knew who was pregnant long before anyone took a pregnancy test. They midwived babies and taped copper pennies on the bellies of the ones who had 'outies' (belly buttons that wouldn't go down) and got results ASAP. They walked new babies around the perimeter of the house in a ritual only they knew of, and would never divulge the secrets of what they whispered in the newcomers' ears, no matter how much we inquired.

They grew herbs in the garden. They knew plants. They made biscuits that made us cry.

They were strange, and wild (untamed). They had unruly hair that they always flushed down the toilet when they brushed or combed it, while simultaneously issuing the admonition to "NEVER let anyone get ahold of your hair."

They prayed and made things come true, like getting people of our jail or getting them jobs. They lived in houses with spirits and weren't concerned. They talked to 'dead' people.

They commanded respect of the men in their lives, and maybe even on some level, awe.

They tended plants, talked to them and made them grow.

They knew things the rest of us didn't know.

While some were kitchen Witches, others were of another breed.

My mother was a stitch Witch. Sewing needles of all sizes, knitting needles and crochet hooks were her wands. She could take a ball of yarn and make a sweater. That's magick. She designed her clothing in the third eye and manifested her visions through the sewing machine. One day she didn't have shoes to match her outfit, so she declared to us that she was going to make a pair of boots. Wait Ma, WHAT?!? The reason this is such a vivid memory for me even though it happened decades ago is because she said it, and a couple of hours later, she had the boots on her feet.

No one had ever seen anything like it. That was the indomitable, unstoppable and astonishingly creative attitude and way of being of the soul that is my mother, currently residing on the other side of the veil helping us out. God bless her soul.

Let me be clear, not one of the Witches in my family line EVER called what they were doing Witchcraft. I didn't know any of it was Witchcraft myself. Magickal was just how we lived.

It wasn't until I read books on Witchcraft and saw in them damn near everything my family was doing that I realized there was a name for what we were doing.

The more I studied Witchcraft and the rules of magick, the more I came home to the realization that we had been practicing magick all along.

Maybe you were too. Maybe you can spot Witchcraft in your family's heritage, traditions and 'Old Wives Tales.' If so, that's a beautiful thing. If not, look harder. I'm convinced almost everyone is in some way related to a Witch. If your mama and grandmothers weren't Witches, what about that weird aunt that traveled the world and wore strange clothes and big jewels and knew everything and was sorta like the mystical one in the family? Yep, she's probably a Witch. Untamed. Doing her own thing, regardless of what people think. And definitely NOT down with the status quo.

The reason I start this book on spellcrafting with a little bit about me and the Witches I come from is to offer the following ideas for your consideration:

- Witchcraft can be as simple as saying a prayer over a home-made remedy and rubbing someone down with it. It doesn't have to be complex. The Witches I'm from whipped up fast and simple magick that WORKED.
- This is a way of being. Witchcraft is an orientation, a way of looking at things, and not so much a specific thing one has to do. From deep in one's being issues forth what to do. I'm convinced these Witches were making things up all the time. It worked because they understood the fundamental principles of the energies and correspondences they were working with.

- Spellcrafting is not linear. It's twisty-twurvy, windy-curvy. Nothing in this book may work for you, exactly as it appears here. Yet you tweak it to the left or to the right and VOILA! Be free to tweak away!
- The Craft is unique to every Witch. Yes, there was a flavor and flair to all the Witches in my family, and still, each one was powerfully her own being. I come from some powerhouse women (which explains a lot lol) and powerhouse men as well.
- It's in the blood. As a woman of African descent on my mother's side, and Puerto Rican descent on my father's side, all the African magicks live in my blood, including Yoruba and Santeria, though I've never been initiated in either one. When I'm in those circles, I understand it, on a soul level. Magick is in our blood.

I'm thankful to the HEAVENS for my first Witchcraft teachers: my forebears.

Note: I write about this in detail on Carolyn Elliott's Witch Blog in a post titled "10 Signs Your Grandmother is a Witch" at www.BadWitch.es

This Book May Hurt Your Feelings

You may be any one of the following possible readers of this book, or you may be none of these…

A Witchy Christian

If you're a Christian who's never practiced magick, never picked up a book on magick and/or Witchcraft and/or the occult and may have been conditioned to believe these are of the devil, WELCOME. This book is for you.

You may find yourself inexplicably drawn to magick, and afraid of what may happen if you answer the call. You may wonder if you'll get sucked down a hole of darkness to the devil's lair if you engage Witchcraft. That was me. If this is you, you may be a Christian who's grappling with your Witchy side, to a lesser or greater degree.

No more. The inner struggle ends now. In this book, you'll find the exact spell I cast for integrating my Witchy self and my Christian self. I pray it serves you as well.

A Practicing Christian Witch

If you're new to Christian Witchcraft, I welcome you. I love you. I appreciate your hunger and your unwillingness to give up Christ or the Craft.

If you're an OG (original gangsta) Christian Witch who's been practicing for years, I'm honored you're here. You're most welcome. I salute you on being a seasoned, practicing Christian Witch. Congratulations! YOU DID IT! You created your own Witchy path from the core of your soul, regardless of other people's opinions. You're on your path and creating your magick like a mofo!

You may be looking for ideas from other Christian Witches on how they practice, or for inspiration to take your Spellcrafting to a whole new righteous level. Rock on Witch! This book is for you. I absolutely freaking love you for who you are and what you mean to the world.

Your very presence shatters illusions and invites creativity. You are a gift to the cosmos.

Magickal Practitioner

If you're a Witch, warlock, wizard or magickal being of another tradition, I welcome you. I'm glad you're here. In my ongoing investigation of magick, I read countless books and have been immersed in rituals with various magickal traditions over the years, including Wicca, Goetia, Theurgy, Yoruba, the Akan and more. I'm richer for the experience. Thank you for being here. I honor and appreciate your Witchy walk.

Curiosity Seeker

Maybe you don't know where you fit in on the issue of Christian Witchcraft and are simply curious. Maybe you're in learn-and-observe mode to decide the direction in which you'll travel. I applaud your honest inquiry and willingness to follow the Voice inside that bought you to this book. This book is for you. I pray it brings revelations, insights, inspiration and clarity.

Christian

If you're a Fundamentalist Christian, or a Christian who's heard much about Christian Witchcraft and are seeking to know more, ***this book may hurt your feelings***, not because this is the intention. I pray to always operate from love.

There's a saying I treasure:

Truth sets us free... But first it pisses us off.

I've had this experience and have heard from countless others who have had this experience as well. The more we discover truth, the more we discover we've been lied to. This discovery can elicit an angry phase when exiting Christianity as it was taught to us.

I understand this angry reaction. I couldn't believe how much I had been lied to over the years. This was the case for those in the cult of Jehovah's Witnesses and for many other strands of Christianity. It doesn't matter. We were all lied to at some point in our lives. Maybe even repeatedly.

Eventually, truth dawns. When we're ready. Open. Available. It just shows up. Bright light and all. It's always been this way, and it will always be.

An Investigator

Maybe you're investigating Christian Witchcraft to see what it's all about. I pray I can answer questions that come up in your investigation. After reading this work, perhaps we will have come to a shared understanding, if not agreement. I don't seek agreement. I seek peace. We are not all here to think, believe, act, speak and worship the same. We are here to answer the unique call of the soul.

If you're investigating Christian Witchcraft, welcome. This book is for you.

If you fit into none of the foregoing descriptions, and you're here anyway, WELCOME. This book is for you.

Whomever you may be, you chose this book and I am thankful.

Welcome Home Christian Witch

Yes, I'm talking to you, Christian Witch, you who tread where others warned you dare not.

We're Christian Witches. We are the ones who step off the cliff into the unknown. We do not know what's on the other side of our step. We only know we are stepping forward with all we are, and we know it is more than enough.

When I started my journey as a Christian Witch, one of the most common statements I heard — from Christians and Witches alike — was "you can't be a Christian Witch" (a reflection of my own deep questioning and doubt of the path my soul had chosen).

Yet my soul longed for something greater than I had experienced. My spirit soared to the heavens and knew there were no limitations. My heart knew better than to give up the Bible and Christ or my wands and my crystals, because of what other people said. I knew not to get rid of my Bible. I am a Witch with Bibles galore.

I used to think I was an anomaly. A weirdo. What Witch reads the Bible? What Christian is Witchy? Am I a heretic?

Yes. I'm a heretic. And a weirdo. And an outlier. I'm all of that. And none of it, and more. No label can encompass the all of who I am. The same is true for all. No label encompasses all of what and who we are as immense beings of power. To me, Witch = POWER. Power to be used as one sees fit. Each one of us gets to choose how we will wield this inherent, infinite power.

I invite you into the heart of Spellcrafting as a Christian Witch in this work, with a prayerful intention to **INSPIRE TO POWER**, to fan the flames of POWER within and to encourage to **STAND** and mark the universe with **MAGICK**! Yeah babyyyyy!

If you haven't yet read the series on Christian Witchcraft, please feel free to pick up the books ***How to Be a Christian Witch*** as well as *Magickal Prayers for the Christian Witch* for background and a foundation for what you'll find here. Though the content here is different, you may benefit from reading the other works along with this one for a fuller, richer understanding and experience. Each book is designed to be complete and whole on its own, and to fulfill the promise of the title. I offer these other works as well for your consideration.

The Structure Herein

This work is structured into 6 parts:

- **Part 1 - Clarifications, Warnings & Disclaimers:** read these first as these form a requisite foundation for the work we'll do together in later stages.
- **Part 2 - YOU:** the most critical and impactful aspect of your spells and rituals.
- **Part 3 - Holistic Magick:** all that is around you is informing your magick, from your environment, to your sleep patterns. Magick is holistic. In this part of our journey together we take a 360 look at your world as it relates to Spellcrafting as a Master Alchemist.
- **Part 4 - Spellcrafting in Christian Witchcraft:** the exact methodology and elements I use to craft spells and live magickal in the Christian Witchcraft tradition.
- **Part 5 - Angel Magick:** because angels figure prominently in all things Christian faith and are said to be in the very presence of God, we explore Angel Magick as it relates to Christian Witchcraft. These vast forces of energy are too powerful and effective to ignore in our magick, rituals and Spellcrafting.
- **Part 6 - Rituals & Spells:** examples of rituals and spells I've crafted that have delivered very specific and astonishingly delicious results. You may be tempted to go directly to this section of the book, but I promise you, if you walk through this work and implement it from

beginning to end, it will take the magick to a whole new level.

Let's begin…

Disclosure

THANK YOU for purchasing this book! Whether you have the eBook or the print version, I'm THANKFUL we get to do this together, you and I.

If you have the eBook version of this book, you'll see quite a few links that I felt helpful to include. Some are affiliate links, and some are not. For affiliate links, please know that we receive a small commission on your purchases if you choose to buy the books using the links provided (at no extra cost to you). Thank you for your support!

The links I've provided are throughout the text, for convenience, so you can hop over to more about the subject matter we're discussing for a richer discourse.

If you have the print version of this book, there are a few links in the back of this book in the Resources section that I pray are helpful. Some of these may be affiliate links, while others are not and simply link to people and things I love.

Any links in this text are to what I love, use and can vouch for. I do not offer anything to anyone that I myself do not love or have not found to be helpful.

FYI, many of my readers acquire both the eBook version and the paperback version of my books on Christian Witchcraft. The reason is so that they have the convenience of hopping to links in the moment with the eBook, and use the paperback or hardcover in their Temple when practicing magick. I myself do not take electronics into my magick space, for energetic reasons. Either way, if you find both versions or either version works for your purposes, I'm thrilled.

So have at it and I pray this adventure we're about to embark upon is a blast!

I

CLARIFICATIONS, WARNINGS & DISCLAIMERS

It would do us well to consider the following clarifications, warnings and disclaimers before getting into the meat of the content offered here.

'Christian' in Christian Witch

The question has come up quite a bit about the meaning of the word 'Christian' in the term Christian Witch, which would be a fair question.

For me, the word 'Christian' denotes one who aspires to the divine ideals as expressed in the life and teachings of Christ: ***Christ Conciousness*** (or to be Christ-like), and NOT one who adheres to a religion. Christ himself was not a Christian.

Christianity is a far cry from the original Christ message, as well it should be. Over centuries, beliefs and ideologies shift and morph with humanity, culture and conditions.

It's my assessment that the Christ we read of in scripture — and the Christ who may have existed millennia ago — is hardly the same as is depicted in the modern day Christian church.

This is not to say that I malign churches. I do not. I am a minister, and quite frankly, I've never met a church or religion or holy place that I didn't love, for one reason or another.

The truth, however, is simple...

Christ and the Christian Church are two very different entities.

Further, there are different ways of looking at Christ, depending upon who you are and what you choose to believe or adhere to. We'll address different ways of looking at Christ here, to answer the very valid question of how one can be a Christian Witch, a term which seems to be an oxymoron.

Before addressing these, let us first consider this quote from Wikipedia under Christianity and Theosophy from Helena Blavatsky, co-founder of the Theosophical Society:

> *"Jesus, the Christ-God, is a myth concocted two centuries after the real Hebrew Jesus died." According to Theosophy, the term "Christ" means the personal divinity "indwelling" each individual human."*
> *Wikipedia on Helena Blavatsky*

This quote perfectly encapsulates the truth we will now examine.

Literal Jesus Christ

We could think of Jesus Christ literally, as a person who walked the planet 2,000 years ago practicing and teaching humanity unconditional love, forgiveness, oneness with the Creator and universal law, and who was able to raise the dead, heal the sick, exorcise demons, rehabilitate those who had strayed from the path and perform astonishing wonders.

There's debate over whether there was a literal person named Jesus or if the Jesus we know of today is more of a mashup of different persuasive characters of the time.

Though there is little to no archeological evidence of a historical Jesus Christ, there is little to no archeological evidence of much we currently hold as true. While I respect archeology, we don't hold to the truth because it's been proven by things we pull out of the ground. We hold to the truth because it's true, proven beyond what archeology has revealed thus far.

For me, whether there was a literal or historical figure named Jesus Christ is a subject of fascinating debate, yet not pivotal to this discussion. I don't base my life on a man who lived 2,000 years ago. I base my life on **LOVE** and universal **LAW**, which are the nature, expression and operation of God.

I don't know if Jesus Christ is a historical figure, and to be honest with you, I don't care. I'll leave it to the archeologists, scientists, historians and Bible scholars to debate over the factual and historical existence of the personage we know from the Bible as Jesus Christ.

The reason I don't care whether he was an actual figure from history, a conglomeration of several figures, or a completely made up character is because I do not take the Bible literally (more on this in the chapter on Bible Magick).

I agree with the wise words of a highly trusted and reputable teacher of Kabbalah, David Ghiyam:

"The Bible is a non-religious manual of energy, explaining the DNA of energy and how energy works."

Taken as a non-religious energy manual, it no longer matters if even one word in the Bible can be proven factual or historical. **EVERTHING IS ENERGY**. The main consideration becomes: what is being revealed about **ENERGY** here? How am I using the **ENERGY** I have access to? What **ENERGIES** am I tapping in to?

Which leads us to the 2nd way I'll mention here of looking at Christ...

The Church Fabricated Jesus

According to what we're told by the Christian church (Catholic and Protestant alike), Jesus Christ was the living, breathing manifestation of God in flesh comprising one-third of a trinity of God the Father, God the Son and God the Holy Ghost.

This take on Jesus was invented by a group of men at the Nicene Council hundreds of years after the death of the person Jesus Christ (if there was such a person). The Nicene Creed can be read online free. If you have not yet examined the Creed, it makes for a fascinating study, especially for the Christian Witch.

This fabrication of a Jesus Christ that is a personal saviour, above all and no longer man, but God, must be recognized for what it is: a pure fabrication.

I do not at all intend to not honor the Catholic Church when I make this statement. This statement is purely for the purpose of facilitating the proverbial scales falling from our eyes so that we may perceive the light of truth. We cannot perceive truth if our minds are muddied with lies.

The Jesus I know didn't ask us to need him as a saviour. A statement in the Bible attributed to Christ is pregnant with meaning:

"Verily, verily, I say unto you, He that believeth on me, the works that I do shall he do also; and greater works than these shall he do; because I go unto my Father."
John 14:12 (KJV)

The entire tenor and tone of the New Testament stories of Christ, for me, forms an empowering mythos designed for me to get off my butt and realize my God nature... to **BECOME** a Christ.

It is important to study the origins of the Christian Church to determine for oneself the veracity of any of these matters. It would appear that many Christians (though not all) are completely ignorant of the origins of their faith, a matter than can be quickly resolved with diligent research with the intention of uncovering and understanding truth.

As a practicing Christian Witch, I've told myself that it's not an option to remain willfully ignorant of matters pertaining to the soul.

Cosmic Christ

Maybe Christ was a man who walked the planet and maybe he wasn't. Some believe he is God, a third person of a Trinity. All well and good.

Beyond that, there is the **COSMIC CHRIST**, or the divine ideal Christ represents.

For me, the divine attributes of the **COSMIC CHRIST** are the pure, unconditional love of God, forgiveness, acceptance of all people, ONENESS with the divine and pure Divine Power.

When one has accomplished this — identical to the Great Work of Alchemy of the Soul — one becomes God.

Becoming God is, for me, the exact same as ascension to Christ Consciousness (oneness with Source) or Buddha-nature, or enlightenment. It is the direct revelation and knowing of one's divinity and oneness with ALL.

Countless humans have had these experiences of oneness with all, especially during unforgettable moments, like the birth of a baby or a captivating sunset on the beach in Maui or other jaw dropping moments when all separation momentarily fades away.

When I speak of being a Christian Witch, I am speaking of my highest aspiration to fully experience, embody and express Christ Consciousness using magick as a means to enlightenment. I believe this is what a Master Alchemist looks like: a **Christ**.

As the above quote recognizes, **Christ is the indwelling divinity in each person**. There is nothing this indwelling divinity cannot do. This is our innate potentiality to become one with Source so that we embody and demonstrate the statement "I and the Father are One."

Christ: The Original Christian Witch

Since some attest that the literal Christ (if there was one) was arrested for sorcery (a little known, revolting fact for some Christians, yet a liberating fact for Christian Witches, read the book ***Magic in Christianity*** for more on that explosive topic), there's a correlation between Christ and Christian Witches.

The Christ we're taught about in the Bible is the original Christian Witch, able to commune with nature spirits (of trees, wind and storm), walk on water, miraculously manifest vast amounts of food from next to nothing, command spirits and demons with a word, and practiced more magick than we can shake a broomstick at.

The Talmud carries a fascinating passage:

> *"On (Sabbath eve and) the eve of Passover, Jesus the Nazarene was hanged and a herald went forth before him forty days heralding, "Jesus the Nazarene is going forth to be stoned because he practiced sorcery and instigated and seduced Israel to idolatry. Whoever knows anything in defense may come and state it."*

According to the Jewish people of the time, Jesus was considered a sorcerer and one who incited his followers to worship other gods (plural), which paints a radically different view of the Jesus Christ that Christians have come to know and love.

I myself also hold an inner knowing that Christ is magickal. A sorcerer of sorts. A being who employs mystical and magickal means for instantaneous and almost unbelievable outcomes.

I speak in present tense when referring to Christ as Christian Witch because this entity is alive and well in the cosmos **NOW**. We have access to this being **NOW**.

Christian Witches is Not a Religion

I have no desire to adhere to a religion. Thus, the word 'Christian' in Christian Witch, for me, does not denote one who adheres to a religion.

With that said, Christian Witches is not a religion (at least not to me anyway, although I honor and respect those who hold it as such). As with all spiritual paths, Christian Witchcraft is a calling. It's for those of us who aren't ready to summarily dismiss and throw out the entirety of the Bible (with all its magick, mysticism and at times mayhem) and who aren't ready to throw out our magickal selves either.

We discovered we didn't have to choose.

We found a way to practice that integrates and honors Christ and the Craft.

On Being a Master Alchemist

A Witch is an alchemist.

One definition for alchemy is "a seemingly magical process of transformation, creation, or combination." Pull out the Tarot trump Temperance (Key #14) and you'll find that it sits as a mediator between Death (Key #13) and The Devil (Key #15). I always found this placement fascinating, as if Temperance could hold the space between transformation (Death) and voluntarily choosing enslavement to the lower nature as the 5 senses (The Devil). To pull off this middle space, Temperance would have to offer the elixir of life… the means to navigate all that is scary and beastly. We can do it. Temperance can help.

How?

Through alchemy.

Temperance is illustrated in the Rider Waite Smith deck as an angel with a red triangle — representing fire — resting on its bosom. The angel is pouring an elixir from one golden chalice to the other, yet we do not know in which direction the liquid is flowing. Up? Or down?

One foot of the angel rests on land, the other on water.

Though Temperance represents a myriad of divine ideas, this card also serves as a reminder on how to practice magick.

Great chefs taste the food, and layer flavor upon flavor with a deft, precision hand that makes us cry when we consume the delicacies placed before us.

That's the kind of magick I desire to perform.

I'm not seeking to throw a bunch of magickal components together in a theoretical pot of stew with everything in it but the kitchen sink.

I desire to practice magick that is performed by the deft hand of an alchemist extraordinaire who knows the elixir's ingredients and measures these with masterful attention born of wisdom.

With each spell and/or ritual, I aspire to create a masterpiece.

I pray you approach your magick as the potent science based art form it is. I pray you become a **MASTER ALCHEMIST**, one who breathes the rarified air of the courageous who dared, even with the inherent hazards.

YES! REACH FOR THE STARS!

BECOME EXCELLENT!

BE A MASTER!

The old adage is vitally true: **ANYTHING WORTH DOING IS WORTH DOING WELL**.

If magick is worth it to you, do it well.

Magick, as meaningful, potent and rich as it is — either as a path to soul ascension or as a means to expand your bank account, and everything in between — ought to be accorded the respect, time, care, energy, attention, resources and training required to **MASTER**.

How to Be a Master Alchemist

I'll offer 5 components (among many) to become a master of the art of magick:

1. **INTENTION** - a master knows why she is doing what she is doing. Check your intentions. Muddy intentions make for muddy results (more about this in the chapter titled "Formula for Crafting a Spell").
2. **STUDY** - I don't know any Witches and/or magicians who are masters of the art of magick who do not have a library of magickal tomes. This is par for the magickal course. **STUDY YOUR CRAFT**. While

there remains a dearth of books on Christian Witchcraft as of the writing of this book in 2020 (a state of affairs I seek to change daily by writing all I know and have learned on the topic, and look forward to reading works from countless other Christian Witches as well), there are mountains of books on all manner of magick and Witchcraft that can be rightly applied to this path. I've carefully curated a selection of books that have been most helpful to me, categorized by subject matter for you in my Amazon store (access to the recommended books list can be found at www.ChristianWitches.com). At the end of this tome, you'll find a list of resources that can amply expand your magickal studies.

3. **PRACTICE** - nothing replaces **DOING MAGICK**. Not talking about magick. Not thinking about magick. Not dreaming of magick. PRACTICING MAGICK over and over and over makes one better and better at magick (provided the results are being cataloged and appropriate adjustments and integrations are continually taking place to OPTIMIZE). I do not subscribe to the saying that "practice makes perfect." Perfect practice makes perfect. Perfecting your results is the goal, not doing the same inappropriate thing over and over.
4. **TIME** - give yourself time. There's a school of thought put forth by Malcolm Gladwell in his book ***Outliers*** that it takes 10,000 hours to become a master. Many have attempted to debunk this theory, with varying results. If the theory is true, devoting 2 hours a day to magick would take you a little over 13 years to master. I say this to put things into perspective, and not to imply it will take you 13 years to master your craft. If you're reading this book, and consider yourself a Witch, it's likely magick is natural for you, which is a gift. There are no hard and fast rules on timing. The idea is to be patient as you practice.
5. **COMMUNITY** - this is why we gather. Witches have come together in covens, ritual gatherings and festivals for eons, in every nook of the planet and in every culture for the same reasons we congregate today: there's strength in numbers and there's power in community. Hitch yourself to a few other amazing Christian Witches and form

a coven, or join us in the Mystery School and have the opportunity to develop friendships with amazing magickal beings. Either way, don't go this road alone. Community doesn't mean you must join a coven. Of course, practice as a solitary Witch, Wizard, Warlock or Magickal Being is performed with great success and may be the way the majority of us walk this path. This fact is well known. And, as a solitary practitioner, being intentional about finding community to plant your magickal self in can exponentially expand both your concept of who you are and your magick. Iron sharpens iron. You can choose how often you'll participate in community, or when or where, from maybe once a year at a festival or convention, to bi-monthly moon rituals with your coven, or daily prayers with prayer partners. There's something very powerful about others witnessing your journey. I think we need that. I think we need others to be the holy, shining mirrors reflecting how far we've come. I think we need each other.

There are many more aspects and components to becoming a master of the craft of magick. These are beginning ideas that have helped me tremendously and continue to feed my spirit and magick.

Now that we have a solid commitment in place to becoming magickal badasses, no matter how long it takes, or how arduous the path, let's move on to…

How to Make Life Your Little Bitch

This book is not just about teaching you how to DO magick. This book is here to catalyze you **BECOMING A MASTER ALCHEMIST**. Doing is not the same as BEING. They don't live in the same universe.

DOING is of the ego.

BEING is of Spirit.

Doing is not negative. The ego is not negative. It's simply human. That's all.

BEING is BEYOND DOING. BEING causes EFFORTLESS manifestation because you're summoning to yourself what you desire by right of CONSCIOUSNESS, and therefore your manifestations are SUSTAINED.

Doing means you have to keep your foot on the pedal. Yes, you could manifest many great and wondrous things with magick. How much of it will stick depends on how aligned you are in **CONSCIOUSNESS** with that which you manifested by magick.

Anyone can do magick.

Not everyone will devote **ALL** that is required to become a **MASTER ALCHEMIST**.

If you're here to just ***do*** magick whenever you want or need to, this book is not for you.

If you're ready to **BE A MASTER**, you're in the right place, because that's what I'm aspiring to **BE** as well.

Who will practice the most potent magick?

A person who does no transformation of self to BE what they are casting for, yet carefully crafts spells according to all the rules of magick (or the grimoire they're working with), says all the right words in the circle with perfect pronunciation, knows every proper correspondence, and can speak ad nauseum about it all?

OR...

A person who chooses and realizes **SELF TRANSFORMATION** as one practices right and true magick?

You have a choice.

Stay the way you are. Do nothing and let life get you, which it surely will. Life will send you lovely letters about how important it is for you to transform yourself... in the form of raucous relationships that wreak havoc in your world, faulty financial systems, a body that's falling apart or not operating at peak, overall system breakdown, stagnancy and/or simply a lingering unfulfilling life experience.

OR...

You could **ENTHUSIASTICALLY** and **PROACTIVELY CHOOSE** to **ENGAGE** in the work of **SELF-REALIZATION** as a **CONSCIOUS**

CHOICE and **HONOR** that **COMMITMENT** to take this delicious life experience **ON** like an amazing **ADVENTURE** of **DISCOVERY** that you **LOVE** to dive into at the deep end of the pool with NO regrets, fears, worries, doubts, procrastination and hesitations that can stop you as you **ASCEND, TRANSCEND, FULFILL YOUR SOUL'S ULTIMATE CALLING** and **BECOME GOD.**

The choice is up to you.

You could either live an UH-OH existence (school of default).

OR...

You could live a **HELL YEAH BRING IT ON** experience in a **BLAZE OF GLORY.**

Either you're going to be life's little bitch or you're going to make life your little bitch.

IT'S HARD EITHER WAY.

It's hard to live by default and let life keep beating you up until you learn all the lessons. This is the school of default. Do nothing and you're a great student in this school of reactivity.

OR...

You could decide to stand and take the reigns, Chariot style (Key #7 in the Tarot), like the Witch you are, and **BE GOD**.

YES, it's hard becoming God. And YES, it's hard NOT becoming God.

Becoming God is so much more fun! Plus, you get to live a much more powerful existence as the **INITIATOR** and **AUTHOR** of your life experience.

You're a Witch.

Witches don't let other people — or life — decide for us. We decide.

Period.

Theurgy

The magick I practice personally is Theurgic in nature. You get to choose the essence and nature of the Magick you practice as a Christian Witch.

Though I don't believe everything on Wikipedia, there's a definition of Theurgy there that works well for our purposes:

> *"**Theurgy** (/θirdi/; from Ancient Greek: θεουργία,* theourgía*) describes the practice of rituals, sometimes seen as magical in nature, performed with the intention of invoking the action or evoking the presence of one or more deities, especially with the goal of achieving henosis (uniting with the divine) and perfecting oneself."*

This is the goal I have in magick: union with the divine as a self realized perfected being.

What does this mean?

In practical terms, it means invoking and connecting with divinity by remembering the truth: this is a spiritual universe with a physical component. The physical component is quantified by Kabbalists as 1%. The other 99% of reality cannot be ascertained through the mechanism of the 5 senses.

If that be the case (we have no way of proving it is not the case), we have a single job on our hands as Witches: connect with the 99% and **IDENTIFY** with the whole of the cosmos. Identifying with the 1% human personality is folly and leads to ultimate spiritual disaster.

We must **IDENTIFY** with something far greater than the human self. This is where theurgic practices and rituals give us a boost. When I connect and identify with Isis (Auset), I am instantaneously lifted out of being a mere mortal and into the lofty realm of the Goddess. When I invite and invoke or evoke the divine as this or that deity, I am understanding my connection with these powerful entities, and hence my correspondence with the same. No one builds deep meaningful relationship with people with whom they have nothing in common. In theurgy, we build relationships and identify with aspects of the divine whom we are drawn to and with whom we have the most in common.

The One Big Dude in the Sky

Traditionally, Christian teeth are set on edge with talk of gods and goddesses.

In the Christian paradigm, there's an omnipotent God in the sky, too big to be comprehended or fully known, thus an intermediary, or several, are required. Supposedly, we humans are just lowly sinners on the ground, in need of saving.

Many have been so thoroughly and completely brainwashed into the monotheistic approach to spirit realms that all mention of anything other in their presence reeks of blasphemy.

In this monotheistic paradigm, angels are considered ok. After all, they're soulless do-gooders who wouldn't dare act contrary to God, with one notable exception (along with the cohorts he purportedly dragged down with him).

Saints are ok too — at least in the Catholic paradigm — because they're considered people who so devoutly gave themselves over to the one God concept and worshipped this God with all they had that they've earned the right to be venerated.

There is, however, no room for gods and goddesses, save the BIG DUDE. Sorry kids, there's not even a BIG DUDETTE. The religion deemed it unacceptable for the Big Dude to have a divine counterpart, or wife.

Strange.

This monotheistic schema sets up an array of complications in the spiritual life of a divine being that it's almost shocking that the hoodwinking has been successfully perpetuated for so long, and on so many of us.

Monotheism: Epic Fail

Monotheism isn't a natural concept. Here's why...

The reason this paradigm (we can call it a lie) is unnatural is because it sucked all the divinity out of the world and up to heaven, to one person: the Big Dude.

For everyone else... good luck.

Not so in the ancient world. Up until about 2,000 years ago, all humans were polytheistic. This is a mystifying fact of all ancient cultures, no matter the locale or practices: there was no 'one God' (with a capital G) concept among our forebears. There were a multiplicity of gods everywhere one turned. The ocean was a goddess or god. The trees and forests were ruled by goddesses and/or gods. The wind, lakes, streams, crops, lightning, thunder, fire and EVERY natural phenomena were under the purview of gods and goddesses. It was natural for us as humans. Divinity was in everything, and we ***experienced*** everything in the natural world as ***divine***.

Monotheism is an idea in its infancy, one I would call an epic fail.

Cave paintings would suggest that we as humans have had a mystical, spiritual component to us that has been recognized, demonstrated and expressed as far back as 60,000 years ago.

Just over 2,000 years ago — with the rise of Judaism, Islam and Christianity — the one God concept was born: a big Dude in the sky you dare not mess with.

A disturbing aspect of our human heritage is how many Christians and Muslims were willing to fight (as evidenced by 'holy wars') over their one

Big God being THE big God.

When we compare 60,000 years of human history to the past 2,000, the one God concept is a new and strange idea.

When the strange change was propagated through the consciousness of humanity, divinity as we knew it left (in belief systems only) the trees, lakes, streams, rivers, oceans, and all of nature, no matter how palpable. Not only were we willing to be hoodwinked into believing that nature contained no divinity, we were eventually convinced that nature held a lesser space than humans, and that we were to subjugate it. This is yet another entry point to the systematic plundering of natural resources on the planet.

If all was divine, as the first nations of the land mass currently called America knew, there would be ritual prayers over the hunt and conversations with trees (or the Standing Nation as they are known in some circles) before cutting them.

If everything in nature is divine, everything in nature is revered.

Even the most logical and scientific among us may have challenges denying the surreal quality of nature. We can all feel and have access to the divine quality of nature, even if not acknowledged. It's called **AWE**.

I remember having a surreal experience of awe on a beach in Maui a couple of decades ago. It was close to sundown. My partner and I had spent the day on the beach and were packing up our things to leave. In the process, the entire beach was enveloped in the most riveting sky colors known to the human eye. In what seemed like an instant, the sky morphed into a kaleidoscope of reds, purples, cyans, yellows, oranges and beyond. It was an explosion of color like I had never seen. What happened next was magickal. Slowly, a hush fell over the entire beach. People everywhere began slowing down, instinctively and intuitively turning to the west. Something from the great beyond was tugging at the heart and soul of everyone on the beach, including the children. We responded by turning, as if on queue, to honor the exact moment when the Divine had whipped Its out crayons. Stunning. Breath taking. I still remember the unfoldment of art. Its etched in my mind. As for all the people on the beach that evening, we didn't collectively agree to be awed at the sunset. A moment before the sunset occurred, we had no idea we would be gifted with a majestic display so colorful and poignant that it caused us to stop dead in our tracks. We gave up our busy-ness, our movement. We were entranced. Together, we were in **AWE**.

If that wasn't the Divine, I don't know what is. And when I say the Divine, you can best believe I am not referring to an old white man with a long beard whose abode is in the sky. I gave up belief in sky gods long ago. When I refer to the Divine, I am referring to beginningless and endless **SOURCE**, undifferentiated, neither male nor female, in which we all live and breathe and move and have our very existence and which is imbued in every aspect and speck of the phenomenal world.

Some in the the Christian Church would have us believe that what we experienced on the beach in Maui that evening was an ACT of God, but was NOT GOD.

I boldly know and declare otherwise.

EVERYTHING IS GOD.

God/The Divine is Omnipresent

The sun is Divine. The moon is Divine. The toad is Divine. You are Divine. I am Divine.

When I perform a ritual by, in or involving the river, I am acknowledging, honoring and revering the truth that Source has materialized as fresh, sweet water flowing through earth's crannies, bringing forth life. This is an aspect of the Divine, though it is not ALL of the Divine. There's more to the Divine than the river. I may refer to this aspect of the Divine as Oshun. If I choose to do so, I now have a name of this aspect of the Divine making it easier to connect deeply with and embody this divinity, thus realizing more of my true God Self.

Oshun is not the only name for the aspect of the Divine that manifests as and holds power over the sweet waters. There are many names for many aspects of the Divine. We get to connect with the aspects and names of the Divine which most deeply resonate with each of us on a soul level.

I am clear that Oshun is not all of creation. Oshun herself does not state that she is all of creation. Oshun is a **POWERFUL ASPECT OF THE ONE**. Oshun is not a person (in my cosmology, others may differ). Oshun is a powerful force, a divine energy representing qualities I get to discover and cultivate within myself, such as beauty, abundance, sensuality, fertility and love. Oshun is the face and embodiment — or the character that my human mind can grasp — who represents aspects of Source I can identify with and acknowledge within myself. Oshun is a teacher, as are all gods and goddesses. If I hang out with Oshun regularly, create an altar for her, and speak with her, it's likely I'll become more beautiful, lavishly abundant and loving. We are greatly influenced by those we associate with who are humans. How much more so for aspects of the Godhead?

There is divinity back of **EVERYTHING**. The entire cosmos is divine.

If one would become a Theurgist, one must dispense with the Big Dude in the sky theory. I call it a theory because it is new and unproven.

My experience of divinity in the natural world has been proven, on countless occasions with myriads of other souls. We are in a shared experience of discovering our divinity. This is a great unveiling.

If we are to come into our **FULL POWER** as divine beings, we must not take a cookie cutter to the dough that is the universe. The egoic mind is a separating, parsing consciousness, which is necessary for life on planet earth. I must clearly know where my arm is and where your arm is if I'm to be in healthy relationship with you.

Yet, the egoic mind — as a separator and distinguisher — becomes dangerous when it applies the same reason and logic to God. It seeks to make us believe that God is here, but not there, as if God were only my arm.

No. We are never to allow the egoic mind to fool us, nor are we to succumb to teachings contrary to nature.

From the tomato to the galaxy, **GOD IS IN ALL, SHOWING UP AS ALL.**

I do not ask you to believe me. I ask you to examine your life experience. I ask you to listen deeply to the still small Voice within. This is truth.

Most of all, I ask you to examine ALL belief systems. A question I ask myself with regard to everything I believe, from is there a devil out to get me to is there one Big God who only exists in heaven is: what is most constructive for my life as a soul on planet earth now? Is it helpful for me to believe there's a devil out to get me at every turn? If not, that belief has to go. It's not a helpful belief.

In a world where you can believe anything, and subsequently shape your reality and your interactions with others based on those beliefs, it would be wise to choose beliefs that are in harmony and alignment with the kind of life you choose to live on planet earth.

Claimed By Isis

For as long as I can remember, I've had a connection, or bond, with Isis. Growing up as a Jehovah's Witness in Harlem would not have exposed me to the concept of Isis. I don't know when I first made conscious contact with her, or she with me. I only know I've been connected to her in an ancient connection that is in no way logical. I'm sure I may have been a Priestess in a Temple of Isis in one or more incarnations.

Either way, the Goddess made herself known to me as a whisper in my soul. I felt as though she had claimed me for her own. I accepted the connection. My soul had made pacts with aspects of the Divine as powerful deities before I landed here, just as it had made pacts with other souls as well.

The soul traverses the Sea of Forgetfulness when it enters a new incarnation. Birth removes conscious memory of the pacts made on the other side of the veil. We start fresh, so to speak. We must remember. We must wake up. This is our soul journey here.

Deities help. Am I a worshipper of Isis? No. I worship the Divine (which is neither male nor female), which is the WHOLE. Isis is a powerful aspect of the whole. I also refer to the Divine as Source. When I perform an Isis Invocation in a ritual, I am **CONNECTING** and **IDENTIFYING** with the aspect of Source that is Isis. Everything is energy. Isis is not so much a person to me as she is a force beyond comprehension... a force of Source.

Deities are vast cosmic forces that anyone can access. We are all children of the divine with no natural restraints on what we can and cannot do spiritually.

YE ARE GODS.

I'm not special. I'm not the only one chosen and claimed by Isis. I'm sure there are millions of us throughout the ages.

Some have been chosen and claimed by Diana, or Thoth, or any number of vast forces that exist in this great cosmos.

I do not see these powers and forces as people, such as ourselves. I intuit and read these vast forces as energy currents with a specific flavor. If that flavor is required in your life, you can call upon the entity of that particular flavor, in an appropriate manner and that flavor will be poured into your life.

This is all quite natural for us. We've been doing this for over 60,000 years. I would say magick is more of a return to who we really are than it is a new awakening.

I would also caution that Isis, or any deity for that matter, isn't sitting in heaven selecting random souls and claiming them, with the soul having no choice in the matter.

No. I want Isis as much as she wants me.

Souls are choosers. That's our divine right. It always will be.

We chose much before we came here. The trick is, we don't always consciously remember our soul choices. We chose the grand themes of this incarnation on a soul level, including:

- Family of origin, including birth parents and those who raise us.
- Place of birth.
- Day, date and time of birth to align with the stars, planets and other powers (including numbers, more about your birth information and what is has to do with your destiny is outlined in specific detail in my book *How to Be a Christian Witch*).
- Soul group we would travel with. Members of our soul group may

appear as siblings, children, close friends and intimate partners.

- The major issues preventing evolutionary ascension to be taken on in this lifetime, i.e. abandonment, unforgiveness, lust or any number of energies that keep us earthbound and prevent, hinder or slow down our process of becoming God.
- The soul markers placed around the globe that remind us of our ultimate destiny.
- The divinities we are connected to, in this lifetime and others.

As we can see, the soul is vaster and way smarter than the human. This is why we cannot rely on our human selves to pilot our soul plane (an essential aspect of theurgic magick). We trust the soul as it's aligned with the Inner Knowing that is Source. The soul is a unique expression of Source, made in Its image and likeness.

YE ARE GODS.

Who do gods and goddesses hang out with? Gods and goddesses.

You're a god/goddess hanging out with gods/goddesses.

We'll talk more about this in the chapter on "Your Spirit Team."

For now, we rest well in the truth that we have more supernatural help in this incarnation than we could ever hope to penetrate the mysteries of.

This universe is chock full of gods and goddesses, made of the same Divinity as you.

Traps in Magick

There are inherent traps in magick. Let's name a few, especially as it relates to divine assignments, challenges, soul mission, the critical distinction between HELP and SUPPORT, as well as the inherent fluidity of the path of the Christian Witch. We'll also consider just how expensive magick is.

Divine Assignments & Challenges

Each one of us has divine assignments. We all have our very specific challenges as well. The assignments and challenges we each own are necessary for our growth and development on the physical plane, as well as for our soul's ascension on spirit planes.

I'm not smart enough to know the full purpose of each divine assignment, nor do I know all the benefits any specific challenge will garner for me. That's not for me to know.

It's for me to face every experience in my world — including divine assignments, challenges and everything else — with grace, love, wisdom, power and faith. Faith is certainty in knowing that it will turn out perfectly for me and everyone, even though I have no evidence of the same or how that will unfold.

An example of a challenge: I may have asked and spelled for greater wealth and am now faced with a tax issue. This is a challenge that will surely teach me how to become smarter with money if I learn the requisite and inherent lessons, which will in turn produce greater wealth. The universe in its infinite wisdom always knows what each of us requires to get the job done.

I don't know what I need. I don't know what challenges I'll receive based on what I've asked for, or based on Higher Self (the True Self) knowing what I require in any given moment. I may not consciously remember all the soul lessons I came here to learn, grow through and overcome.

I don't know all the divine assignments that will present themselves throughout my lifetime.

When met with a divine assignment, it's not uncommon to be confused or overwhelmed at the enormity of the task. I remember listening to a minister many years back who received the divine assignment to podcast the Bible. He didn't know where to begin. He had no idea of how the divine assignment would be fulfilled. He also had never created a podcast before.

When Helen Schucman began to receive material from an inner voice she perceived as Jesus that would later become the book ***A Course In Miracles***, the enormity of the task was not immediately apparent. Can you imagine being the scribe for *A Course In Miracles*? Yes, she had help, and yes, it was still a huge deal.

This is the stuff of Spirit.

Divine assignments run the gamut from writing books to starting a healing practice to becoming a practicing Witch to creating a retreat center and so many more that we would literally have to name billions of divine assignments. There are divine assignments for every person on planet earth. Whether we take them on or not is a choice.

This is a good time to address where divine assignments come from. I believe they come from within one's own soul, in concert with Source.

What's clear is that at certain points on the journey, we're inspired or called — or compelled even — to do certain things that seem superhuman, or outside of our current sphere of possibility. This has happened to me on more occasions than I can count. It's likely happened for you as well. Exactly where the inspiration comes from is a matter of discussion, and may not be the most important aspect of the matter.

If you're inspired or compelled or divinely led to do something, it's for a reason. The reason may go far beyond your current paradigm.

You're drawn to Christian Witchcraft, otherwise you wouldn't be reading these words right now. There's a reason. Is this a divine assignment? What does it mean for you? Only you can answer these questions.

This is where a warning comes in with regard to magick. Do not attempt to spell away challenges, especially challenges that are connected with a divine assignment. We don't like challenges, because they don't feel good. A Witch who's amazing at magick may be tempted to cast a spell and do away with certain challenge with a quickness.

This may not always be the best approach for our long term soul ascension.

Divination helps us here. We can peer deep into the core essence of what we are facing in any given moment, causing our magick to be that much more effectual, with the help of our divinatory tools. When we are divining, we are literally seeking the Mind of the Divine. Aligned with Divine Mind, we will always spell for the highest and best, even if the spell work doesn't turn out as we expected. The results will still be for the highest and best for **ALL**.

Soul Mission

Your soul is here on a mission. You came into a body for a reason.

The full spectrum of our incarnation is often hidden from us. We don't consciously know all the in's and out's of why we're here. This is what we get to discover. This is the journey of the soul, the hero's quest.

Do not be tempted to practice magick to get rid of something annoying or painful that is indeed part of your soul mission.

Example. You may be here on a soul mission to help souls come home to Source. Part of that soul mission is creating spiritual places of residence for those who may find themselves temporarily homeless. A soul who does not know it is home could result in a body that is not in a home.

Part of this soul mission causes you to be homeless for a period of time, or at several junctures throughout your life. This is actually my story. Being evicted, having my dream home go into foreclosure and moving constantly were all part of my soul mission and were **NECESSARY** to develop in me humility, compassion for the homeless, patience, and more lessons than I can shake a broomstick at. Of course, while I was in the experiences, I wanted out as FAST AS POSSIBLE. I was doing magick to spell for beautiful homes.

The beautiful homes didn't arrive **UNTIL** I learned the requisite lessons. This is what I love about practicing magick with an intention to be a **MASTER ALCHEMIST**. We are not attached to a specific outcome on the physical plane. We are first and foremost here for **ASCENSION**. ASCENSION as a soul may mean hunger, homelessness, and pain in the body temple, temporarily. These are not useless problems producing unnecessary suffering. These are tools of the universe to shape and mold us into **GIANTS**.

Adversity is the carver of souls. Adversity causes us to pay attention. Adversity is an indispensable aspect of SOUL ASCENSION. Adversity teaches us things that we could learn in no other way. Spiritual gangstas are wrought of adversity.

With that said, understand the issues at hand before attempting to spell all your problems away. Understand the connection between the current very unpleasurable (even revolting) experience and the grander **SOUL MISSION**. Then practice magick accordingly. **SPELL IN HARMONY WITH SOUL ASCENSION** and not to avoid it.

Help vs. Support

Help is doing for others what they are to do for themselves. It's rescuing or saving others. It's getting in other peoples' lane and minding other peoples' business.

Conversely, support is giving what you're inspired to give to others as they do their own work.

For example, if the universe, in all its infinite wisdom, put before you 50 bricks to move so that you grow requisite muscle to fulfill your soul mission, or receive what you've requested, your best option is to get to work moving your bricks. If I jump in and move 49 of your bricks, I just helped you in a way that does not allow you to learn your lessons and grow your muscles. A problem is born.

Conversely, if I keep you company as you move your bricks, cheer you on, pray for you and maybe do a sing-along with you as you move all 50 of your bricks, that's support. No problems are created and only victory is celebrated. I give you a big fat high five when you're done your work. Now you are perfectly poised and ready for your next steps, whatever they may be.

The bottom line: we each have our own unique work to do. We get to jump in and do it, with **ENTHUSIASM**, no matter how enormous the divine assignment, how difficult the challenge or how gargantuan the soul mission.

If other people continually 'save' us from the work that only we can do, how are we to become the mighty giants we're born to be?

Fluidity Does Not Mean Floppy

This warrants stating in a book like this, especially with the current state of Christian Witchcraft, where much is fluid and open and not much is solidified into a uniform way of practicing, as can be the case with other magickal systems.

Christian Witchcraft is fluid and open to interpretation. It's a deeply personal path with no rules, dogma or rigidity. I love the path for this very reason. And I also see the inherent trap in fluidity.

Fluidity can imply being ungrounded or lost upon the waves of the sea. For me, this is why it is imperative for the Christian Witch to have an anchor, or to be solidly rooted in ***something***.

I found my solid root in Love and Law, as outlined in my book *Christian Witches Manifesto* (which is now a gift included in paid membership on my YouTube channel).

Though my anchor serves me well, you don't have to subscribe to the same anchor to effectively utilize the Spellcrafting and ritual creation in this book.

I would offer that of supreme importance here is for you to **ANCHOR** yourself. What are you rooted in? What do you KNOW to be truth? What keeps you grounded?

This wisdom from Christ serves us well:

"Whoever therefore hears these my words and does them, I will liken him to a prudent man, who built his house upon the rock;
25 and the rain came down, and the streams came, and the winds blew and fell upon that house, and it did not fall, for it had been founded upon the rock.
26 And every one who hears these my words and does not do them, he shall be likened to a foolish man, who built his house upon the sand;
27 and the rain came down, and the streams came, and the winds blew and beat upon that house, and it fell, and its fall was great."
Matthew 7:24-27 (DARBY)

Make truth your rock solid foundation.

Yes, this path is fluid, not floppy.

As Christian Witches, we seek and aspire to be solidly grounded in truth. The fluidity of our path serves as a clarion call to our greatest creativity and courage!

The Cost of Magick

Magick will cost you. It's extremely expensive.

Let's draw a clear distinction.

It doesn't cost much to buy a magick book, cast a few spells, and see what happens.

That's not the kind of magick I'm talking about here.

I'm talking about a whole-souled surrender yourself to the Divine with magick as a means of soul ascension. The Great Work.

I have found, my beloved Witch, that magick as a means of catalyzing the Great Work of alchemy of the soul has cost me everything: friends, family, money, homes and more.

Why? Because I was choosing for the soul, rather than for the human. I could have done things more expediently. I could have cut corners. I could have tried to rush the process. Every time I tried these tactics, I was slapped unceremoniously by the universe back to square 1 to do the job and do it in the way it was meant to be done.

Living this way is the best and most free way to live, yet it's also the most expensive. Nothing in your life will be spared. Nothing will be the same after you choose to open this metaphorical Pandora's Box. I didn't have a clue of how sweeping the practice of magick would be in my entire world. The broom left no corner untouched.

This is an expensive path. Are you ready to pay what it costs?

New Age Pitfalls

There's a strange phenomenon that has been unfolding in the world of magick and the occult over the last two decades or so.

As humanity entered a new phase of increased focus on spirituality as a means to navigate fast-paced, technologically driven, modern life on planet earth, movies such as The Secret, among others, taught the masses about ancient spiritual laws that had been heretofore only discussed, practiced and mastered in occult circles or mystery schools.

As we moved deeper into this new age of enlightenment, the internet became the supplier of a glut of information on almost every spiritual topic and magickal tradition, from the practices of shamans in Peru to the rituals of the Yoruba and everything in between. A few mouse clicks will return to any seeker as much information about a chosen spiritual path or magickal tradition as they desire to gorge upon.

I view this unfoldment as a gift.

Yet, a distinction is in order: information in the hands of the initiated is a gift while too much information in the hands of a fool becomes his undoing.

Information does not equal wisdom. Wisdom is applied knowledge. Information is words wafting through one's head. Too much information and we are lost. Information is cold and soul-less.

Wisdom is warm, arising from having walked out what we know from digesting it, practicing it, and receiving results. While wisdom is full circle, information is the starting point.

Excess information entering a big head that is not accompanied by a heart centered consciousness just leads to a really smart person who can spout and quote everything about magick, yet does not practice. They know everything, yet they ***know*** nothing.

This is not the focus nor the purpose of this book. This book of magick is created and intended to be used, put to the test, argued with, challenged, acted upon and ultimately become yet another tool and/or instrument in the hands of the master for self-gnosis, Spellcrafting and ritual creation mastery and badass magickal results.

The danger of having access to this much information without the nuances and subtleties that only come from a teacher or from years of walking one's own initiatory path is that we may be missing the most vital aspects of the magickal tradition in question.

I'm a purist. I thought I'd let you know that, so you understand where I'm coming from in the writing of this book and the crafting of these spells. You get to choose for yourself how you'll approach magick. Some Witches are eclectic. Some are pure to a particular tradition and do not stray.

You choose.

There is no right or wrong choice. There are only the choices that work **FOR YOU**.

Now let's examine 5 pitfalls of this new age:

Wishful Thinking

Wishful thinking, as defined here, is any thought process that divorces work or exerted action from the outcomes we desire. In wishful thinking, a desired result is put on a vision board, perhaps accompanied with a candle spell or two, and lots of visualization, yet there is **NOT THE REQUISITE ACTION** or **WORK** on the 3rd dimensional plane to facilitate that desire coming into the 3rd dimensional reality.

REQUISITE ACTION means the required **ACTION STEPS** and

WORK to MATCH the DESIRED RESULT. If one is asking to be a billionaire, there are REQUIRED ACTION STEPS and WORK that EVERY billionaire engages in daily. This will not change. This is called the CURRICULUM for becoming a billionaire. One cannot sidestep critical aspects of the process, especially DIVINE RIGHT ACTION and expect to receive the desired result.

There seemed to be a general shift away from hard work somewhere in the late 90's or early 2000's. I'm a child of the 60's, so hard work was a mantra. I don't agree with hard work exclusively, nor do I agree with magickal thinking that dismisses hard work. Neither are desirable or efficacious.

I know a lot of hard working people who absolutely do NOT have their desired outcomes, and I've observed a lot of wishful thinkers who are lazy and non-committal (more on that below), including myself at certain moments.

It didn't work.

I would offer that the beautiful blend of magick AND action brings about breathtakingly stellar results.

Mixing Shit Up and Calling it Eclectic

Mixing shit up due to failure of study and lack of commitment and calling it 'eclectic' is not the move.

There's a vast divide between true eclectic Witches, and mixer-uppers.

Eclectic Witches are Witches who have weaved into a beautiful tapestry deeply meaningful elements from magickal traditions and spiritual paths into a whole and dynamic spiritual practice and magickal way of being that issues froth from the soul. True eclecticism is beauty and creativity. It's inspiring. It's informed. It's experiential.

I guess you could call Christian Witchcraft an eclectic path because we beautifully harmonize elements of the Christ path, the Bible and other holy books with Witchcraft, magick and the occult for a surprisingly delicious and satisfying magickal way of being.

Mixer-uppers, on the other hand, are people who may be in a bind, a pinch, an unwanted or desperate situation, then watch a YouTube video here and there, and decide they're going to throw this together with that, and voila! hope something good comes out.

Mixer-uppers have no depth in any particular path. They're surface and untested. There's no solid foundation in a deeply meaningful spiritual practice that feeds the soul.

A friend of mine who doesn't practice magick had an unexpected financial challenge arise. While searching YouTube for spiritual help with this pressing matter, she watched a video about how to call on Papa Legba for help with finances. It involved traditional elements of Voodoo, such as the crossroads, pennies and an offering to Papa Legba.

Knowing what I know about Papa Legba, and I am NOT a Voodoo Priestess, I wouldn't touch him with a ten foot pole without knowing exactly what I was doing. He's not one to be trifled with, as is true with almost every deity one would call upon.

My friend performed the steps in the video, with no knowledge of Papa Legba or Voodoo, and received pretty untoward results that are still lingering. She has to work through it spiritually. She added more to her process than she began with.

This story, along with countless others I've heard of or observed in people who are not committed to any particular path or magick as a whole, or who are not truly desirous of **DOING THE WORK** to master a specific magickal tradition, yet who want instant results in a 'push a magick button, say these works, twirl around 5 times and out spits your dream life' sort of way, highlights how NOT to become a Master Alchemist.

Non-committal

You get to choose which path you'll travel: committed or non-committal.

A committed Witch is one who has **DECIDED** that they're living a magickal life, and who has committed to that path, whatever that means for that Witch. It's a sacred vow. That's why initiation is often involved. It means study, practicing magick, receiving results and making corrections. It means giving the rest of one's life to this experiential undertaking. It involves BEING and DOING. As mentioned, the spiritual path as a Witch has demanded nothing short of **EVERYTHING**. MY ALL. That's the magick. Hurling your **WHOLE SELF** into the abyss of the unknown because that's what your soul bid you do now. WOW. THAT'S LIVING!

Then there's the non-comittal way to go about it. Because the essence of being non-committal is unworthiness, nothing worthy can come of being non-committal. Unlike the uncommitted — which is simply a person who's decided not to commit themselves to a particular path for their own good reasons — the non-committal person actually has an inability to commit.

There are many things we may or may not commit to on the path of magick. These are all within the purview of our Divine power of choice. Yet, we know we are committed to magick and being a Witch. Exactly how that unfolds is each Witch's story of becoming.

The non-committal people (of which I was one for quite a while, so I understand the malady) are people who have an inability to commit, are always second-guessing self, change their minds often, are flighty, and cannot be relied upon. Their foundation is not solid, so they change with the wind. Because I'm an air sign, a lot of the foregoing was my challenge. Because that was not the person I desired to be, I made a **COMMITMENT** to myself to be the **Witch I AM BORN TO BE** and to utilize **MAGICK AS A SPIRITUAL PATH** to **ENLIGHTENMENT** come what may, while I burned all the effin bridges behind me.

Laziness

I was stricken with a malady. It's name is *'don't feel like it.'* If stricken with this malady, one will not get up and do the important, and even critical, action steps to create desired results. People with the *'don't feel like it'* malady are lazy. I learned many hard lessons from living in lazy-land.

I carry these golden lessons with me now.

The first big lesson I learned was that I'll never feel like it. Doing the work to create the desired result is not an option. The work must be done. If I wait until I feel like doing it, or feel inspired to do it, or feel happy about doing it, it will never get done. The most successful people in the world have come to the realization that they must take the action steps to create the desired result every day whether they feel like it or not.

The next big lesson I learned from laziness is that no one is going to do the work for me. No one can live my experience except me.

Lazy people like to have everything put on a silver platter and given to them. They want someone else to do their work. This laziness streak can be insidious and cleverly masked.

Case in point: I noticed myself not learning herbology for spell work. I deeply desired to learn it, yet I observed myself not taking steps in that direction. The core of the issue was revealed one day while I was writing. In fact, I was writing a section of this book and included all the necessary ingredients for a working, except the herbs. I'm being as transparent as I can with you. I initially wrote in the herbs section that I didn't know herbology well enough to provide the proper herbs for the working. When I looked at that sentence on my computer, I knew it was a lie. In addition, I knew it was inappropriate for a person who's teaching magick not to understand herbology. My first reaction was to go look up herbs on the web and find 5 or 6 that would work. I did that. In addition, I combed the regions of my mind and life experience for herbology for what I knew about it from practical experience. There was quite a bit already in my mind on herbology from growing up with the Witchy potions of my mother and grandmothers. I knew loads already. My life experience had been my greatest teacher on herbs and plants. I have a green thumb. I've cared for and grown enough plants to fill a forest. I love all things green. I keep about 60-70 essential oils at all times and have an intimate relationship with these energies because I've actively sought out a relationship with each plant. I've traveled to Peru on multiple occasions — and continue to each year — for experiential learning in plant medicine under shamans who have been practicing for over 30 years. I've ingested more plant medicine than I can recount here, a not always pleasant experience. As a matter of conversation, some of the experiences were downright unpleasant, if not revolting. The results are beautiful though, which is why we're still crazy (like a fox) enough to keep chugging Ayahuasca or munching mushrooms.

Yet, it was in my mind that I didn't know enough about herbology to recommend this or that to someone else.

Why do I have this confession in the 'laziness' section? (It could just as easily go into a section on unworthiness or resistance or overwhelm.) Because it wasn't that I didn't know, I was being mentally lazy. The invitation in that moment was to go deep into my inner world, find and bring out the plethora of pertinent information, order it, and present it in a digestible format that serves and benefits others, all the while being EFFECTIVE.

Lazy. Don't feel like it.

I had to cast that off immediately. The 'don't feel like it' malady is a clever devil that may not be overt. It expresses as the covert little ways we seek to not do the work. Go to a website instead and find a ready made spell.

My tendency was to look up what herbs are effective for which working, rather than persist in the deeper work my life experience had been urging me in all along: become a master herbalist.

I'm like you. I know what I'm supposed to be doing. You know what you're supposed to be doing. No one has to tell you. We all know, deep within our bones, what we're supposed to be doing. I'm to be taking the steps to become a master herbalist so as to take my entire life experience with plants to the master level. Maybe you've been called in a particular direction as well, and have yet to answer the call.

For me, it's the lazy streak that gets me, and the occasional appearance of the '*don't feel like it*' malady I long ago prayed to shake off and actively sought to slaughter. If I see remnants pop up, I realize my work is not done. I reach deeper into my alchemical bag of treasures to transform myself.

Funny how one sentence can reveal so much, if aware. You may read this and think something else. Each person knows what it means for them. The Inner Voice is speaking to each of us.

Bottom line: don't want it easy. Do the work. Even when you don't feel like it. Magick is that important, and it's well worth it. ***You're well worth it.***

Irresponsibility

Another trap of the New Age is the tendency to not take 100% responsibility for self. One of the biggest places this shows up in the lightworker/magickal community is with astrology. I've heard advanced lightworkers make statements like "Mercury is retrograde, oh Lord, no wonder my computer is acting up."

Yes, there's a thing called 'cosmic weather.' Yes, I pay attention to astrology. And, I take astrology as it's considered in the east. In the east, a person who goes to have their fortune told from one who reads the stars is seeking insight and understanding to add to their decision making process, rather than taking the reading as an absolute and unchangeable outcome.

If a person in the east goes to a reader of the 'stars' and finds out that on Thursday a terrible accident will happen, that person may elect to stay home on Thursday. When they wake up on Thursday, they make a nice cup of tea and enjoy being home that day. They fully expect a perfect day with no accident, because they averted the disaster that the stars warned of. The way I see it, this is using cosmic weather appropriately, as an early warning system, or as a source of greater and/or helpful information which will prove useful in an overall decision making process. Cosmic weather consists of helpful elements, not determinants.

Having a deterministic view toward cosmic weather or divination or anything in magick takes responsibility away from self (where it always rightly lives) and places it (along with the matching power) outside of self.

Responsibility and power are inextricably linked, a dynamic duo that will never divorce. When a person becomes President of the United States, the power is great, as is the attendant responsibility.

A teacher of mine says that if there's spare responsibility floating around, grab it. When you do, you just simultaneously gained the power married to that responsibility.

Going With Intuition

It would appear some in the magickal community are not clear on the distinction between 'go with your intuition' and 'make shit up.'

These are not the same.

The main issue is that the person who makes shit up and says it's intuition has not established a deep, rich, soul stirring spiritual practice such that they know exactly when the Inner Voice is speaking, versus one of the many possible voices of the egoic mind. It's not always easy to discern the difference, which is why we have divination. Literally we desire to divine our answers, which means harvesting answers from the Divine Self, and not the lower mind.

These two minds are in no way aligned. Herein lies the difficulty for most of us humans. We have two minds. The ego mind — powered exclusively by the 5 senses — only knows lack, separation, emptiness and not enough. It is designed to be a conduit between the 3rd dimensional plane of sense perception and the interior subjective reality. The 5 senses are like antennae to navigate the 3rd dimension, and are not meant to be decision making tools. The 3rd dimension is so compelling that we can be tricked into taking what we see in the 3rd dimension as reality. Remember, it is not. The 3rd dimension is the 'shadow' world, not the real world. The real world cannot be perceived by the 5 senses.

Divine Mind continually communicates the best and highest for self and all with each of us within. Divine Mind is not on board with the ego's agenda for separateness and littleness. Divine Mind is one with all. Divine Mind is ALL. We are tapping into **DIVINE MIND** when we cast our divination.

Further, we get to clearly intuit and attune to the Voice of the Divine by the practice of meditation. Developing the habit of quieting the surface mind at many pauses throughout the day — and not just when formally meditating in the morning or evening — is a powerful practice for Self awareness.

The more we quiet the surface mind, the more we hear directly from

Source. The Divine is the REAL YOU. The ego is the fake you. You get to decide, moment by moment, which one you'll side with.

Not Honoring Systems

All magickal systems have protocols, rituals and ways of doing things.

There's a system for Santeria. I don't know that system. I honor it. I wouldn't pull from it a few pieces here and there and throw it into my spell work. Not to say that it wouldn't work. If done well, it probably would work.

Honoring a system means approaching the system with respect and reverence. It means understanding that there may be centuries and even millennia of magick associated with a particular system, such as magick from ancient Kemet. Humility helps. We do not foster a hubris that would have us believe we are above having to learn a system in order to use it for our advantage. We understand, as Master Alchemists, the requisite time, energy and attention for mastering ANY system of magick and we pay our dues. We're happy to pay our dues.

I honor every magickal system I know of, because I honor myself.

Honoring a system, on the other hand, does not mean being a slave to a system.

Here's how I see it (and I welcome challenging conversation on this) when approaching any system of magick I may or may not have heard of, or know about:

- **Reverential state of mind**. To me, reverence is acknowledging the divine aspects of a thing, and knowing that what I'm approaching is a revered aspect of the ALL. Approaching all magickal systems with reverence helps me to not act like a toddler who grabs things, sniffs at them for a second or two, puts it in the mouth to learn what it is, then drops it and is on to the next. We're called to spiritual maturity. For me, maturity includes reverence. I never met a magickal system that didn't deserve my reverence, and I've met with and studied a LOT of magickal traditions.

- **Learn**. No way around it. Study. Every day.
- **Decide**. Decide if this is a casual course of study, or if this is a deeper course of study AND practice. While I LOVE studying all manner of magickal traditions, I haven't decided to devote myself to all of them. I've studied lots of magick that I wouldn't practice. I don't know that one can be devoted to many systems at the same time. Perhaps you can. I'm challenged with that. I like doing deep dives into the systems I'm most called to, which have been different at different times. I remember I had a deep dive Wicca period. I was searching. Wondering if this was the path for me. I read book after book. Studied. Learned. Attended and engaged in rituals. Checked in with myself all along the way for resonance. I decided it wasn't for me. Yet I don't think I would have come to such clarity on it had I not gone through that process.
- **Initiation**. Is this path resonant to such a degree that it warrants the time, energy, attention and devoted resources to be initiated? My first initiation was a solitary initiation in which I devoted myself to walking out my life as a Witch and received a new magickal name. Several initiations followed over the years, and I'm sure many more are in the making. Each initiation was a beginning and an ending. It was the beginning of true, deep and lasting devotion to a particular path, and the end of searching. The search had yielded certainty. You'll know into which path(s) you're to be initiated. You can't not know. If you're called to be initiated in Christian Witchcraft, our **Mystery School** may support you in that endeavor. And of course, not every system of magick we're drawn to will become an initiatory path for us.

Stealing bits and pieces from magickal traditions — absent of deep understanding — and using them in any way one sees fit in the moment is not advantageous. For me, this is nothing short of theft. There's a plethora of spells online that grab a piece from one thing, a piece from another thing and mash it all together in an attempt to create a whole, without first having a deep understanding of each of the constituents.

I think this phenomena may be due to the availability of information on just about every magickal tradition, whereas previously, only initiates would be privy to the information. Yes, we're deep in the information age. This isn't license to do everything that we have information about. As alluded to earlier, there's a great divide between information and understanding.

Example: grabbing an incantation from a Solomonic grimoire, added to a ritual to Oshun at the river, on a Wiccan holy day. This may be an extreme example, yet I've seen stranger.

The solution: have a deep understanding of what you're doing and why. If you don't yet have the understanding, **TAKE ACTION ANYWAY**, just follow the protocols and instructions of the thing you're doing until you're wise enough in that system to make necessary personal adjustments.

In all subjects one undertakes to study, one must first understand the BASICS of the system, practice these over and over, and then, once mastered, one can put a spin on it. I see people put a spin on things too early, and then pass their spin on as truth, which results in nothing more than a bastardization. This is not the practice of the Master Alchemist.

There are no shortcuts in magick or in spirituality. Yes, there are hacks, and smarter ways to do things. When these are available, take them.

If you are truly devoting yourself to the practice of magick, go deep. Don't be surface. **GIVE YOURSELF TO MAGICK**. Learn. Practice. Grow. Master your craft.

Stupidity

There are copious amounts of stupidity on the web, along with more access than ever to it. We each and all have full access to all the stupidity out there.

Because stupidity is has become ubiquitous and pervasive, the question we must ask ourselves is: how do I identify stupidity and immediately trash it?

Before answering that question, let's define stupidity for the purposes of this conversation:

- **Practices that have no real basis in how the universe actually works** (according to LAW). This is not a random universe. This universe operates by LAW. I see a lot of ideas online that do not align with universal law.
- **Doing only what 'feels good.'** Some of the most potent magick and spiritual practices don't feel good in the process, though they yield exquisite results. The ego is having a field day with people who have a requirement that things feel good, and who take 'not feeling good' as a sign that they shouldn't go in a particular direction, even after having received clear divine guidance to go in that direction. FYI: Source doesn't change Its Mind.
- **Getting 'values' and 'principles' mixed up.** Everyone has values, including criminals. A value proposition for criminals is: 'don't rat each other out.' Principles, on the other hand, are unfailing energy currents that work the exact same way for everyone, regardless of creed, color, religion, sex, or any other factor. Principles — such as discipline, trust, responsibility, accountability, to name a few — determine outcomes. A criminal could have a value system that includes robbing banks and feel justified in doing so. The principles of responsibility, accountability, honesty and others will determine the outcome. Please understand principles go beyond the criminal justice system or ANY human system. Principles are universal and cannot be tamed or controlled by human minds. Principles move the wheels of karma and destiny. To understand this in greater detail, there's no greater book than ***The 8th Habit*** by Stephen R. Covey (God bless his soul).

There's a lot more stupidity out there on the web than I can put in one book. Suffice it so say: **BEWARE**.

The best ways to detect and trash stupidity are INTUITION and

DIVINATION.

Studying Ad Nauseam

Studying ad nauseum and asking endless questions **WITHOUT TAKING ACTION** are traps wrought of fear.

Year after year of study — with no magickal practice — is not how we become Master Alchemists.

A Master Alchemist takes the scientific approach. (I detail this approach in my book ***How to Be a Christian Witch*** so we won't do deep into it here.) In short, the scientific approach is one of **INFORMED ACTION** for results. One then catalogs the results and moves forward again, with the feedback loop of prior actions. This process is repeated until mastery in producing desired results is achieved. This will take years, so...

MOVE FORWARD NOW WITH WHAT YOU CURRENTLY KNOW. Don't worry, you can't break magick. One of the things I love most about magick is that anything you can do you can undo. You're a creator. So **GO FOR IT. NOW.**

Yes, study. Yes, read books. Yes, associate with other magickal practitioners and Christian Witches. Yes, belong to groups or courses or schools or covens.

AND NEVER LET THESE PRECLUDE YOU FROM TAKING ACTION NOW WITH WHAT YOU CURRENTLY KNOW AND HAVE AT YOUR DISPOSAL.

MOVE.

Don't be rash. Don't be impetuous. Don't rush and don't be hasty.

Simply MOVE confidently forward with what you know and have NOW.

Study doesn't create results. Practical application of our studies through informed **ACTION** creates results.

If Malcolm Gladwell is right, and it'll take 10,000 hours to master magick, wouldn't you rather get started now?

Bible Magick

In this book — being a manual of Christian Witchcraft — you'll find a good number of Bible references.

Let's take a moment to clarify a few things about the Bible as it relates to this text.

For me, the Bible is not a literal, historical or factual book. I don't take it literally. I've found the Bible to be a huge book of magick, metaphor, allegory, mysticism, astrology, numerology, symbolism, angelology, demonology and more, divinely designed to stir up latent energies within the soul so that we ascend.

The Bible (and every holy book I've ever read) is a gateway to supernal realms.

I consider the words of a Kabbalah teacher who's also a Jewish Rabbi: "Anyone who takes the Bible literally is a fool." I concur.

If we stay at the surface level of the Bible (the literal story) we miss the deeper, richer and TRUE meaning of what we're reading. The depths are where the gold lies. I HIGHLY recommend acquiring the ***Metaphysical Bible Dictionary*** available through Unity. It contains metaphysical meaning of Bible texts, legends and characters. We discover that all Bible characters essentially represent **DIVINE ATTRIBUTES** or a **SET OF DIVINE PRINCIPLES**. We can intuit these divine attributes by reading the story as a pointer to a greater truth rather than as the truth itself.

For instance, the Bible character Abraham represents a host of divine attributes, including hospitality, faith extraordinaire, and the willingness to heed the divine prompting within at ALL costs. These are qualities each of us get to cultivate for a full experience of transcendence.

Seeking to deeply understand the Bible (and every holy book) at its **ESSENCE** is the goal, not just memorizing Bible stories, as I was pressed to do as a child. I know a lot of church people who can recount every story in the Bible, yet their understanding of the spiritual and energetic mechanics behind the same is blunted.

We desire to use the Bible as a sharp double edged **SWORD**.

Also to be noted is that many books in the Hebrew Bible (including Genesis to Deuteronomy) were heavily revised, edited and even invented, including an editing in the mid-fifth century when Jerusalem's governor Nehemiah and the priest-scribe Ezra reshaped the religion and history of the Jews.

I do not consider it a negative fact that the Bible has been heavily edited, revised, and in some places, invented. This is because I don't take the Bible literally, which in no way reduces it's power or efficacy for spiritual transformation or for its use in magick.

The simple truth is: the Bible is a spiritual book, with the power and purpose of any and all spiritual books, and that is to point to deeper truths that guide the soul home.

How to Read the Bible as a Christian Witch

As a handy guide, here are a few points of reflection and meditation one could utilize when reading the Bible for magickal purposes:

- **What's the context?** What's happening in the story?
- **Who?** Who are these people and what was going on in their lives? What does each person represent in the Metaphysical Bible Dictionary?
- **How?** How does this apply to me right now? Ask Source within.
- **Angels and demons:** who are the supernatural figures in the story?

The Bible is full of angels and demons. We gain useful insights for magick and life from these entities.

- **Astrology:** are there astrological references? An easy marker that appears REPEATEDLY in the Bible is the number 12. In the movie Zeitgeist (if you haven't watched it, it's well worth renting or buying on YouTube) the recurring theme of 12 in the Bible is explored as code for embedded astrology.
- **Numerology:** are there numbers in the passage, and if so, what are the meanings of the numbers? The Bible has an entire book titled Numbers. The entire universe is built on numbers (or mathematical equations as far as we now know in 21st century science, although we're always learning more). The Fibonacci Sequence (also known as the divine mean) is a mathematical ratio that applies to everything in nature.
- **Magick:** is there magick in the passage or reference to magickal rituals or implements? There's more hidden magick in the Bible than we can shake a broomstick at, and it's our job as Christian Witches to find and use it. (Psalms is particularly potent.) Many of the healings of Christ include magickal words and/or elements, yet they're not recognized as such to those who have never studied magick.
- **Metaphysics:** if the Bible (and every spiritual tome for that matter) is really a metaphysical book, that would mean that everything in it is referring to some aspect of **CONSCIOUSNESS** or **ENERGY**. It's up to us to decode it. I've found no better and more comprehensive tool for the job than the ***Metaphysical Bible Dictionary.***

As for exegesis of the Bible, I don't need or want it. I rarely believe what I'm told anyway. I'm seriously seeking to rid myself of ALL beliefs. I'm a truth seeker. I desire ***gnosis***... of Self as the cosmos. Gnosis does not come from what other people tell us, even if those people are pastors, reverends, ministers or any other person we've been conditioned to view as an authority figure.

As an ordained minister, it may seem strange for me to teach not to listen to ministers. My position: **FIND OUT FOR YOURSELF.** You're a fully actualized, **DIVINE BEING** with absolute **SOVEREIGNTY**.

This doesn't mean it isn't helpful to listen to other perspectives about the Bible, or to read books and consider all sides of a matter. The Bible itself offers a charge to anyone willing to take it on:

"Study to shew thyself approved unto God, a workman that needeth not to be ashamed, rightly dividing the word of truth."
2 Timothy 2:15 (KJV)

To me, this sounds like becoming a Master Alchemist who knows exactly what's true and what isn't. At the end of the day...

YOU ARE THE AUTHORITY in your life and world. YOU as in the REAL YOU (SOURCE) and not the superficial personality wrought of the ego mind.

Rhema Word

In church, I've heard it taught that a 'rhema word' is the utterance of God within the heart that conveys wisdom in that moment for a particular issue or question, as the person reads the Bible in an ascended state (or 'prayed up' to put it in church parlance). A rhema word is the understanding revealed beyond words on a page, and beyond what any human mind could logically come up with on its own. It is the direct communication with supernal realms as our consciousness touches a holy book, almost as if the holy book were a portal. I believe all holy books can act in this fashion.

Rhema word can also mean 'second utterance,' the 2nd word spoken by God in the heart, with the first word being before us on the page.

Seek a 'rhema word' on everything you're reading and/or studying in the Bible.

In addition, expand your Bible examination to include the **Pseudepigrapha**, the **Lost Books of the Bible** and the **Gnostic Gospels** (many of which can be read free online at **Sacred-Texts.com**) and any other sacred texts you're mystically drawn to.

Note: I have a practice of reading the same verse in several Bible translations and/or versions, in order to gain a broader perspective, deeper meaning and better understanding. This can easily be accomplished at BibleGateway.com.

How Did Magick Get Sucked Out of the Bible?

My mother stuck a Bible in my hands when I was about 3. It came with these warnings:

- Never put your Bible on the floor.
- Never write in your Bible.
- Never let your Bible become dog eared or tattered.
- Read your Bible every day.
- Read the entire Bible every year.
- Do what the Bible says.
- The Bible is the infallible word of God.
- As soon as your Bible shows signs of wear and tear, replace it.

Granted, I grew up in the cult of Jehovah's Witnesses, who are fanatical Fundamentalist Christians, so the rules were quite likely excessive. At the same time, I've heard from others who grew up in a Christian household or a Bible reading home that were given pretty much the same instructions.

Of course, I was far too young to understand what the whole thing meant as it was happening. Over the years of trying my best to read the entire

Bible every year (I never made it straight through) there were many things I noticed about the Bible and had questions about. The questions were never fully answered in a way that satisfied my soul and my mind. Either the religion was asking me to suspend logic to believe something that was completely illogical and unreasonable, or it was asking me to view as very normal and reasonable something that was not.

It was this very issue that revealed to me, over many decades, the distinction between spirituality and religion. One big distinction, among many, is that religion asks us to believe while spirituality ushers us into knowing.

Spirituality doesn't ask me to believe anything. It requires that I step squarely on the path of my soul for the purpose of ascension as I follow the Inner Knowing (True Divine Self) no matter what. I don't have to believe anything because everything I require will be shown and proven to me, such that it satisfies my soul AND my mind. I'm an air sign, and air signs don't do well with commands to believe things that are completely illogical.

I needed to know more than the religion was telling me.

Is that you? Is that what bought this book to you?

If so, you're in the right place. Not because I claim to have all the answers. I do not. You're in the right place because your soul magnetized this material to you for purposes beyond what you and I can know right now.

I love the spiritual path.

So, because I wasn't keen on believing what they told me, and because from what I could tell from the Bible as a little girl growing up, it seemed to not be very far off from the mystical fairy tales I loved. The Bible was full of stories, as far as my little mind could see.

Stories that are no different in fantasy content from Harry Potter, Game of Thrones or the Last Airbender.

I would read the Bible and see magick. I didn't have the languaging for it at the time. My little self had yet to read magick book the first, and Harry Potter had not been dreamed of yet. What I knew intuitively is that the Bible was not what they were telling me it was, and that, to me, the Bible was for magick, replete with:

- Talking animals: of course animals can talk, Balaam's talking donkey is perfectly acceptable to a 3-year-old, not to mention the most infamous talking animal of all time, the serpent in the garden. (Numbers chapters 22-24 and Genesis chapter 3.)
- A man who could survive 3 days in the belly of a whale deep in the ocean. (The book of Jonah.)
- A raging sea that is only calmed after being fed a disobedient prophet. (More from the book of Jonah.)
- 4 men who could walk in flames and not be so much as scorched or singed. (Daniel chapter 3.)
- Angels and demons. Throughout the Bible.
- Angels killing people. (2 Kings 19:35)
- A man who did not die but ascended into heaven on a flaming chariot led by flaming horses who suddenly appear and disappear. (2 Kings chapter 2)
- A dead man who came back to life after his body comes into contact with the bones of a dead prophet. (2 Kings 13:20-21)
- Zombies: raising a vast undead army from a valley of dry bones. (Ezekiel chapter 37)
- Blind people being healed and others who are temporarily blinded. (Gospels and Acts chapter 9)
- A prayer and praise induced earthquake that freed God's people from prison and turned more into believers. (Acts chapter 16)
- A man who saw a vision, wrote it out and it became the book of Revelation. (The book of Revelation... if that's not magick, I don't know what is, or maybe it's a shrooms trip, or many shrooms trips.)
- Necromancy (Matthew chapter 17 and 1 Samuel chapter 18)
- People controlling the weather, wind and water with great staffs, cloaks and/or words of power. (Exodus chapter 14; 2 Kings 2:8; Mark chapter 4)
- People who were instantaneously transported by angels. (Daniel

chapter 14 in the Revised Standard Version Catholic Edition. You can also read this account in the Apocrypha in the book titled *Daniel, Bel and the Snake.*)

- A man who could sit amongst wild lions and not be eaten. (The book of Daniel.)
- People walking on water. (Matthew chapter 14)
- A demon who kills 6 husbands of a virgin. (The book of Tobit)
- Women who became impregnated without a male father, or who were barren and suddenly became pregnant. (Genesis 21; 1 Samuel chapter 1; Matthew chapter 1; Luke chapter 1)

If you were born and bred or reared on the Bible, you know all these stories (and far more than these) well. We read them over and over.

Now, let's say someone gave you a book chock full of these stories, but didn't tell you it was a Bible or a holy book.

What would you think?

Any rational person reading this book, without knowing it was a Bible, would likely come to the conclusion that:

- This is an epic fantasy.
- This is a book of outlandish stories that couldn't possibly be true.
- This is a book of allegories, metaphors, myths and legends that point us to deeper meanings, much like Greek Mythology (those gods were always up to something, weren't they?).

No one reading such a book would take it literally anymore than we take the Chronicles of Narnia or the Lord of the Rings literally. We understand perfectly well that these fantastic stories are allegories.

Yet we've been told to take the Bible literally, down to the last iota. We've been instructed that the Bible is the infallible word of God, though there's damning archeological evidence proving that this is simply not so.

I do not make these statements to in any way demean the Bible, nor do I seek to reduce it to being a novel.

To the contrary, the Bible has always been for me one of the biggest books of magick and mysticism in the world. I love it. I'm intrigued by it. Enamored of it. The beauty is, no one can crack the code of the Bible and all it means. There's no way I would pass the Bible up because I'm a Witch. It's precisely why I haven't passed it up… ***because I'm a Witch.***

Naysayers

Because this is a work of Christian Witchcraft, and we discuss and use the Bible, I acknowledge that there will be naysayers. I now respectfully address those who say:

- The Bible is the irrefutable word of God. Period.
- The Bible does not include the Apocrypha and the Pseudepigrapha. It's 66 books only. The rest are spurious.
- The Bible is too lofty for human understanding.

I completely understand this point of view, because a long ways back, I held this identical point of view for one reason and one reason only: it was what I was conditioned to think and believe.

I have since gone beyond the teachings of my childhood, as I pray we all do. I have dared to venture far beyond what I thought previously, thank God. I have ceaselessly studied, investigated, grappled with, questioned, interrogated and examined all the matters I speak of here.

This is my life's work.

With that said, I can conclusively state that there is ALWAYS far more than we've been exposed to or come to believe. In these matters, I have found that putting the truth out there for examination will be met with those who are attached to what they want to believe, more than they are committed to discovering the truth.

Regardless of what I believe, **TRUTH IS TRUTH**. My beliefs don't change **TRUTH**. The best thing I can do with myself is uncover the **TRUTH** and **ALIGN WITH IT**.

How Does One Come to Truth?

Excellent question, and one we must answer on the spiritual path.

There are many camps when it comes to truth and what it is. Some say there is no effable truth. Others say the Bible is the only truth. Others say science is truth.

They may all be right, and, as always, there's more.

I love the story of 5 blind men standing around an elephant. Because each blind man was in contact with a different part of the elephant's anatomy, when asked what an elephant is, the answers varied wildly:

The blind man who was touching the elephant's tail said "I know what an elephant is, it's like a whisk broom."

The blind man who was on his knees with his arms around the elephant's leg said "No, no, an elephant is just like a tree trunk."

The blind man who was softly holding one of the elephant's ears in between his two palms said "No, you all are wrong, an elephant is just like a fan."

The blind man who was running his hands over the smooth tusk said "Absolutely not, an elephant is just like a horn of plenty."

The blind man standing at the side of the elephant running his hands across its enormous body exclaimed "Are you all fools!? An elephant is a great leather wall."

We understand the allegory.

No one has the corner on God, or the Bible, or spirituality.

Yet many people have their piece of it in hand and are willing to fight and kill anyone who doesn't believe an elephant is a tree trunk.

This must end.

Since none of us may have the whole irrefutable truth, why not agree to:

- Respect others and what they believe as you believe whatever you choose to believe. You can do whatever you like with your mind. So can everyone else.
- Listen to others and learn. If we find ourselves in a space where there

are others who believe differently, why not take the opportunity to learn?

- Be open and exploratory rather than rigid and a know-it-all. This is an approach to life that is inquisitive and discovery based, rather than approaching life as if we know everything… we do not (and life will surely check us on this one, over and over again if it must, until we get the point).
- Be kind. There's no law against being kind to people who see things differently.
- Be peaceful. Make peace, not war, especially when it comes to spirituality.

Will this book give you the irrefutable truth? I don't know. That's my most honest answer. It may be true for you, and it may not. Either way, I'm thankful you're here.

Ultimately, how do we come to the truth?

- We must be willing to suspend what we BELIEVE.
- We must be deep in prayer, meditation and spiritual practices to intuit truth. (More on this in coming chapters.)
- We must be willing to give up everything we think we know so we can be stretched in new, different and sometimes strange directions. Who's effecting this expansion in our consciousness? **SOURCE**.
- Truth has a ring to it. An open heart can intuit that clarion call.

I don't know what's true for everyone, or if there's an ineffable truth and if there is, that it can be known.

Thankfully, we don't need to know it all. There's a saying that serves us well:

I don't have to know. I know the Knower.

Having decoded the ultimate truths of the entire universe is not a requirement for practicing magick or for living a magickal life. That's what this book is about: moving forward with what you know now, giving it your all, and trusting that the 'next' will be given you at the perfect divine time. This is one of the principles upon which I rest my entire life. It has never failed me.

Growing Up

Growing up doesn't mean getting rid of magick, though I'm sure you've given up belief in the Easter Bunny, Santa Claus and countless other characters. You didn't give up belief in them because you didn't like them.

We loved those characters. We gave up belief in them because we grew into a greater understanding of the world and our place in it.

As Witches, we didn't give up the magick of our childhood. Magick is real. We gave up our beliefs about magick and how it works. We were operating on elementary levels of consciousness, and have, prayerfully, integrated the Inner Child in our continual expansion and ascension.

Conversely, the grown ups who dispensed with the magick of their childhood have a propensity to be jaded, stuck, stagnant or live the lackluster existence of a life without awe, wonder and imagination.

Dorothy at one time believed in a wizard that could grant her the ability to go home. She wasn't wrong, she just didn't have the complete picture. The wizard didn't have the power to send her home, only she could do that for herself. The wizard, beng fake ass, helped her come home to the truth that she was her own Magick Maker. She's supreme in her world. We know how the story ends. A Witch had to help her out.

As magickal beings, we knew better than to give up magick itself. We came into a greater understanding of the energies **POWERING** magick, and what these represented. Once we were opened to the greater mysteries, we could embrace the invisible behind the scenes effecters of the magick we were witnessing in childhood.

The magick didn't go away. This universe is full of magick. Magick is in everyone, all the time, as well as being all around us. It's an energy in the universe just like countless other energies in the universe, including those science has yet to discover.

Disclaimers

This book speaks of consciousness shifting substances and practices, hence these disclaimers:

- **There's no medical advice here.** Nothing in this book is intended to replace the care and/or guidance of your chosen health care professional. Nothing here is intended to diagnose, treat, cure or heal any medical condition.
- **There's no advice here.** This is not a book of advice. This is a book of my own experiences, and those of others. It's a book of inspiration, ideas, practices and helpful steps, should you choose to utilize them. Your Inner Knowing from Source is the final arbiter of what's good and right for you.
- **Keep yourself safe at all times.** Do not embark on any process, protocol or ritual in this book unless you have created around yourself a safe space in which to do so. Do not practice magick with people you do not thoroughly trust.
- **Magick doesn't 'fix' things.** Don't look to magick to correct things that are to be corrected by other means, such as changing thought patterns, clearing emotional toxicity and/or changing one's habits. These are to be addressed anyway, whether we practice magick or not.

- **No guarantee on spells.** The spells may or may not work for you, for an untold number of reasons. You must do the experiential work of deciding what works for you, and become the alchemist of your own soul and world.
- **No shortcuts.** There are none to mastery. Being a **MASTER ALCHEMIST** is **ALWAYS** going to mean taking the proverbial **HIGH ROAD**, which is longer and more arduous. Not many people are on this road of mastery, so it's never crowded. You may wonder why one would purposely choose a longer, more challenging, lonelier path. Because the results are literally **OUT OF THIS WORLD**.

II

YOU

There is no greater effect on your Spellcrafting, spell casting, magickal results and entire life experience than YOU.

Who Are You?

We would do well to answer this question, for maximum success in magick. ALL of who you ARE is crafting every spell. ALL of who you ARE is bringing forth the results of your magick. We cannot escape the largest, most potent aspect of your magick: **YOU**.

Two people can perform the exact same spell or ritual and receive radically different results. Why? Because of the "YOU" factor.

You can't turn off who you ARE. Who you are is being poured into every spell, or at the very least, seeping in.

If this be true, it would be wise to BE the VERY BEST version of self, which will naturally lead to better and better magick. Not only will this approach lead to better and better magick, it will lead to better and better EVERYTHING... health, wealth, relationships and blissful attainment of destiny.

There's a master level distinction we must highlight here.

BEING the best version of self does not mean striving to be something, or seeking to continually make yourself better, or always improving self, or getting better and better.

NONE of that is BEING.

BE YOUR BEST SELF RIGHT NOW. This is the invitation.

There's nowhere to get to that will be better than where you are now.

Give up striving.

Give up constant improving.

BE.

BE is not DO. DO is inherent in the egoic, surface mind. It seeks to get us to be busy, to always keep 'doing' something. Why? Because DOING gets in the way of BEING.

Don't be busy trying to be your best self. **SIMPLY BE YOUR BEST SELF NOW**.

How?

By realizing your **INHERENT PERFECTION RIGHT NOW**.

There's nothing wrong with you. There's only something attempting to hide the perfection that is you. Remove the veil, and voila! You're perfect RIGHT NOW, you just may not be able to see it.

This stops striving. This stops all self-development. This ends all self-improvement. In essence, you couldn't improve your real self if you tried. You're already perfect. What's better than perfection?

The reason we think we need to improve ourselves is because we are looking at ourselves amiss, not unlike the bulimic person who sees a fat person in the mirror. In reality, the person's ribs are protruding because the person is so skinny, yet the person's mind will not allow them to see reality.

All of us have this strange 'seeing' which is actually a faulty perception of self:

- We see guilt in self when all that exists is **HOLINESS**.
- We see shame in self when all that exists is **INNOCENCE**.
- We see unworthiness in self when all that exists is **PRICELESSNESS**.
- We see not enough in self when all that exists is **ABUNDANCE**.
- We see stupidity in self when all that exists is **INTELLIGENCE**.
- We see weakness in self when all that exists is **POWER**.
- We see faults in self when all that exists is **PERFECTION**.

I could go on and on. The message is clear: we have distorted perceptions of reality, especially when it comes to self.

If we do not sort these matters out, the magick suffers.

These distorted perceptions are described in *A Course In Miracles* (ACIM) quite clearly, as well as the very clear solution. The solution is **FORGIVENESS**. Forgive ALL. To FORGIVE is to GIVE FOR. GIVE up faulty perceptions FOR right seeing.

It's giving up illusions for reality. ACIM teaches there are 2 worlds: the dream world, and the real world.

The dream world is the 3rd dimension, perceived through the portal formed by the 5 senses. This world is an illusion, a shadow, smoke in mirrors. The Toltec wisdom book *The Four Agreements* written by Don Miguel Ruiz refers to this world as the 'dream' that we're called to awaken from.

This is actually good news in magick. If you know that the world about you, perceivable through the lens of the 5 senses, is not the real world and exists as a sort of shadow world, it's easier to change it. This world is a movie, being projected from consciousness. The movie is what you see before you in your world. You can change it at any time by means of magick. The projector, your consciousness, is behind you in the movie theater. One knows full well that to change a movie in a theater would not mean attacking the screen. Changing the movie being projected onto the screen would require going to the point of projection and changing it.

The movie is the 3rd dimension you desire to change with magick.

The projector is your consciousness.

This is why magick, in the way I engage and teach it, is alchemy of the soul. It's me changing me. It's me aligning with the cosmos using nature as a helper. In the system of magick I teach, it does not benefit anyone to attempt to change the screen. It is pointless and time and energy wasting. It is attention misdirected. This is a travesty, considering how powerful we are, and how much we could really change the WORLD if we were crafting and casting spells in harmony with the laws of nature.

This system of magick requires self-examination, first and foremost. Next, correction of faulty perceptions is essential.

If you're not willing to FIRST examine self to become self-aware, to live as if **KNOW THYSELF** were your sacred charge at all times, and to correct faulty belief systems, errant perceptions and old systems of thinking, this magick is not for you. Alchemy is not for you. Becoming a master is not for you.

We don't get what we want. We get what we **ARE**.

The fact that we're receiving WHO WE ARE — and not WHAT WE WANT or WHAT WE SPELL FOR — is all unfolding by the laws of the universe, such as:

- The Law of Mentalism: ALL IS MIND.
- The Law of Attraction: LIKE ATTRACTS LIKE.

Though there's a richer, more in depth discussion of universal law in a later chapter, let's address these 2 foundational principles now as it relates to you and magick.

The universe is one great big Mind. Your mind is in this cosmic Mind and is continually interacting with it in an energetic flow that cannot be turned off. ***A Course In Miracles*** states that there are no private thoughts. This is because every thought we have, conscious and unconscious, is being broadcast throughout the cosmic Mind. Thoughts are energetic and carry frequencies. A FREQUENCY holds INFORMATION, like a radio wave carrying the information of a particular show, which can be picked up by a receiver.

Thoughts are also ELECTROMAGNETIC. There is a MAGNETISM to every thought. These magnet thoughts we're having are bringing before us the precise people, situations and circumstances that **MATCH** the **FREQUENCY** or the information encoded in the signal we put out. (For now, we'll leave children out of this discussion, as I often hear the question 'well, what about innocent children?' I don't know. What I do know is that not having the answer to that part of the puzzle doesn't preclude me from working with the law and coming to conclusions in my own life, so that's what I choose to do. It works.)

I apply these ideas to magick. Let's integrate these so we have a practical working system.

If the entire universe is MENTAL, and my mind is continually communicating with the cosmic Mind, and the signals I'm sending out are full of information that are finding their match and returning the same to me as my life experience, I can change what I receive by changing the signal I send out. (Though there are multiple dimensions to this process, and other factors, such as soul path, karma and destiny, we'll proceed with what we've stated thus far.)

In other words, everything I see begins and ends with me. This is the approach I take, since it is the stance of ultimate power. While I'm not the Ultimate Power in the universe, I do have ultimate power over **WHAT I CHOOSE TO PUT OUT AS AN ENERGY SIGNAL.**

This all seems to make perfect sense, yet the opposite runs rampant in magickal communities. Here are violations of the 2 simple laws we've highlighted:

Hexes

Who am I hexing? If I'm sending out an intention to harm another, according to law, I'm sending out a signal that will find its match and return to me. In Wicca this is referred to as the 3-fold Law of Return, which states that whatever bad you send out returns to you 3-fold. I completely understand this law. Yet, I've also seen posts all over social media that say something to this effect: "I don't live by the 3-fold rule. You send something bad to me, and I'll return it to you." If we knew and lived the laws of the universe, we would know that there's no such thing as sending anything to anyone else while totally escaping its effects on self. In this faulty mindset, the murderer can only see that he ended an enemy. He does not see the black mark he's placed on his own soul.

Revenge Spells

I'm not concerned with what other people do.

Here is a **TRUTH**: Other people have ZERO creative ability in your life. PERIOD. Source did not create you to be subject the whims of others.

Each person is created **WHOLE** and is the **SELF-INITIATOR** of their reality through the all-important power of **CHOICE**.

No one can do anything to you. The opposite would appear to be the case in the movie, yet it cannot happen in ultimate reality. In ultimate reality, you are the director, screenwriter, producer, executive producer, and star of the movie that is your life.

Yes, we can think others are out to get us. Is this the path of power? Is this kind of thinking forwarding our magick or is it a weakening influence?

For me, these are just 2 examples of mis-directed magick. You may differ in your approach. The beauty of magick is that there's room for everyone. You get to choose what you'll do, and what kind of magick you'll engage. I'm sharing with you my take on it. Use what works for you and leave the rest.

Know Thyself

To conclude this chapter, the power of self-introspection, self-awareness and self-gnosis as a Witch cannot be overstated. It'll be emphasized throughout this book, perhaps more than in any other book I've written on Christian Witchcraft. Why? Because we're talking Spellcrafting here. We're talking creating rituals from the core of your soul. We're talking going into the cauldron of your heart to pull forward the righteous magick that's lived there since before the beginning of time.

In the Christian Witches Mystery School, the first lesson is **KNOW THYSELF**. In the ancient temple at Delphi where seekers lined up to see the oracle, there was a sign that hung over the entrance: **KNOW THYSELF**. Before consulting any oracle, our charge is to know and understand self.

This includes knowing one's:

- Habits (good and not so good)
- Conditioned thoughts
- Habitual, patterned, robotic responses (versus BE HERE NOW)
- Toxicities (emotional, mental and relational)
- Emotional triggers
- Gifts and strengths
- Talents and skills
- Weaknesses and blind spots
- Desires with clarity
- Destiny and purpose and how to fulfill it
- And a whole lot more than I can add to this list.

The Wheel of Destiny Inventory in a coming chapter presents an opportunity to score all aspects of your current life experience, for better or for worse. It's a tool for awareness. We can't transform anything we're unaware of. We can't improve anything we don't measure. This is an assessment for magickal beings.

The Ritual of Light and Shadow is another tool presented later in this book, for the express purpose of fulfilling the magickal maxim to **KNOW THYSELF**.

I pray you engage these tools regularly and with earnest to take your magick to the stratosphere as the Master Alchemist you were born to be.

2 Selves

There are 2 selves, figuratively, inside each of us.

One self is the ego self, the false self, the self that knows only the input from the 5 senses. While this self is not bad, it's simply not true. It's now who we really are. The ego has built up a personality over time that is a false front, a covering over the majesty of the soul.

The ego's agenda is:

- Separation
- Littleness
- Lack
- Guilt

Feeding into the ego's agenda will always result in emptiness. The ego does not know enough to grant us fulfillment, or even so much as lead us to the place where fulfillment abides. This is because the ego is always looking outside of self, and all the deliciousness is found **WITHIN SELF**.

The **TRUE SELF** is Source. Ye are gods. Source expresses individually as souls. Souls inhabit bodies for evolution, or soul ascension.

The TRUE SELF doesn't have an agenda; It's simply pure love energy. Aligning with the TRUE SELF is what I believe Aleister Crowley referred to as the WILL. There's a place inside where the TRUE SELF's Will dwells. We are doing magick from this space of power within.

What is Will? Imperative. It's the dynamic force and power of the soul, the engine of destiny. It's the drive we have inside to do great things… like write poetry, design a clothing line, compose a sonata, paint, dance, sing, create an app that changes humanity, or any and all manner of divine impetus we sense pulsing within.

Something inside of us wants to leap out. Let it.

This is soul work. If the soul stays in the driver's seat, we know we are living from the TRUE SELF. If the egoic personality is in the driver's seat, we are living a fake existence.

Who's Doing the Magick?

I find it fascinating that the more uncomfortable the human is, the more the soul is ascending. Hence, the possibility of a conundrum.

Do I satisfy all the creature comforts of the human self, backed by the ego and its endless needs from a space of emptiness and lack?

Or, do I do the soul work of ascension and focus my magick on matters of destiny?

Both can be accomplished, yet self-awareness and truth must be present for it to succeed.

There's some magick I do for no other purpose than to make my life better.

The soul doesn't care about how big your mansion is, nor does it care whether you drive a hooptie or a Benz. The egoic personality cares about these things. I'm okay with that, as long as I KNOW MYSELF and am operating in TRUTH.

There's no problem with doing magick to satisfy the wants of the human.

The problem arises when self-awareness and truth are absent.

The human me may want a big beautiful home, yet the soul may know that if I had this, I would be distracted from the creative work I'm engaged in and love because I'd have to take care of a big mansion and all that goes along with it. The soul as the TRUE SELF knows taking care of a mansion is not in my best interests.

This was my exact situation, more than once. I lived in big beautiful homes, because I love big beautiful homes. Let's face it, they're eye candy. Then, I'd get into the big beautiful home, and I'd have to furnish the big beautiful home, maintain the lawns of the big beautiful home, take care of the swimming pool of the big beautiful home, and on and on.

Call me a slow learner, but I did this 3 times and it never worked.

I'm like you, a great manifestor.

I put my mind to it, back it up with magick, and go to work by taking the action steps required. If more money is required, I acquire more clients or grow the income in creative ways.

Then, I get what I wanted. But did I really want it?

Who wanted it?

Each time, some aspect of the human self wanted it, which would not have been a problem, had it not been antithetical to the impetus of the soul and the creative work I'm engaged in on a daily basis.

As I write this, I'm a nomad, with few possessions, and have never been happier, freer or lighter. My kids are grown and I literally live anywhere I'm inspired to be. When I got rid of my latest mansion (5 bedrooms, 4 baths, 3 car garage and swimming pool) and 80% of the stuff in it (gave it away or sold it), I remember crying at the storage shed where the few things I desired to keep currently live. I had never felt freer. Tears streamed down my face as the realization dropped into my spirit that there was no place I had to be. I was totally and completely free!

All I can say is this: be careful what you spell for.

You will likely get it.

But then the question will be: is this what the real me really wanted?

Always on the Path

What I love about soul destiny is that we're always on the path. We can't not be on the path, even when it looks like we're as far from destiny as it's possible to be.

EVERY STEP is a destiny step.

So me magicking and manifesting the mansions was part of it. I received loads of valuable wisdom that I get to keep. I might add that it's not a shabby way to learn. Being in a mansion is nice. I just realized that it wasn't necessary, and it was actually a distraction that seemed to get in the way of the creative work my soul desired to be immersed in every day: writing.

So even when it seems as if we're off the path, we never are. The cosmic GPS can re-route us from where ever we are. In addition, this beautiful universe uses EVERY BIT of our learning for good. Nothing is wasted.

My mansion manifesting powers are currently focused on creating a retreat center, a call of my soul.

Even with our seeming detours, there's no judgment. The soul isn't judging the human.

So relax. Let yourself play. You can't get it wrong because there is no wrong.

Divination

Hence the role of divination. Divination is communing with the Divine, and receiving the answers from Source (the TRUE SELF). Divination reveals motives and the hidden drivers behind any particular desire.

We have desires. We want what we want. AND... we want what we want for a REASON. Best get it touch with that reason before the reason is returned to you in the form of the results of the spell.

This is intention. Intention is a boomerang, as are thoughts.

I'd like to know, as best I can, what I'm throwing out, because it will return. This is law. I can't plant acorns and expect or receive string beans. The seed has information packed inside.

INTENTION HAS INFORMATION PACKED INSIDE. If you are the one crafting and creating the spell, it's your job to know your true intentions and motives, including the hidden unconscious drivers of our actions.

This is how to be a Master Alchemist.

Your Ashe

You have a sacred magick all your own, which forms your magickal fingerprint. No one else can perform the magick you can, although they may do the exact same spell.

Ashe (also spelled ase) means sacred energy, the energy which underlies the whole universe. It is a word originating from my ancient African ancestors, who migrated from Kemet (Egypt) westward and carried sacred wisdom with them. It is the power of the cosmos. It is the creative energy of all that is manifest and unmanifest.

The word ashe can be used in many ways. A spiritual community I belong to is a beautiful home to Yoruba Priests and Priestesses, from which I've learned much by simply listening, observing and attending a bembe (sacred ritual). One of the things I hear often is the word ashe. It can be used in different contexts:

- Ashe - said after a prayer to confirm agreement and completion of the spoken word, much like the word Amen, from ancient Kemet (Egypt).
- Ashe - said when someone in the community says something powerful and we agree.
- She has ashe in her voice - said when someone is speaking and the speaker's words originate from and are backed by the power of the Divine.

- Ashe - the power of the Divine coursing through an individualized expression of Source, also known as a soul, and making its presence known through a person.

I'm sure there are many more ways this broad term could be used. I equate Ashe to:

- Chi - the vitalizing life force energy that flows throughout the cosmos, including everyone and everything. Chi can be balanced or harmonized within one's self, home and/or office and other spaces by utilizing the principles of Feng Shui. To me, chi is another way of saying ashe.
- Prana - a term from India denoting the substantative life force moving through all and infusing all with life. Pranic healing is facilitated by healers who are deeply and profoundly in touch with this energy.
- Ruach - literally means spirit, breath or wind and is considered the spirit or breath of God in a religious context. Ruach is a Hebrew word with a Greek equivalent: *pneuma*. In the New Testament, pneuma is the Holy Spirit.

Without going too deep into these terms, we'll stay on topic by understanding their relationship to ashe: all are varying terms for the universal energy creating all, sustaining all and generally powering the entire cosmos. While the energy is undifferentiated, it also courses through everything created, sustaining all life.

Your Magickal Superpower

Why are we speaking of ashe here? We will refer to ashe, in this context, as your magickal superpower, the unique sacred energy emanating from your soul.

Every Witch, Wizard, Warlock and Magickal Being has a unique way of doing magick. No two are the same, even within the exact same magickal system. There are no 2 Yoruba Priestesses alike, just as there are no 2 Hoodoo Rootworkers alike.

The same holds true in Christianity. There are no 2 Catholics alike.

And it goes without saying, there are no 2 Christian Witches alike.

While each of the foregoing traditions have rites, rituals and protocols, the actual souls engaging those rites, rituals and protocols are each unique expressions of Source. Therefore, we can surmise that the outcome for each may be slightly or even vastly different.

It's your job to get in touch with your ashe: the sacred cosmic energy coursing through you as an individual. It's almost as if the cosmic energy is dough (undifferentiated) and each soul is a cookie cutter shape. We are shaping and molding the energy of the cosmos with the entirety of our consciousness.

Because the purpose and intention of this book is to become a Master Alchemist, an imperative arises: get in touch with your soul and its unique brand of magick (which may be very different from the magick you've been practicing… or not).

For me, magick from the soul forms the magickal superpower. Each of us can get in touch with our magickal superpower (ashe) through introspective spiritual practices (meditation, stillness, chanting, yoga, prayer, etc.) and by practicing magick.

You're Superhuman

An example comes to mind. My magickal superpower is being able to easily communicate with higher order spirits (angels, archangels, ascended masters, enlightened ancestors). It's almost as if these beings are speaking with me in normal conversations, without casting circle the first. While I LOVE reading the old grimoires about Solomonic magick and find ceremonial magick intriguing as can be, my magickal ashe (or superpower) is being able to speak with entities like I speak with humans.

We all have superhuman abilities. We all have gifts deposited in the soul before we took human form. It's time to go within the soul and bring those gifts OUT!

If there's a desire and decision to take these inherent magickal gifts of the soul to superpower levels, we must develop these gifts by practice and mastery.

WE GET TO DO THE WORK.

Nothing comes from nothing. Do nothing, and our inherent soul gifts do not flourish. Nurture the gifts and watch the magick happen!

Your ashe is your unique magickal superpower. Engage it for this work and you will be astonished at the results.

Bio Hacking

*Note: my book **How to Be a Christian Witch** delves deeply into how to clear emotional toxicity with specific practices that will complement the work of this chapter very nicely. If you don't have it, it's well worth investing in. I make a point not to regurgitate what I've already written in one book in another, so that fresh content is always being presented, as best I can. There may be some overlap, which happens when it's necessary to state particular information for the purpose of the discussion at hand so you always have a complete work in your hands with the current book.*

This book on Spellcrafting would not be complete lest it contain a healthy discourse on your physical body as it relates to practicing magick.

Yes, I'm a bit of a bio-hacker, though I don't think a Witch has to be in order to practice great magick. There are Witches that never do any of this that can cast a spells and change the whole world. This is my process, that I'm choosing to share with you. I take a holistic approach to magick and life.

It may seem obvious that we'd want to be as healthy and as strong as possible, yet masters pay attention to and master ***subtleties***. We're going for **MASTERY**.

Our **DEVOTION** to optimal spiritual, emotional, mental and physical health cannot be overstated.

Some rituals require endurance: standing for long periods in a magick circle, or challenging breath work during extended chanting sessions, or imbibing plant medicines and being able to withstand the physical effects.

The bottom line is: **MAGICK WILL CHALLENGE YOU ON EVERY LEVEL.**

Your body must be up to snuff. We're not talking about being an Olympic athlete here. We're addressing the **MINDSET** that is a **TOTAL COMMITMENT** to being **YOUR BEST SELF**, including **YOUR BODY.**

Non-negotiable Health, Wellness & Vitality

Be non-negotiable about your health. It will not only serve your magick, it will serve all the people who love and adore you, and it will serve your entire life existence on planet earth. It's not easy to live your destiny from a hospital bed. Nor is it ideal. We can prevent many problematic issues in the body temple with a few core commitments firmly in place:

1. **CONSCIOUSNESS OF HEALTH** - remember our first law of the universe: **ALL IS MIND**. Without a firm, undeniable, unshakable **HEALTH CONSCIOUSNESS**, maintaining health in the body temple will be impossible. (More on how to do this below.)
2. **MASTER YOUR BREATH** - I put breathing before food and water since you can go a number of days without the later 2 and only a few minutes without the first. BREATH is our lifeline to Source. BREATH is life force. BREATH is magick. BREATHE WELL. (More on how to do that is below as well.)
3. **HEALTHFUL DIET/FASTING** - as of the writing of this book, there are 4 dis-ease states that have taken hold in humanity on an unprecedented level. I call them the 4 Horsemen of the Apocalypse: heart dis-ease, cancer, stroke (due to hypertension) and diabetes. The very gladdening news about all these is that they can be helped with diet. (More on diet below.) Disclaimer: this is not medical advice. See your health care practitioner.
4. **WATER** - lots and lots and lots of water cleans everything out and

aligns us with the planet, which is over 70% water.

5. **DECREASE/ELIMINATE TOXINS** - a host of dis-ease states are caused by inflammation, which is part of the body's immune response to toxins.
6. **MOVEMENT** - I deign to use the word exercise. For one, I don't like the word, much less actually doing it. MOVEMENT however, agrees with me (I realize this may just be semantics, but work with me as I work with my subconscious mind lol). (More below on how to integrate movement into your daily round.)
7. **SLEEP** - good sleep is not an option. It's a MUST for optimal health and optimal spiritual practice.

Because of my holistic approach to health, and the powerful health practices I've baked in to my daily rituals, I've been able to release over 70 pounds of fat (I ballooned to over 200 pounds after giving birth to my 3rd child). I feel strong, powerful, energetic and healthy. Next year, I'll be celebrating the 24th anniversary of my 36th birthday (do the math) with no dis-ease states and no medications of any kind. I FEEL AMAZING. I pray to look amazing as well.

An amazing body and mind can do amazing magick.

Back Door Subconscious Hack: Bake It In

If you're saying to yourself, 'Val, this is all fine and good but, I have kids and life. How am I supposed to change everything around to do everything in this book?' there's an answer.

If you're already doing everything in this book and your magick is smoking like gangbusters, AWESOME!

Here's how I do it. Prayerfully it may help.

BAKE IT IN.

BAKE IT IN means making it part and parcel of what you do ANYWAY, without adding yet another item to an already full day.

An example is my yoga practice. While I immensely enjoyed going to the yoga studio, it just wasn't practical for me to go as often as required to maintain the kind of yoga practice I desired to maintain, and to get the RESULTS I was after: an amazing, flexible, lean, strong, healthy, powerful body (add in a few muscles too), considering it took an extra 3 hours to travel to the hot yoga studio, undress and dress, shower and practice.

At one point, my business office was only a few blocks from an amazing hot yoga studio. After leaving my business for the day, I would walk to the yoga studio for a 90 minute class that started at 6 PM. After completion of class at 7:30 PM, lying in dead corpse pose after class for a few minutes was the norm. Then a shower and Uber home. This entire circuit took about 3 hours.

Not everyone has the time to do this. The good news: it's not required.

You have your body with you at all times. No yoga studio required. I'm not saying to swear off yoga studios, because I certainly am not. I love a good yoga studio.

What I practice and am proposing for your consideration: if you bake in yoga poses throughout your day, you could get pretty much the same results. Then maybe you go to the yoga studio on the weekend, or twice a month, or whenever you desire to be around like-minded beings who are contorting themselves into pretzels for the greater good.

Example: while I'm in the shower, I have to wash my feet anyway. I'm already standing. Why not do tree pose to wash my feet? When brushing my teeth, why not do balancing stick or some other standing pose? I'm standing there anyway. While putting on underwear, why not do standing head to knee. My knees are there anyway. I may as well put them to good use.

The point is: we have a million opportunities throughout the day to **BAKE IN** healthy habits.

It was easier for me to get way more done when I didn't try to force myself to add yet one more thing to an already full day, or try to significantly change my habits.

Habits are difficult to change, so getting yourself to do something else — especially if that something else is going to the gym every day — will be an uphill climb, demonstrated by the huge rise in gym memberships in January and the empty gyms by March. Everyone who's sane wants to have healthy habits. We just don't always stick with the new healthy habit we've declared (at least I've been challenged with this, you may be an ace).

To help myself along, I BAKE IN the new habit with something I'M ALREADY DOING. This is a back-door subconscious hack that works wonders. The beauty of this method is that it makes us more mindful throughout the day of what we're doing for health. For instance, if I just did yoga poses in the bathroom, I'm less likely to slouch in my seat as I write this book. It's a total win-win all the way around!

Don't take my word for it. Bake in a few yoga poses, or dance moves or stretches with everything you do getting ready in the morning every day and see what happens in 30 days. You may amaze yourself with how much you can transform without adding anything additional to your schedule or existing commitments.

Health Consciousness

What is health consciousness? Health consciousness goes far beyond thinking healthy thoughts.

As we now know from many sources, including science and especially the work of Dr. Joe Dispenza (whom I adore and have experienced untold revelations from), every thought is energetic, and is on a frequency. As we've discussed, frequency carries information.

Add to this the third law of the universe as handed down to us from ancient Kemet (Egypt) all is in **VIBRATION**. The whole universe, including you, is continually **VIBRATING**. We're all VIBRATING at a particular frequency, or within a range of frequencies. The lowest vibrations are fear, worry, doubt and the like, while the highest vibration states are love, enthusiasm, bliss, beauty, fulfillment and the like.

When we speak of love here, we are not speaking of an emotion. Love is a state of being and is the creative energy of the cosmos. This energy fuels all, heals all, and if need be, kills what no longer serves the whole. God is love. Therefore, being love is being God.

Let's go deeper within the body.

In addition to the foregoing, every thought can set off a chemical reaction in the body. Thoughts of fear, lack and limitation set off certain chemical reactions, while thoughts of abundance, beauty, joy and an overall peaceful mind set off other chemical reactions.

Your body is a chemical factory capable of creating thousands of chemicals. These chemicals affect mood and all manner of bodily functions.

It goes without saying that an overall peaceful mind will produce a much healthier body. This doesn't meant that if we have disruptive thoughts thrown in here and there that these alone will cause disruption in the body temple. It also doesn't mean that if we have a peaceful mind we'll never get ill.

What we can count on is the Law of Cause and Effect: cause is always in consciousness (the unseen) while effects appear in the 3rd dimensional plane (the seen). What goes on consistently and persistently in our consciousness is what will outpicture — in one form or another — in the world of effects with regard to our body and everything else.

We are seeing the effects RIGHT NOW in the body temple of our past PERSISTENT PATTERN OF THOUGHTS, BELIEFS (thought + emotion, the power house combination) and ATTITUDES about health, or lack thereof.

The good news is: WE CAN CHANGE OUR PERSISTENT PATTERN OF THOUGHTS, BELIEFS and ATTITUDES AT ANY TIME.

It's a choice.

When we make a new choice, we have new outcomes. I proved it to myself with regard to my body. I've suffered in the past from all manner of ailments that were cleared up, not with medication or visits to doctors, but through my own **DECISION** to change how I was thinking and feeling on a CONSISTENT BASIS. This was a decision to heal my mind, first and foremost. Healing in the body temple happened to follow.

One thought of dis-ease will not make one unhealthy.

A PERSISTENT PATTERN OF UNHEALTHY THOUGHTS, FEEL-

INGS and BELIEFS will absolutely culminate in unwanted conditions in the body temple.

YOU HAVE A CHOICE.

Here are a few of the fear thoughts I had to eradicate from my consciousness to experience greater and greater health:

- What if I get _______________ (fears I have around 'getting' something or 'catching' something). In reality, nothing can be 'got' or 'caught.' Let me restate that this book is for **MASTERY**. If you're seeking to become a MASTER, there's a state of being that goes with it. The state of being that informs the MASTER is: **IF IT IS TO BE, IT'S UP TO ME. MASTERS ARE 100% RESPONSIBLE.** Masters do not 'catch' things. Masters understand that if something shows up in the body temple, which it well could, it is the result of **CONSCIOUSNESS** and nothing else. With this truth, the MASTER is equipped to go into multiple dimensions of CONSCIOUSNESS to CORRECT the issue, or to at least know what the issue is about as one works through it. Be uncompromising with yourself on this one. Otherwise you're likely to give up too much of your power to the victim that can sulk about inside.
- Fears around an untoward diagnosis from a doctor. This could make one avoid going to a health care practitioner when it would be highly advisable, or could cause one to ignore the feedback from a health care professional.
- Avoidance. Aches, pains and symptoms in the body temple that are ignored due to fear that they may be pointing to something far worse.
- Fear of getting old. I'm maturing. This is natural. I'm either going to enjoy it or not. My not enjoying it is not making it not happen, so I choose to enjoy my **FLOWERING**.
- Fear that we already have some terrible something. This is the house that hypochondria built. It is the imagination gone wild in an inappropriate direction. Avoid it at all costs.

There are too many fears to list out here, so I'll stop the list here. These are a few of the fears I've encountered and refuse to let myself wallow in or consider without a **CORRECTION** in **CONSCIOUSNESS**.

Here are the correction thoughts to be meditated upon daily, all day, along with accompanying EMOTIONAL states:

- **I'M HEALTHY AND STRONG!**
- **LIFE LOVES ME!**
- **I LOVE MY BODY AND IT LOVES ME.**
- **I LOVE HOW STRONG I FEEL.**
- **I LOVE HOW FLEXIBLE MY BODY IS.**
- **WOW! MY BODY DOES AMAZING THINGS!**
- **I'M IN AWE OF HOW WELL MY BODY FUNCTIONS FOR ME EVERY MOMENT OF EVERY DAY.**
- **I FEEL HIGH ON LIFE!**
- **I FEEL AMAZING!**
- **I LOVE LIFE!**
- **I AM HAPPY TO BE ALIVE!**
- **I JUMP OUT OF BED!**
- **I LOVE WALKING OUTSIDE!**
- **I LOVE DEEP BREATHING! I DO IT ALL THE TIME!**
- **I LOVE HOW AMAZING IT FEELS TO WIGGLE MY TOES! MY TOES ARE A MIRACLE!**
- **WOW! YOGA LOVES ME! YOGA SUITS ME! MY BODY LOVES YOGA!**
- **I'M SO THANKFUL TO BE SO HEALTHY AND VIBRANT! IT'S AMAZING!**
- **I'M IN AWE OF HOW YOUNG I FEEL!**
- **WOW! SEX IS AMAZING!**
- **WOW! THIS FOOD IS AMAZING!**
- **WOW! THIS LIFE IS AMAZING!**

Energetically, this is about **LOVE, LOVE, LOVE, THANKFULNESS,**

APPRECIATION and **GRATITUDE**!

Whatever the wording you use, **CONVINCE YOURSELF YOU ARE THANKFUL TO BE AN INFINITE BEING WHO IS HEALTHY, HAPPY, POWERFUL, BEAUTIFUL/HANDSOME, FLEXIBLE, YOUTHFUL, STRONG, SEXY, AGILE, IN LOVE WITH LIFE AND FULL OF BOUNDLESS ENERGY**.

Make these (and every desirable state) your **PERSISTENT, CONSISTENT PATTERNS OF THINKING AND FEELING**. Your body will produce matching chemical compounds and **AMAZING RESULTS**.

Your body is a magnificent tail that's doing whatever the mind tells it to do.

DIRECT YOUR MIND APPROPRIATELY.

One more consideration to take your health consciousness to a whole new level: **THINK LESS THOUGHTS.**

No matter how positive you attempt to make your thinking, if you think a lot, you'll spiral downward. It's a given. MORE THOUGHTS = MORE PROPENSITY TOWARD NEGATIVITY.

The average person has 80,000 thoughts per day. Rather than making your major focus thinking great thoughts (which is a challenging yet worthy undertaking) simultaneously challenge yourself to **THINK LESS. HAVE LESS THOUGHTS**.

How?

Meditate.

How? BAKE IT IN.

The book that forever changed my consciousness with regard to thinking LESS is currently in the top 10-20 all-time fave spiritual tomes I've ever read. ***The Power of Now*** by Eckhart Tolle was the book that got me to **TRANSFORM** myself by thinking less.

How?

I took to heart the fact that we don't have to be thinking all the time. Eckhart Tolle teaches that there's a way out of the robotic habit of letting our minds use us.

The book was the push I required to **DO SOMETHING ABOUT MY**

MIND USING ME.

I began a simple practice of using a SUSPEND command. It looked like this:

I decided to stop my mind AT WILL throughout the day with one word: SUSPEND. After my SUSPEND command, I would be intentionally still in my mind with NO thoughts. It's like taking a mental deep breath. At first I could be thoughtless for 15 seconds before thoughts would rush back in. Then I practiced and was able to raise it to 30 seconds. I continued to practice and practice. Each time I was able to suspend my thoughts, even for a few seconds, I felt lighter, freer, more Divine.

I kept doing it until I could still my mind for longer and longer periods. I still practice today.

I no longer have to use the SUSPEND command to get my mind to stop.

I simply breathe and let all thoughts go.

This too is BAKED IN to how I operate during my day.

It works wonders.

The habit of thinking less will allow you to naturally be more healthy because your body doesn't have to respond to 80,000 thoughts in a day.

Master Your Breath

Whatever your breath is doing, your mind is also doing. Breath, mind and spirit are interwoven.

Breathe deeper and slower and you may notice your mind no longer racing.

I was a 'panter.' We can tell if we're panting or not by placing one hand over the belly and one hand over the upper chest. Breathe normally. Which hand is moving up and down? If the hand over the belly is moving up and down, you are breathing deeply. If the top of the chest hand is moving up and down, you're panting.

In my twenties when my life was a series of putting out one fire after another, racing from this thing to that, and generally melting down on all fronts, I was panting the whole time.

I didn't know I was panting. It was an unconscious habit. I looked for the solution and found it in books on spirituality that taught me the connection between breath work and peace.

Being the spiritual lab rat I am, I gave it a whirl and found yet another tool to consciousness mastery: **BREATH**.

The beauty of all these practices is that they're ACCESSIBLE.

Your breath is with you always, so just like your body, it's simple to change (not easy, yet simple).

The first step for me was to begin breathing deeper and slower as a habitual WAY OF BEING.

Yoga helped. As did **BEING PRESENT IN THE MOMENT** and not racing to the future (habitually working out in my mind what I had to do, when, how and with whom) and languishing in the past over events and actions I wish I'd done differently.

It's pointless to pour that much energy into things over which I did not have complete control. I had zero control of what 'might' happen and zero control of what already happened.

There are other things over which I have 100% sovereignty and dominion: **MY CONSCIOUSNESS AND WHAT I CHOOSE TO DO WITH IT IN ANY GIVEN MOMENT**.

The past and the future are inherent enemies of the NOW.

NOW is the magick.

NOW is where **ALL YOUR POWER** resides.

NOW is when you can take deep breaths.

NOW is when you make the decision to change.

NOW. NOW. NOW.

All the magick is in the **NOW**.

For me, there's few better ways to stay in the **PRESENT** other than **BREATHING DEEPLY INTO THIS DELICIOUS RIGHT NOW MOMENT**. YUMMEEE!

When you breathe deeply, you may notice physical changes. Here's what I notice about myself when I stick to conscious breathing:

- **I tingle**. This tingle signals a connection to Source and reminds me that the potent energies of the universe are flowing through me, including the power of magick.
- **I relax**. When is relaxation not a good thing? Even when I have something REALLY challenging to do, being relaxed (as opposed to wound up, tight, tense and constricted) is always a bonus.
- **My heart rate slows down**. My heart thanks me for every deep breath I take.
- **My blood pressure decreases**. That's super helpful.
- **Happy hormones are secreted**. More serotonin and the bliss hormone anandamide in the system is a beautiful thing!
- **Unhealthy hormones are decreased.** Less adrenaline and cortisol coursing through the bloodstream is also a beautiful thing. While these hormones are naturally created in the body and are helpful in certain instances, they are not to be present always. The persistent presence of hormones that are meant for emergency purposes only is antithetical to health. I ONLY want adrenaline to pump out when I need it and NOT coursing through my system all the time because of the way I conduct my life: as an ongoing emergency.
- **Clearer thinking**. I think better when I deep breathe and clear my mind of clutter.
- **Better decision making**. A cluttered mind is not the best decision-making mind. Deep breathing is a key to making more beneficial decisions.
- **Better skin/less wrinkles**. Stress is abated when I breathe deeply, which will release frown lines, a tight jaw and tension in the face, head, neck, shoulders and back.
- **Less stress**. The ability to not 'flip out' over seeming disasters. I'm much less prone to stress. This is due to a holistic approach to life and magick.
- **Expulsion of toxins**. I've heard that 80% of the toxins in our bodies are expelled through EXHALATION.
- **Happiness and spontaneous eruptions of joy and bliss!** Ok, who

doesn't want that?!?

- **Expanded abundance**. Deep breathing is EXPANSIVE breathing that opens up the mind and pathways to greater EXPANSION of GOOD. Abundance naturally assumes its rightful space of being EVERYWHERE present when we're no longer constricting or outright blocking it. Abundance is not going to kick your door down and demand presence in your life. The second we stop constricting it, abundance flows NATURALLY and is EVERYWHERE PRESENT ALL THE TIME.
- **Connection**. To everything.
- I **LOVE** more. I **APPRECIATE** the people and the beauty of my life more.

Deep breathing took me out of panting and out of emergency. Crisis modes of operation gave way to proactive presence.

Healthful Diet

Most, if not all, dis-ease states can be helped with a better intake of nutrient rich foods.

Unfortunately, the soil in the North American continent is depleted of naturally occurring nutrients and is largely no longer soil, but dirt.

With this knowing, we're armed to add nutrients to our diets in all manner of ways, so that we still give our bodies all the nutrients required to form the building blocks of health.

Your body is likely the most amazing magician you know, after all, it can turn a potato into a brain. The magick of how your body transforms and alchemicalizes your intake to give you a result is beyond miraculous.

Let's help the body along!

How?

Put the best nutrients in and leave the garbage out.

I had to make the commitment to eat nutrient dense foods (which never seemed to taste as good as empty calorie foods). I started eating for the bacteria in my gut rather than strictly for my tongue. Over time, the taste in my mouth changed to enjoy food that whole my body enjoys. One quick example: beets are actually delicious to me now, whereas before the change, I couldn't stand them.

Conversely, I had to make a decision to NOT eat what I knew was harmful to my body, including fast food. Sugar was a big issue for me as well. I had a sugar addiction like you wouldn't believe, with Oreo cookies hiding under my bed for late night snacks and Pepsi in the fridge at all times.

This changed for me over time. The results have been stellar. I released over 70 pounds and have never felt better. I transformed by making one simple change each year on January 1. This is what one permanent change in diet looked like year over year:

- One year I gave up pork.
- One year I gave up beef.
- One year I gave up white sugar.
- One year I gave up white bread.
- One year I gave up soda.
- One year I gave up chicken and turkey.
- One year I gave up Oreos (yes, this was big for me lol).

If I had told my body that all these changes were to be made at once, I would have had a full scale revolt on my hands. There was no way I was giving up everything at once. I can say, after 20 years of making these year over year changes, the effects are CUMULATIVE and AMAZING.

We don't have to suffer and it doesn't have to be hard.

With AMAZING nutrition — whether that's nutritional supplements and nutrient rich foods — the body temple will be that powerhouse you require it to be for your stunning life as a badass Witch. Not to mention, your skin, hair and nails will be GORGEOUS.

Now that we've addressed eating, let's address it's opposite.

Fasting

Several years ago, I undertook a fast called the Master Cleanse. It was all the rage then, so I decided to try it out to see what the health benefits would be.

Before sharing that experience, it's important to note that I grew up in the cult of Jehovah's Witnesses and made my exit after 26 years (a riveting story fully detailed in my book ***Confessions of a Christian Witch***). In that faith, there's no talk of fasting. It's not encouraged, not taught, and not practiced, a fact I find intriguing, considering how beneficial fasting is, especially spiritually. Yet I must acknowledge that the cult is about obedience and strict adherence to a religion and not spirituality.

With that said, I wasn't familiar with fasting until I was a grown woman. The intuitive Voice led me to seek it out. Since delving into fasting, I've been led to engage in a variety of fasts, including:

- **40-Day Grape Fast** - yes, 40 days of only grapes for food; plus liquids such as huge amounts of water, green tea and green smoothies. Life-changing.
- **Daniel Fast** - fruits and vegetables with water.
- **Master Cleanse** - a complete detox — especially for ridding the organs of mucous — consisting of a lemonade mixture (made of water, organic lemon juice, Grade B Maple Syrup and cayenne pepper) along with a salt water flush in the morning, and a detox laxative tea at night. (If you have the eBook version of this book, the exact methodology is here along with a video with step by step instructions. The book is here. If you have the paperback or hard cover edition of this book, Google Master Cleanse diet.) I've done the Master Cleanse several times over the years, with varied lengths of the fast from 7-14 days. Game-changer.
- **Water Fast** - only drinking water.
- **Dry Fast** - no food and no water (usually only for 24 hours).

PLEASE NOTE: these fasts are not here as recommendations of any kind. This information is presented to share with you what I did. As always, go with your intuition. See your health care practitioner if required. I put this warning in for good measure as a fast is a large undertaking for the body, mind and emotional body. I don't know you, your body or any health issues that may be present. You are the one in charge of your health and body. Proceed accordingly. Take deep care of and hold great regard for your whole self. Do not put your body or health at risk. This is a self-loving path.

Fasting is a discipline existing in all manner of spiritual traditions, magickal paths and religions. At one point, I fasted weekly on Wednesday. Simply no food from sunrise to sundown, in similar fashion to fasting during the Islamic observance of Ramadan.

I fast to:

- Connect with the divine on a deeper, more visceral level because the body is denied. Physical senses must be transcended.
- Remind myself the body is not the master. It's a great servant. The body is to be the tool of the Divine Self, not in charge.
- Give my digestive system a much needed rest.
- Give my entire body a much needed rest to.
- Clear my mind.
- Clear toxic emotions, become aware of emotional eating, and clear the drivers of emotional eating.
- Reveal the shadow self (see below).
- Pray more. More prayer is required to not think about yummy food when you haven't had any for days or weeks.
- Open the third eye. On day 3 of my 40-Day Grape Fast, it was almost as if I could see all the way to heaven. I remember walking on a Washington DC sidewalk not far from my office when I looked up and had a very real sense that I could see all the way to heaven. I walked around in somewhat of an in-between state that day. I could SEE so clearly. Everything was clear. I realized that I did not know how

cloudy I was in mind and/or third eye until all the fog cleared. Much of the fogginess came from what I chose to ingest.

This is just a short list of the wonders I've discovered in the ritual of fasting. As with every practice and ritual in this book, you'll have to make it experiential (should you choose to do so) to see what emerges for you. I honor the Divine Self you are.

A word on emotional eating… I didn't consider myself an emotional eater until about day 24 or 25 of my 40-Day Grape Fast (by far the WORST days of the fast). I almost quit. Why? Because I observed myself becoming depressed at the prospect of eating only grapes and not the delicacies I was accustomed to. I'm a big foodie, so delicious, healthful food is fun for me. I became aware during the fast of how much time I spend thinking about food, eating food, and planning what food to eat next. This was an enormous expenditure of time and energy on FOOD. It was then that I discovered that I was an emotional eater, gaining pleasure emotions from food, or the prospect of food.

I'm not saying it's not a good thing to gain pleasure from eating. Delicious food is a pleasure I'm not yet willing to give up, although one day I may (by becoming a breatharian, but that's a topic for another day).

What I do know is that it's not okay to lose joy when fasting because one is choosing to temporarily deny self of delicacies. There's the issue: deprivation of food = loss of joy and depression.

A master does not lose joy when fasting. If anything, joy could be increased.

Christ went 40 days and 40 nights in the wilderness with no water and no food and met his shadow self and conquered it. Yes, the legend goes that he was tempted by the devil. I view the devil in this story as a metaphor for the shadow self.

The shadow self is CLEARLY seen when fasting. You can rest assured it will rear its head. You then get to decide what you'll do about it.

Water

Water is an element in magick and is critical in every working. It is represented on the altar at all times and is essential to Spellcrafting.

We are water beings living on a water planet. Water sustains life. Our body's cells are literally swimming about in liquid. The more we understand our watery being, the better our health, including mental and emotional states.

Water is full of crystals. The work of Dr. Masaru Emoto, when he was in this life, opened my eyes to a way of looking at water I had never conceived. In his book *The Hidden Messages in Water,* he revealed his experiments with water and what happened when water was prayed over. Depending upon the energy the water was exposed to (the high vibrations of prayer or the low vibrations of hate speech), crystals either formed perfectly or were distorted.

The crystalline patterns of the water in the body are either perfectly shaped like beautiful snowflakes, thus aiding us in being healthier and more vibrantly alive, or they're jagged-edged, causing problems and unwanted issues in the body temple.

There's a solution. Just as we as Christian Witches pray over the water on our altar or the water placed in the corners of our Temple, praying or uttering words of beauty causes the crystalline structures of the water in our bodies to be more beautiful and perfect.

You are a water being. Pray over, or express words of appreciation over your water before ingesting, as I'm sure you do.

I only set my water on top of highly charged words on magick books or on words of power. I have Dr. Emoto to thank for changing my entire consciousness around water.

Decrease/Eliminate Toxins

Dis-ease starts with 2 deadly issues:

1. Increasing toxicity
2. Nutritional deficiency

Fix these two issues and you'll be a LOT better off.

BOTH can be addressed with LIFESTYLE CHOICES. I'm an avid activist when it comes to ridding our minds, emotions, bodies, homes and the planet of toxins. We are being inundated with chemicals.

To address and heal this rampant malady, I have a group and a business dedicated exclusively to ridding ourselves of dangerous chemical toxins, especially in personal care products. Because this issue is so close to my heart, I am a Marketing Executive for an online wellness shopping club. We have hundreds of members who are becoming healthier and healthier each day by systematically clearing toxins and intentionally integrating high quality, nature based home and personal products and ingesting nutrients and healthy snacks. I love it. Fell free to join our Facebook community (the Wealth & Wellness Vortex Facebook Group) by sending me a text (text wellnessvortex to 47177 and you'll receive an invite into the group).

I'm PASSIONATE about health and wellness. I'm PASSIONATE about green living. I'm PASSIONATE about the environment. I'm PASSIONATE about how our food choices affect the entire ecosystem of the planet. And I'm PASSIONATE about the health of our Earth Mother.

Witch also means WARRIOR. We get to take on the things we're PASSIONATE with a holy fervor and say NO to the things that destroy us. WE get to do something about the world.

Movement

I grew up watching my father do Jack LaLanne exercises on strange machines wearing what looked like a suit made of aluminum foil. Yes, my father was fit. He went to the gym often besides working out at home. It also looked crazy to me. That could be when I swore off exercise. So no, I don't use the word exercise, and I try my best not to exercise.

I MOVE a LOT. EVERY DAY. YOGA. DANCE. STRETCHING. WALKING. I LOVE to move. Our bodies were made to MOVE.

I am a writer. Writers sit for long stretches of time and do nothing but write. Writing could be a way to become sedentary, if allowed. I don't believe writing in itself is sedentary. Everything is what you make it, considering we're reality creators.

So for me, writing isn't sedentary. It's one of the most active endeavors I could engage. I'm using my mind, my body, my superconscious and my breath. I'm using my muscles as I sit straight. I'm using my emotive states and feelings. Writing is an inflow and an out breath. It's exquisite.

I get up at least once or twice and hour and move. I move in my seat, with head rolls and shoulder rolls. I keep it moving. We are made to move. Everywhere in nature where there is no movement, bad things happen.

The same is true of your body. Even if what you do requires you to be still, you can integrate movement into your workplay (I call writing workplay).

Here's how:

- **Set an intention to move.** Intention powers results.
- **Stand every hour for several minutes**. A standing desk is an option, or a desk that adjusts from standing to sitting.
- **Sit on a ball.** Those balancing balls keep you moving even if you're sitting and are working core muscles as you sit.
- **Stretch in your seat every 30 minutes or so.** Stretch your crown to the heavens, back straight. Stretch over to one side, then the other. Stretch our your legs, circle your feet around and flex and stretch out

your toes. Your body will thank you. (Set chimes on a device to remind you to get up and move or stretch until it's locked in as a habit.)

- **Lightly jog**. When you do get up, lightly jog to the bathroom or to the kitchen, or where ever you're going.
- **If you find yourself on a line, do a couple of yoga poses while standing there.** We're not talking about doing a full on triangle pose in the bank, which could result in the summoning of security. You can do simple yoga poses standing in place such as mountain pose with no one being the wiser and without making a spectacle of self.

Your spine is not only the conduit for your nervous system, it's also the conduit for your awakening from being ruled by sense consciousness to being led by Divine Mind. This happens by way of Kundalini energy rising up the spine as 2 serpents winding upwards in a criss-cross fashion, crossing at each chakra and culminating the rise by meeting face to face at the third eye.

It is said by some Bible commentators that the "silver cord" of Ecclesiastes 12 refers to the spinal cord, or to a cord that literally tethers the soul to the body. When the cord is snapped, the soul is freed of its clay companion. What we know of the spine and the spinal cord is that these being in peak state is essential for life and health.

Bend your spine daily in 6 directions:

1. To the left by bending your body over to your left side.
2. To the right.
3. Back bend.
4. Forward bend.
5. Twist around to the left.
6. Twist around to the right.

Listen to your body about how deep to go in each bend.

Whatever you do, **MOVE YOUR BODY**. A lot. Where there's **MOVEMENT**, there's **FLOW**. Where there's **FLOW**, there's **LIFE**.

Sleep

More will be addressed about critical components of a good night's sleep in the chapter titled "Blackness" on the benefits of being in the dark.

After discovering the work of Shawn Stephenson, author of *Sleep Smarter*, my mind was blown about how little I knew about sleep. My ignorance was a huge problem, considering that quality of sleep is more important than diet and exercise combined. WHOA. I knew I had to learn more, and make some serious changes.

What I'll offer here are elements of a good night's sleep that are not covered in a subsequent chapter and are specifically practices I implemented that reshaped my sleeping world:

- **Be cold**. If we observe nature, temperatures fall at night. We're naturally supposed to be a lot cooler at night than we are during the day. When I made my sleep quarters way colder, I feel into deeper more restorative sleep states and stayed there. Turns out, I was too hot at night.
- **Night time hygiene.** There are studies that say we fall asleep faster and sleep better if we've had a warm bath or shower 1-2 hours before going to bed. I was a day time shower lover. I sWitched to night time showers and love the change. Plus, there's less to do in the morning, so I jump into my day sooner.
- **Lavender Essential OIl**. My friend, my lover, my everythang lol. I hold to the belief that Witches can never have too much Lavender. I slather it on me. It makes for a luscious pillow spray when added to water.
- **Nudity**. Freedom of movement in the bed feels yummy and refreshing.

There are more must-haves for me when it comes to sleep (coming up shortly), but this is a good starter list.

Your Nervous System

You can make several changes in how you do what you do, yet they will not have a dramatic effect on your health, body and ultimately your life, until your nervous system is re-wired for the new change.

In the days in my development when I didn't understand this process, I was easily frustrated at the paltry results that would follow a significant breakthrough in awareness. Yes, I had a new awareness, yet my results didn't always match the seismic shifts in knowledge.

A major issue was at work, and still is.

If the transformation is not below the neck, it's not permanent. The change cannot be made in the head only. The change must be **SYSTEMIC**. It must be a living, breathing, pulsing, dynamic knowing in the entire being.

This can take time, or it can be instantaneous. Shocking experiences can create instantaneous transformation that's sustainable. Shocking here means out of the ordinary to such a degree that our consciousness is permanently changed. I don't think shocking has to mean unpleasant or negative, although it can be. Shocking can be enjoyable, it's just that the experience is vastly different from the customary.

Examples of shocking experiences:

- Giving birth or watching a birth.
- Travel to foreign countries.
- Plant medicines.
- Skydiving.
- Rock/mountain climbing.
- Being in the wilderness overnight.
- Sweat lodge.

There are many more shocking experiences than these, but we get the picture. The idea is that you are taken so far out of your norm that your system MUST re-wire itself to accommodate the new information.

Once your mind is stretched, it can never go back to what it was before, hence an instantaneous, permanent transformation. Congratulations! You're a Master
Alchemist! You just permanently changed yourself in an instant.

To sum it up, sustainable transformation cannot be a thought or new idea only. Permanent change happens below your neck and must be **SYSTEMIC**, to include the nervous system, hormones and your entire emotional body.

Now that we've addressed a bit of bio-hacking to make us into freakin WARRIORS, let's proceed to the energetic structure of the body temple.

7 Sheaths

There are 7 sheaths around your physical body that comprise the aura, here referred to as the auric field. These sheaths exist layer by layer from closest to the body to furthest from the physical body.

We are all walking about as if in an energetic bubble.

We create the constitution and flavor of this energetic bubble with who we choose to be as demonstrated by consciousness, including thoughts and emotions.

The reason we examine these now is because they are related to Spellcrafting. How? Once again, **ALL OF YOU** is crafting magick. We're not simply going for being good at magick. We're going for **BEING MASTER ALCHEMISTS.** A Master Alchemist knows well the spiritual, mental, emotional and physical constitution of the body and uses this powerful insight and revelation to perform the highest magick and transcend lower dimensions. If you desire to leave the body and travel the astral plane, it would be wise to know how to do it. This is the beginning.

7 Energy Sheaths

The 7 sheaths — from closest to the body to the outermost sheath — are:

- **Etheric Body** - this sheath is closest to the body and is shaped exactly like the body. It is the energetic conductor between subtler energies and the the physical body. Corresponds to the Root Chakra (red in color) - sustenance, survival, belonging. Mantra: **I TRUST**.
- **Emotional Body** - this sheath is larger than the body and follows the general outline of the body. This sheath is the most difficult to clear and holds toxic emotions as energy blocks or dark spots. It's also where energetic excess weight is stored (if a person has issues releasing pounds, it could be related to an energetic issue, such as unforgiveness and the burden of obligation). Corresponds to the Sacral Chakra (orange in color) - creativity, sexuality, sensuality, fertility. Mantra: **I CREATE**.
- **Mental Body** - this sheath is not exactly shaped like the body. It is where mental issues are stored. Cleansing this body could release the inability to meditate or to achieve mental stillness and peace. Corresponds to the Solar Plexus Chakra (yellow in color) - the seat of WILL and POWER. It's CRITICAL for Witches, Wizards, Warlocks and Magickal Beings that this chakra and corresponding sheath be POWERED, ALIGNED and in FULL ACTIVATION. The causative power of magick is the WILL. One's WILL emanates from the Solar Plexus Chakra, where our will and the Divine will are one and the same. Mantra: **I WILL**.
- **Astral Body** - this sheath is not shaped like the body and is the connection to the astral plane and beyond, and can be considered a bridge from lower, denser states of consciousness to higher, finer states of consciousness. When one goes about the astral plane, one does so in the astral body. The astral plane is a complex, timeless dimension, filled with all manner of spirits (more on this later). Corresponds to the Heart Chakra (green in color) - love, wisdom, power (these form

the TRIUNE forces of the Divine Being and form a Trinity). Mantra: **I LOVE**.

- **Etheric Template or Double** - an energetic template or blueprint of the physical body on a higher plane of vibration than the Etheric Body. Corresponds to the Throat Chakra (bright blue in color) - expression, creativity, communication, speaking truth, words, sounds. Mantra: **I EXPRESS**.
- **Celestial Body** - a high vibration sheath connected to ALL THAT IS and is associated with enlightenment, dreams, psychic abilities, telepathy, vision and all things related to the Third Eye Chakra (indigo in color). Mantra: **I SEE**.
- **Ketheric/Ketheric Template/Causal Body** - cosmic consciousness, also known as Christ Consciousness (especially important in Christian Witchcraft). Crown chakra (purple in color) - divine connection, angelic communication, super-conscious states of being. Mantra: **I AM**.

Notes:

- If you conduct research on the 7 subtle bodies (highly recommended), you may find slight variances in the names for each sheath. Seek to intuit the true essence of a thing beyond what it may be called in English (or the language you speak). Words are pointers, and not the thing itself. We do not desire to get caught up in a label and miss the essence. This applies throughout magickal practice and occult studies.
- In the Vedic tradition from India, there are 5 sheaths around the body, also known as Koshas. Study these if you're led. Though there are a different number of bodies stated in the 2 systems, at the core, they are the same. As a mystic, we become accustomed to seeing the correspondences in all spiritual systems, and can easily translate between the system we may operate in and another system. I do this at holy houses all the time. We're all essentially doing the same thing. If a master visits a Catholic Church, this one will be able to intuit the

correspondence between incense there and what's used in a Hindu temple, even with varying scents and applications. ***What is the essence?*** The essence is identical though the application and names may vary widely. We do not get caught in the web of differentiation. We're able to see correspondences because we view the universe as it truly is: ***a harmonic whole***.

- Each of the energy sheaths has a wide range it operates in, and is dynamic.
- The first 3 sheaths constitute a system for navigating life on the physical plane successfully. These 3 sheaths are also responsible for the formation of your ego personality. They begin to form at conception and are no longer needed after the physical body has been released (in what is called death). The upper 3 sheaths are for navigating supernal realms. The Astral Body is the bridge between the lower 3 bodies and the upper 3.
- Of course, there's more to your energetic body than these 7 sheaths. This is a template so that we can begin to understand our multi-dimensional, cosmic existence.
- While the base of each of the above 7 mentioned chakras is located inside the body temple (though the emanations can extend beyond the body), there are additional chakras above and below the physical body. Above the head are 4 chakras. Below the Root Chakra is an Earth Chakra, for an even deeper energetic connection to the earth mother. For those who have tapped into these chakras through meditation and ascended states of awareness, they are operating on the ***12 Chakra System***.
- There are hundreds of chakras throughout your being, including chakras in the palms of your hands, in your feet and at all 13 articulations in the body: ankles, knees, hips, shoulders, elbows, wrists and where the head meets the neck.
- To understand the subtle bodies and the chakras, you must experience them for yourself. It may not be a good idea to endlessly study. An excellent approach is to make it EXPERIENTIAL through your

spiritual practices, rituals and daily way of being. This is the best method of discovery. It turns out grandma was right: ***experience is the best teacher.***

Understanding the function and essence of these subtle bodies, their connection to the chakras, and their role in magickal life is a huge advantage in Spellcrafting. When one gains knowledge, it is not yet wisdom. Wisdom is garnered from putting knowledge to right use in order to receive results. The results give us wisdom on how a thing actually works.

Until then, we remain somewhat in the dark, even with knowledge. We may know a lot, yet we don't REALLY know a thing until we can demonstrate it.

Now that we've taken a brief look at our multi-layered, energetic nature, we can proceed to assessing our world.

Wheel of Destiny

Now would be a good time to take a heart-full inventory of self and the self-created world we currently find ourselves in.

For this exercise, you'll require only your grimoire, and your true and honest intention to lovingly give attention to EVERY area of your life for the purpose of AWARENESS before beginning to craft spells and create rituals.

Here are the 7 areas we'll address in the inventory, known as the **Wheel of Destiny**:

1. **Faith** - what you hold as sacred in your spiritual unfoldment.
2. **Family** - the people closest to you.
3. **Fitness** - your body, diet and health habits.
4. **Finances** - your abundance, money, wealth and resources.
5. **Friends** - covens, communities, business partners and people in your world beyond family.
6. **Fulfillment** - your destiny or purpose on the planet.
7. **Fun** - ways of curling your toes in sheer delight, entertainment, how you unwind or decompress.

Constructing the Wheel

In your grimoire, draw a large circle with lines that create 7 slices. Here's an example:

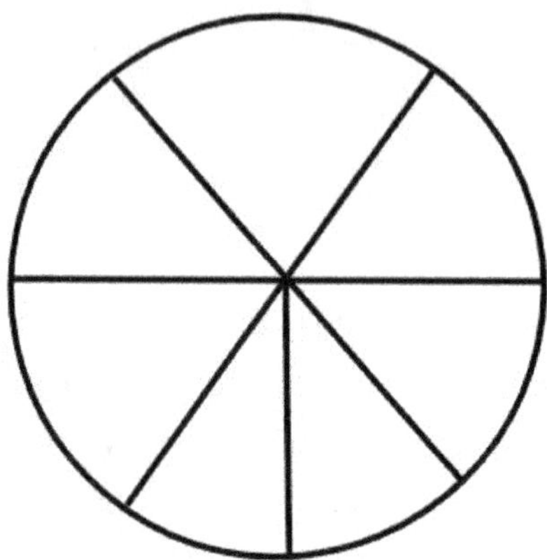

Wheel of Destiny

I usually construct the Wheel by drawing a circle, then drawing a Y inside the circle, followed by a horizontal line in the middle of the circle. I then extend the axis on both lines in the upper Y to the bottom outer edges of the circle. I formed it in this way because it created the largest slice of the pie at the top, which I labeled 'Faith.'

Construct the circle with lines in any way you like that will yield 7 slices of the pie.

Labeling the Wheel

In each slice of the pie, place one of the 7 above mentioned areas of your life in any order you like. All of these areas work together holistically to form a whole that is your current life.

Scoring

You'll now give a numerical score to each of the slices of the pie from 0 to 5 — based on how desirable your current experience in this area of your life is — with zero being the worst possible experience and 5 being the best.

A perfect score is 35, which means every area of your life is exactly as you desire. If that were true, you probably wouldn't have picked up a book on how to craft spells, since magick is about creation and transformation, so I'm guessing there are things you'd like to create or change, to one degree or another.

How to Score

Do NOT let your conscious mind score the areas of your life. Go to your heart. Ask Divine Mind within to give you the TRUE NUMBER for each area of your life, which will in essence be vastly different from what you think it is.

Remember, our minds trick us into believing that we're good with something we know in our hearts we are not. Our minds want us to believe that we're better than we are, or that things are peachy when they're not. This is the rationalization part of the brain, and is useful when it comes to mathematics and useless when it comes to self-gnosis. Rationalization is not your friend in spirituality. It could be one of your greatest enemies on the path of unfoldment.

Don't rationalize. Don't think too long. Don't trick yourself.

Simply ask your heart what's really going on for you in each area of your life experience, for INFORMATION PURPOSES ONLY, and not as ammunition to beat up on self for not having a better life.

Self-Love

This exercise must be conducted from the deepest well of self-love you can draw from inside yourself. The ONLY way we can tell ourselves the truth about what's really going on with self and in our world is with **DEEP ABIDING SELF LOVE**.

Otherwise, we won't look at self because we'll always find something to judge.

For instance, if I'm habitually late to everything (which at one time I was), it could be showing me that I'm afraid. If I don't accept this information as loving feedback from a loving universe to help me be better, I'll keep beating up on myself about being late all the time. I used to live in this cycle in multiple areas of my life. It was torture.

I no longer willingly torture myself. I pray and practice rooting into self love, no matter what.

Self love is the answer to everything.

NOT narcissism. Self love. They are worlds apart.

Feedback Loop

Now that you have the loving feedback loop of knowing that your family life may be a 4, but your fitness is a 1, you get to decide what to do about it, if anything.

I don't always jump into action when I receive a feedback loop from the universe about the true state of my consciousness in any given area of life. Sometimes, the awareness itself is the necessary catalyst for change. If I know, according to our earlier example, that the habit of being late is a result of fear, it shifts something in me. There may be no further action required. We cannot always assume that awareness equals having to take a specific action to rid self of the thing we just became aware of.

I view awareness as the blinding light of a fiery love that melts anything and everything that isn't divinity.

This is not to be considered a pass to NOT work on issues we become aware of. If the fitness area of life is indeed a 1, immediate corrective action, habits and thought processes may be critically necessary to transmute this area, lest some greater untoward result present itself later on.

You'll know what to do when trusting Divine Self as the sure Guide.

Frequency

You can conduct this assessment every 6 months or so. I've used it over and over as a quick assessment tool. What I love about this tool is that it's dynamic, just like life. Life is in flux. It isn't static. We require tools that acknowledge and work with the dynamic action of life.

Date each Wheel of Destiny you create and complete. This will be valuable information later on. Keep each completed Wheel in your grimoire, along with notes.

Simplicity

Don't let the simplicity of the tool be a misrepresentation of its power and efficacy. The best things are simple. Over-complication is another word for ego. Truth is simple.

We desire **SELF GNOSIS**. We can get that in a few minutes with this tool. The magick of this tool is in the IMPLEMENTATION of it, as is true with everything.

Underlying Factors

Let's get into the underlying factors of WHY a specific area of life may be a 1 or 2 rather than a 5.

The bottom line is: it's in the mind.

The first law, as we've discussed, is the **LAW OF MENTALISM**. The universe is mental. All is mind. Therefore, everything in the Wheel of

Destiny, and the resultant scores, can be traced back to something in the MIND.

If we always approach the Wheel from this perspective, we'll get to the true underlying factors in every case, and create lasting change. That's real magick.

An example. I receive a score of 1 from my heart in the area of finances. Before jumping up and buying the latest financial software, or blaming my boo for spending too much money, or being mad with myself for having such a low score when it comes to money, or casting a spell for more money, I could instead:

- **Meditate on it**. Allow wisdom about this area to bubble up from the heart-well. Answers will begin to reveal themselves.
- **Observe myself for 30 days.** I could lovingly observe myself with money for 30 days to become aware of underlying emotional triggers and tendencies, and what they cause me to do in the financial area of my life.
- **Journal on it.** Writing out thoughts and emotions in a stream of consciousness about money could bring more revelations than you bargained for.
- **Decide**. Decide what to do differently in this area, now that greater insight and self-gnosis have arrived.
- **Supernatural knowing.** What downloads am I receiving from Source about my situation?

Doing this kind of ground work in consciousness will cause us to spell craft from a much more expanded and informed state of consciousness, which will yield **INFINITELY BETTER RESULTS**.

While we still may buy the financial software or craft a money spell, we definitely will NOT engage in blaming the boo, nor will we engage in beating up on self.

We will move right on with the task at hand: **TRANSFORMING CONSCIOUSNESS** by means of magick.

I would offer that if you craft a spell simply because you don't have enough money, that kind of magick will yield one result.

If you craft a spell from a place of knowing WHY YOU DON'T have the money you desire, that my be the most powerful magick you can engage.

This is INFORMED MAGICK.

This is SELF AWARE MAGICK.

This is PRACTICAL MAGICK.

This is EFFECTUAL MAGICK.

III

Holistic Magick

Magick is holistic. Here's how.

Holistic Magick

This book seeks to fully honor the intrinsic holistic nature of magick. We cannot divorce what we do from who we are, any more than we can divorce our head from our body and expect to survive the ordeal.

Your world is the context that informs your magick. We cannot ignore this and go straight to the circle (and expect to have permanent success).

Because everything we are and do has a subtle (or not so subtle) influence on Spellcrafting, we'll acknowledge many subtleties here, with the intention of awareness.

To sink deeper into the holistic nature of magick, we'll invite science and spirituality to blend beautifully, and we'll develop the practice of looking at ALL aspects of our life experience to determine if these are harmonious with what we're spelling for and the magickal lives we get to lead as **MASTER ALCHEMISTS** who practice **CHRISTIAN WitchCRAFT**.

But first, a cautionary tale.

A Warning for Christian Witches

Several years ago, I was visiting the home of a friend in our spiritual community who was embarking on her initiatory process of becoming a Yoruba Priestess.

She told me she was washing the entire inside of her home — including walls and floors — with an herbal solution for ridding her life of unwanted energies that would in any way thwart or hinder her accelerated ascension. She was 'prescribed' the healing ritual by her spiritual mother, who was head of the house she was being initiated into.

This was a massive undertaking, considering she'd been living in her house for years. I sat in her living room and looked around. There were so many items to move that it was overwhelming to even think about, let alone follow through and complete the mission in excellence.

I would love to see this type of undertaking in Christian Witchcraft.

Not to say that it would involve washing one's entire home with a sacred herbal wash, but in the knowing that my whole house must be cleaned for me to proceed at my highest and best.

As Christian Witches, me may benefit from 'whole house' cleansing and purification. Yes, we talk of sacred herbal baths in the magickal community, and the importance of purification, cleansing and clearing.

Could we take it to another level? Maybe so.

Lots of people want spells. Many of us will engage in ritual, herbal baths.

Not so many people would want to wash their entire house down with an herbal bath (including me). Yet, that may at times be just what's called for.

When she told me what she was doing, I sat there with my mouth open. This was many years ago, when I did not yet have a firm handle on the concept that **EVERYTHING** in my world informs my magick.

In the conversation with her, Source was giving me a powerful message. *Look at **EVERYTHING**. Be willing to **WASH YOUR ENTIRE HOUSE**.*

House = consciousness.

Be willing to wash, purify and cleanse my entire consciousness, from top to bottom, moving all the mental furniture, especially the furniture I love, releasing quite a few prized possessions in the process.

In Christian Witchcraft, there's no requirement to do this. There's no house mother giving you a reading and telling you what to clear. There's no requirement to clean your entire house. You can pretty much start this path and do anything you please.

I will admit that this is the beauty of this path: you can completely make it up as you go.

I will also acknowledge that this is the danger of the path: that you can completely make it up as you go.

Even on my best day, my consciousness is not 100% on point. With no expressed tradition, protocols or efficacious guiding principles in play, I could make up any damn thing and call it magick.

We must be careful as Christian Witches.

We get to study the underlying principles of magick, other magickal traditions, spirituality and the nature of the cosmos itself so that we root our magick in a foundation grounded in spiritual law and truth.

We're all subject to engage in flights of fancy here and there, which is a-ok. However, if one is to become a Master Alchemist, a firm foundation of truth must be present, otherwise the house cannot stand. This is us building our house on rock, not on sand.

360 Vision

Looking at one's life holistically means intentionally utilizing 360 degrees of vision. It means looking all around, at everything in one's consciousness and in one's world. Nothing escapes our attention.

While this may seem demanding, it's required of the master.

There's no area of mastery that overlooks the 360 principle. If a person desires to be a black belt, a certain discipline, physical practice, diet and mindset are required to achieve the goal. The same applies if a person desires to be a championship skater, Olympic swimmer, or champion chess player. The identical principles apply to becoming a Master Alchemist.

There's no getting around ruthless examination of self and everything in our world.

This is not to say that one is to become hyper sensitive, or always atop the watchtower in over-scrutinizing, watch-dog fashion.

It means nothing escapes our attention. Nothing in our lives is off limits and out of our purview. We're not blindsided because we're willing to look at it ALL.

Hold an INTENTION to see. ***A Course In Miracles*** offers Lesson 27 for our consideration: "Above all else, I want to see."

Hold an intention to see ALL of SELF, meaning consciousness, and ALL that's unfolding as a result.

Though deep awareness can be at times a slap in the face, it's vital to the master.

I'd rather know than be ignorant.

We are reminded of our supreme magickal maxim: **KNOW THYSELF**.

With 360 vision, we get to throw open the cupboards in consciousness and discover the dust bunnies hiding out in corners; we get to fling open the closet doors of the mind for a good examination and all-out spring cleaning. We get to toss what's rancid out of the refrigerator, knowing that the only way it survived this long was because we didn't seek out and examine the contents at the back of the shelf, untwist lids on jars, stick our nose in and be repulsed at what we discovered. No one has an issue with quickly eliminating that shit. In the trash it goes. We get to do so the same in consciousness, our true house. Let's wash the walls and floors, from top to bottom.

Be ruthless with eliminating trash in your consciousness. **TAKE IT OUT**. It doesn't belong in the sacred domain that is I AM.

"Know ye not that ye are the temple of God, and that *the Spirit of God dwelleth in you?"*
1 Corinthians 3:16 (KJV)

Science and Magick

As Master Alchemists who study and practice the Magickal Arts & Sciences, it could greatly benefit us to study all manner of science, history, archaeology and more, to inform our path.

Let's turn our attention to science momentarily, and the place it holds in magick and Spellcrafting.

The non-local nature of consciousness has been proven in the laboratory of science, even as it had been proven long ago in the laboratory of life experience.

Books abound on this topic, but no scientist is dearer to my heart and resonates with me more in the current moment than Rupert Sheldrake, the scientist whom I feel has found the smoking gun overlap of science and spirituality. We knew the overlap existed. He's proven it.

Let's be clear, we don't need science to tell us what's true.

Because I love science and have always found it fascinating, I appreciate when science comes to the exact same conclusions spirituality has already revealed. There's a maxim that says science scales the great mountain of knowledge, only to find the yogis, gurus and saints already sitting there. For me, science affirms what we already know. It does not prove it. I do not require proof of the truth.

Rupert Sheldrake speaks and teaches on the idea of morphic resonance, an invisible field in and around everything and everyone that's encoded with information. He also speaks of panpsychism: the idea that everything has consciousness, from the sun to the worm.

This would appear to be the exact same truth found in the first of the 7 Hermetic principles of the universe stated in the book the ***Kybalion***:

"All is mind. The universe is mental."

This means there's a consciousness, for example, associated with cassia, one of the 50 fundamental plant medicines in China. When I'm crafting a spell that will employ cassia, I'm literally tapping into the consciousness of cassia, asking it to lend its specific attributes to the working.

The idea of panpsychism, for me, made scientific proof of the practices that have been in my family for generations, from healing with Castor Oil to drinking pot liquor for ailments (the juices in the pot after cooking leafy green vegetables like kale, mustard greens and/or collard greens).

The mustard greens have a consciousness.

The castor beans used to press out castor oil have a consciousness.

Witches have known this all along.

Rightly proven science aligns with spirituality, and thus with magick. Let's consider the scientific method (this also appears in my book *How to Be a Christian Witch;* I'm including here as well as it's pertinent to our discussion).

The Scientific Method

1. Ask a question.
2. Do background research.
3. Construct a hypothesis.
4. Test the hypothesis with an experiment.
5. Analyze data and draw conclusions.
6. Report results.

Or:

1. Make an observation.
2. Ask a question.
3. Form a hypothesis, or testable explanation.
4. Make a prediction based on the hypothesis.
5. Test the prediction.
6. Iterate: use the results to make new hypotheses or predictions

Here's how the scientific method (using the 1st model listed above) can be applied to magick:

1. Ask a question: what is the highest and best ways and means for me and my family to experience greater wealth, abundance, riches and prosperity?
2. Do background research: look up the angels, planets, times and correspondences that apply to wealth, abundance, riches and prosperity.
3. Construct a hypothesis: if I invoke the Archangel Gadiel on the New Moon in Taurus to gather intelligence on wealth creation, and I act on this angelic guidance, I will start to experience greater prosperity during that moon cycle and continually increasing far beyond.
4. Test the hypothesis with an experiment: conduct the magickal operation.
5. Analyze data and draw conclusions: did the magickal operation work as expected? What can I change for even better results? What can I add? Subtract?
6. Report results: carefully record all results in my grimoire. If appropriate, share with the coven.

It was important for me to understand the connections between science and magick. Not because I needed it. But because I'm a Libra, and air signs have the added burden of trying to make sense of things. It won't do for me to simply be told that something works. My mind will continue to press with questions... *how does it work*? And *why does it work*? And *does it work that way every time, or are there variables?*

There are answers to every question. The answer begs discovery by sending forth the question.

By studying science, including botany, herbology, astronomy, astrology, numerology, Gematria, psychology and more, we arrive at being better informed Witches.

I grew up in the cult of Jehovah's Witnesses, a sordid tale of intrigue I reveal in the book ***Confessions of a Christian Witch***. One of the most debilitating habits of fundamentalist Christianity is the charge to its adherents to ignore history and science. This is one reason I believe some atheists view Christians as crazy. Who would continue to believe something that's been proven by science as untrue in the name of religion? Still, we see it every day. Case in point: Jehovah's Witnesses do not believe in the existence of dinosaurs because it turns their belief in the creation story being 6 days of a literal 1,000 years each on its head. It would be the undoing of their religion's foundation, or would at least require a massive overhaul or restructuring.

Because the entire Jehovah's Witness story has been proven by science to be hogwash, they must caution and warn their adherents to ignore science as a tool of the devil. They teach that the only real science agrees with what the Witnesses hold as core beliefs. This is a twisted and treacherous game of control, built on manipulation of the mind.

The travesty of this is that many, if not all of religion's teachings are dismissed offhand by some as completely unusable fantasy because they have been proven untrue by science.

This is a travesty.

Religion's original aim and purpose was not to be scientific. The word religion comes from two root words, meaning to re-link. Religion was meant to re-link us with the Divine after our entry into the 3rd dimension.

In short, religion's refusal to accept certain damning advances in science and archaeology has made it laughable in some circles as a security blanket for those with little hope — or sense — to hold on to in a world so confusing they must be told what to think.

Not so with Witches.

We go anywhere, study anything we're drawn to, and come to our own righteous conclusions based on the wisdom and guidance of the Inner Voice from the Divine.

Science and magick align. We'll use this fact to our advantage.

Blackness

Now we'll address the nature of darkness and why it's important to us as Witches.

First, introduce more blackness into your life.

Blackness is the total and absolute absence of light.

I heard an experience from someone I highly regard on YouTube about his attendance at a 'Dark Retreat' (a retreat where attendees stay in complete darkness for a number of days).

He spoke of eating in the dark, brushing his teeth with no idea how much toothpaste he was squeezing out onto the toothbrush, and taking a crap without knowing if he had sufficiently wiped his bottom. He did everything in complete darkness for days.

He was forever changed.

I can attest, and perhaps you can too, to the absolute nature of pure blackness. It's still yet moving. Deep and unending. It brings up our worst fears; the ones lurking in the dark of our unconscious.

Why would we be talking about blackness in a book on Spellcrafting for Christian Witches?

Good question… one I will attempt to answer now, as best I can.

After addressing that question, we'll also look at why we don't have enough darkness in our modern lives, mostly due to use of technology. We'll also look at a few ways we can reclaim more blackness in our every day — and night — existence.

Blackness makes us better, in very profound ways.

The Nature of Darkness Itself

We quickly learn, as did the spiritual experiencer I spoke of earlier in this chapter, that blackness is the VOID spoken of in Genesis out of which Source formed EVERYTHING.

Blackness is infinite possibility, from which any and all can emerge. We don't have this experience of KNOWING blackness is really the ground of all being until we're immersed in utter blackness for long enough for us to intuit its nature.

I think a lot of us run from pitch blackness.

I did, until I started coming to grips with the inherent power in darkness. Not that there's power in the darkness, but that darkness is POWER ITSELF. Infinite power. Creative power. Pure potential.

The nature of blackness is no-thing-ness, which is the nature of Source, the vast undifferentiated energy fueling and informing the entire cosmos, creating all, destroying what's no longer useful to life, and healing what requires it.

Genesis chapter 1 says that in the beginning, darkness was over the surface, or the face of the deep. The Genesis account says water was present, but no light.

The first thing Source brought into existence was light, stated in verse 3 as a command: "Let there be light." And then there was light.

Though I do not take Genesis as a literal account of creation, nor do I view it as a book of historical accuracy, I do acknowledge that it contains keys to creation.

Before there was anything, there was darkness. Light was created. Darkness was not. Darkness simply was. If we took away everything, there would only be darkness left.

To me, this is super magickal!

If I take a cue from Genesis about creation, I could use the power of darkness to create as well. I could go into the void and bring forth anything. You can too. We are creators.

Scientists say that dark energy is 68% of the universe, dark matter is 27% while all other matter, including the earth, is only 5% of existence. These scientific findings coincide almost exactly with Kabbalah, which states that the world of matter, perceivable by the 5 senses, comprises only 1% of reality, while 99% of existence is beyond our 5 senses. This also aligns with the fact that the conscious mind is responsible for 5% of our results, while the subconscious mind is responsible for 95%.

If one believed in coincidence, which I do not, a fascinating consideration lives in Chapter 1 of the Tao Te Ching by Lao Tzu:

"The Tao that can be told is not the eternal Tao.
The name that can be named is not the eternal name.
The nameless is the beginning of heaven and earth.
The named is the mother of ten thousand things.
Ever desireless, one can see the mystery.
Ever desiring, one can see the manifestations.
These two spring from the same source but differ in name;
this appears as darkness.
Darkness within darkness.
The gate to all mystery."

Does this sound the tiniest bit like Genesis chapter 1? Both sacred writings begin with darkness. Lao Tzu even states that darkness is the gate to all mystery. What are Witches about if not mystery?

There's a vast unseen darkness at play here. Since it's the overwhelming majority of existence, we do well as spiritual seekers to understand its nature, not just from the vantage point of science, but as an experiential undertaking.

Willfully placing self in the pitch black for many hours per 24-hour cycle will provide this vital experiential understanding.

Blackness Conditioning

Realizing that blackness is the void and is almost the entire universe, we now are confronted with our conditioning about the dark, so that we take it on and free ourselves.

I grew up being bathed in duality teachings: light and dark, with God being the light and the devil being everything dark.

This is the reason why I believe so many Witches have a hard time coming into their full power and practicing magick after years of indoctrination in Christianity. There's a brainwashing that must be addressed and tackled.

The world is NOT made up of two opposing forces of dark and light, with a big face-off coming at the end of the world between God and the devil.

Darkness is simply the normal state of the entire universe until light is introduced. Darkness is not evil. Darkness is the void.

Remember, light was created. Darkness was not.

You'll have a hard time going along with all of this until you experience it for yourself. That's what this book (and all my work) is really about... wisdom born of experience. We can talk about all this til the cows come home. The final say will be what you yourself experience.

Put yourself in a dark retreat for many days and see what happens.

Put yourself in the dark every night for many hours and see what happens.

Light Spills

When the spiritual experiencer I spoke of at the beginning of this chapter went into the dark retreat, he was given instructions by the facilitators on where everything was located, including where his food would be placed at mealtimes and where the bathroom was in his quarters. He was given a blindfold to ensure he stayed in complete darkness.

He was told that if he wanted fresh air, he could pull back the thick black curtains at the window and open it for fresh air. As long as he was wearing his blindfold, he would avoid a 'light spill.' The retreat leaders referred to any contact with light during the dark retreat as a spill.

I thought about light spills. It's a fascinating concept to me, when our entire orientation seems to be toward light, not light avoidance.

Imagine being in a dark room for days on end, with yourself. No technology, devices, television or anything that can be viewed. Audio was the only option for anything other than being with one's own thoughts, or lack thereof.

He said he's never been the same.

Genesis Sleep

I thoroughly enjoy the work of Shawn Stevenson, author of *Sleep Smarter* mentioned earlier. He places huge emphasis on sleeping in pitch black darkness, and gives several reasons why, and strategies to achieve sleeping in somewhat of a cocoon of darkness. One of my success coaches has put almost all of these strategies to use, with supreme results.

To sleep in the Genesis state means to sleep in total darkness by sealing off all light. Here are a few ideas:

- **No devices.** Turn off and eliminate devices in sleeping quarters. Shawn Stevenson even advises enjoying 2 hours prior to sleep with no devices, or at least with devices in night mode. Devices emitting blue light are particularly problematic.
- **No television.** The habit of sleeping with the television on introduces all manner of suggestions to the subconscious mind when the sleeper is especially susceptible. Some say they can't sleep without it. A television is a created device and is not natural to us as Witches. My mother called it the 'idiot box' for good reason. Television is one of the most widely used tools of mass conditioning. As Witches, not only is television highly suspect, one must be VIGILANT with what we watch when we do choose to watch it.
- **Black out curtains.** Once you've eliminated all light inside the room,

seal off all windows in your sleep space where light can enter from the outside.

- **Blindfold**. If you cannot achieve complete darkness in your environment for whatever reason, a blackout sleep blindfold of high quality is an excellent gift to self.

You get the idea. Create your space into a BLACK cocoon where you sleep in the Genesis state. The benefits cannot be overstated. As was mentioned — according to the work and research of Shawn Stevenson — sleep is more important than diet and exercise combined.

DMT and Darkness

There's a direct link between darkness and the production of DMT in the brain. Dimethyltryptamine (DMT) is naturally produced in the body and can be found throughout nature. It's responsible for the psychoactive nature of plant medicine experiences that can be had when one ingests Ayahuasca, where an ego death unfolds and one is put in direct connection with transcendental realms of consciousness, resulting in an experience of BEING versus doing.

There's an excellent article here on Steemit which provides the physical and hormonal processes that take place in the body to produce DMT and its resultant effects on consciousness. I highly recommend reading it and absorbing the material, as this has effects not only on our magick, but on our overall health, sleep, well-being and neuroplasticity, with the added benefits of reducing pain, possibly eliminating addictions and creating a sense of inner peace. (Of course, none of these are medical claims. You'll have to find out for yourself what effects DMT has on you.)

I DO NOT recommend taking DMT if you're unfamiliar or without guidance and support. I've experienced many Ayahuasca journeys, all of which have taken place in a ceremonial context with experienced shamans. Ceremonial protocols have been in place for eons with plant medicines of all kinds around the globe, for good reason. If you were all of a sudden knocked out of who you thought you were (as I've experienced in Ayahuasca journeys), it can be jarring, not to mention terrifying. Support is a beautiful thing. There were even medical staff present at my experience. It turns out, a person in our group — who was attending the same retreat myself and a friend were attending in Peru — required the help of the doctors present. In that first experience we also had access to a licensed therapist, who met with each one of us privately before our first journey. He asked thorough questions, one of the first being if there was anyone I'd lost lately, and if I'd had significant life changes, such as divorce or a move. The nature of his questions was to help each of us uncover unconscious grief and traumas that will more than likely surface in an Ayahuasca journey.

The good news is you don't have to travel to Peru and find shamans to experience the liberating effects of DMT.

You can do that in the darkness. Yes, you can produce your own DMT experiences without substances of any kind. Give yourself enough darkness, and you'll begin to approach and delve into profound states of consciousness.

A good start is to give yourself several hours of complete and utter darkness at night. A full on experience can be had if you're brave enough to give yourself utter and complete darkness for 14 days straight.

This would approach the practices of Taoists, who refer to the dark room as the Perfect Inner Alchemy Chamber. We are seeking to be Master Alchemists, so this aligns perfectly with our work. One of the Taoist teachers I am forever thankful for and continue to learn from is Mantak Chia.

Tibetans have long used 'dark retreats' for healing, conducted under the auspices of a teacher.

In ancient Egypt the Kemetic people used darkness in the pyramids for rites of passage and sacred ceremonies, knowing the blackness held mysteries present nowhere else.

Though we live in an advanced world offering many stylized versions of a dark retreat, truth be told, you could go into a cave and have a dark retreat of your own, free of charge. Be safe of course. I mention this to keep this practice as pure and simple as it is. The purpose is simply you in darkness for profound inner world alchemy. How yummy!

Sensory Deprivation Chambers

I'm insatiably curious, so when I heard of sensory deprivation tanks (or chambers) and all the mental and emotional health benefits, I was all in!

I first entered a sensory deprivation tank in Virginia, right outside of Washington, DC a couple of years prior to the writing of this work. The tank was in a spa-like facility, where several different kinds of tanks were offered. One tank was a huge, open tub for one, while others were a huge bath for 2, or a tank that resembled a pod with a lid that could be closed. Each tank was filled with salt water, making it impossible to sink to the bottom (important for me since I don't swim). All lights are turned off, and all sound is muffled. The room is completely black. The water is the exact same temperature as the body. One enters the water completely nude (or with a swimsuit if desired), lays outs, eyes closed, and simply lets go.

The experience is immediately foreign. After a few minutes, the part of the brain that regulates orientation and spatial relationships has nothing to hold on to, so it can't orient to anything. The resulting experience is that of floating in space.

After a while in the tank with my eyes closed, I couldn't tell if I was on my side, on my back or upside down. It was all so disorienting, which is exactly the point.

Though the tank can induce a profoundly meditative state, it can also induce panic, which is also exactly the point. We have a choice. To meditate or to panic. So it goes in life.

I loved the sensory deprivation tank so much that I got a membership and returned several times. Each time I entered the tank, I went deeper… healing spaces and places in me I didn't know required healing.

All this occurs in complete and utter darkness and salt water, much like the womb we all marinated in before making our appearance.

Ego Death Through Darkness

In this context, ego death simply means the death of who we think we are. We think we are humans, or mothers, or fathers, or teachers, or black, or white, or Norwegian or this or that. We have mental and emotional layers of cultural conditioning that inform who we think we are. Jamaicans have different layers of cultural conditioning than Swiss people.

These mental constructs exist in the 3rd dimension, and nowhere else. Since we've been exposed to the idea from both science and spirituality that the 3rd dimension is only 5% of reality, it would follow that only 5% of me is a black woman from Harlem. The other 95% of what I am is far beyond that.

In ultimate reality, we are not anything that can be perceived by the 5 senses. In fact, the veil of the 3rd dimension is actually hiding what we are in ultimate reality. We want to get past this veil as quickly and as often as possible, to live from the expanded dimension of ultimate reality.

In ultimate reality, what we are cannot be put into words, as stated by Lao Tzu. In ego death, we experience the disintegration of thought constructs that maintain a sense of an individual little self (who we think we are), so that we can experience what we TRULY are.

Night Paralysis

To put a bow on this chapter, I'd like to share my darkness induction experiences.

When I was a pre-teen, right around the time when Witch powers begin to manifest, I remember having terrifying night paralysis episodes.

They weren't terrifying in and of themselves; they were terrifying because I didn't know what they were and was frightened out of my tiny little 12-year-old mind.

I don't recall the very first one, I only recall that these were a recurring issue I had no control over, with no idea where they came from, or when they would strike, or what I could do to prevent the unwelcome and scary nighttime visitor.

The episodes were happening in an apartment our family had recently moved into. We were only in that apartment for a few months, while waiting for our new home to be completed. It was a long 4-bedroom apartment in a building between Broadway and Riverside Drive in Harlem where I grew up.

There was a bedroom close to the front door, and since I was the oldest, I got to choose my bedroom first. I chose that one, since it was away from the rest of the bedrooms down the hall. I would enjoy my solitude away from my dumb little brother I thought smugly to myself. It was the perfect plan.

Now that you have the backdrop and context, let's go inside myself during an episode...

I awaken from a deep sleep. I don't know what time it is. I only know it's pitch black in the room and I cannot move. I am completely paralyzed from head to toe. I don't try to move, because I know I can't. I'm tingling all over. I'm terrified. I lie there waiting for something to happen. It doesn't. Can I get up? Am I conscious? What's happening to me?!? When will this be over?

I lose time. Eventually, I fall back to sleep, having no idea of how long the night paralysis with its accompanying altered states of consciousness has lasted. Was I under for 10 minutes? Or 2 hours? How would I know?

I had so many questions. I couldn't make heads or tails of any of it. I was clear that there was NO ONE to tell about this in my world, seeing that I was in the cult of Jehovah's Witnesses. Every inexplicable, paranormal or supernatural event or episode had one author: Satan the devil.

Thought you saw and angel? Nope. It was the devil. Had a clear premonition ahead of time that later came true? That was the devil. Know psychically what's going on with other people and later have it confirmed? Definitely the devil.

These people had one answer and one answer only for anything not of the 5 senses: the devil.

This is a strange paradigm for people who claim they love Jehovah God and are utterly devoted to him above all else, considering that the devil is receiving credit for telepathy, psychic abilities, dream messages, angel visitations and all other gifts from God. The whole supernatural world got thrown into his domain. This is idolatry as far as I'm concerned. I wonder if fundamentalist Christians, in a twisted, backfiring sort of way, aren't the biggest devil worshipers going? He gets massive attention and credit, and is continually spoken of. He's so significant in the religion that you can't hear about God without hearing about him. It's almost as if God had an evil twin.

All I knew back then in my tiny little mind was: I had to find answers, and I couldn't ask the people around me.

There was no internet. There was no one to ask. There was no way I could even procure a book from the library that would help me, even though we went there often and I was an avid reader. My mother was the non-negotiating judge of what I could and could not read. If the reading material was benign to Witness beliefs, like books on bird watching or the Sahara desert or some other innocuous subject that extolled the virtues of nature, with no conflicting science added in, it was approved. This kind of literature could be used to back up the Witness story of Jehovah God being the Great Creator. Much of science, history and archaeology denied or disproved the Witness doctrine, and was typically banned.

It was clear I was literally and symbolically 'in the dark' about these night paralysis episodes.

For a short while, I entertained the thought that the devil must be visiting me at night.

I dismissed the theory when it didn't hold up under tougher examination. If the devil is the fount of all evil, and is single minded in his aim to steal my soul from God for his evil purposes, why isn't he doing anything to me at night? He isn't even so much as speaking a word about stealing my soul. He isn't even making his presence known.

The devil must be slacking on his job. I'm not sure how it works, but if I was in the soul-stealing business, I think I'd get on with the job and make it happen as quickly as possible.

Never heard from the devil. Still haven't.

Which made me realize back then that the Witnesses definitely did not have this thing all figured out like they'd claimed.

There were gaping holes in one of the most significant parts of their story: the devil concept.

I was being ushered into the truth and out of mental darkness, at a tiny age, via PHYSICAL DARKNESS… DARKNESS THAT DID NOT CONTAIN A DEVIL.

I found no conclusive answers then.

It wasn't until I became an adult woman who had left the Witness world and had began associating with the Witchy community that I heard others who had the exact same night paralysis episodes. The only difference between me and them was that they were not terrified by them because they had understanding.

I learned first hand that ignorance breeds fear.

From the vantage point of this now moment, I pour love on my little self of decades ago. She was having all kinds of Witchy, paranormal experiences for which there was no explanation, other than the devil.

As a grown Witch, I've continued to have these experiences. I welcome night paralysis. It's euphoric, and I've learned how to work with these energies in my body. I notice healing and cessation of aches and pains. I'm clear these are beneficial episodes which closely resemble experiences I've had with magic mushrooms.

Now, I welcome the darkness.

"And ye shall know the truth, and the truth shall make you free."
John 8:32 (KJV)

IV

Spellcrafting in Christian Witchcraft

A collection of elements and considerations for Christian Witchcraft.

What is Magick?

What is magick? A simple question that defies a simple answer. For purposes of this book, we'll keep it simple and go with Aleister Crowley's definition:

"The Science and Art of causing Change to occur in conformity with Will."

Will is defined by Aleister Crowley as one's true destiny. I call it the divine urge, or divine unction. It's the compelling direction of our life that could be defined as one's true purpose, or reason for being. Divine Will is the True Will.

Divine Will is not the mandate of the Big Dude we spoke of earlier.

Divine Will is what we really want to be doing, at the core of self.

For me, a magickal act is one that aligns with and supports my true WILL, my reason for being, or my great divine assignment, or the purpose for which my soul landed here.

You are here for a reason.

I am here for a reason.

That reason is not ***for*** other people, though it ***involves*** other people. I'm not here ***for*** my kids, yet my kids are ***involved*** in the fulfillment of my overall destiny. If it were not so, they would not exist in my world. I sense the universe is full of wonder and awe, and at the same time, it's practical and mission driven. Nothing exists without a purpose.

This doesn't mean that the only reason to practice magick, or the only instances to practice magick would have to be destiny related.

Let's look deeper.

I don't know that any of us could do something, or participate in something that's ***not*** destiny related.

Everything you're participating in now, from who you're in relationships with, to what clothes you love to wear, to what you love to eat, is all being chosen by you ***for a reason***.

At first blush, some of these reasons may seem downright antithetical to your purpose. Yet are they? Me choosing a bad relationship partner was just what I required to bring me to a deeper experience of true unconditional love, which is absolutely required for my destiny.

I would say that in some way, everything that's important enough to do magick for is some expression of a divine unction toward something greater. That something greater will ultimately equate to something useful on the path of destiny.

For me, we're all walking the path of destiny. Everything that I encounter on this path is ***for*** me; and is somehow helping me to unfold what I came here to fulfill.

Acts of WILL aren't limited to being magickal acts. Acts of will can be 'mundane' as well. We practice far more mundane acts each day than magickal acts. Brushing teeth. Showering. Putting on shoes. Making coffee. All these acts — even though 'mundane' — are taking us somewhere. They are the seat belts and radio and such in the car that's driving us to destiny. They're all interrelated; not separate from the whole of our being. How we do one thing is essentially how we do everything. This would mean that a significant improvement in one area of my life will automatically significantly improve another area.

Countless issues in my world have gotten substantially better with no direct focus on that particular thing, and no magickal intervention whatsoever, even though I'm naturally a magickal being, probably just like you.

The bottom line for me: **everything is magick**.

In addition to being acts of will, ***I also view magick as a creative power and ability that everyone possesses***, whether they choose to develop it to its fullest extent or not. Everyone's creating all the time. We're creative beings, so we can't NOT create.

With Aleister Crowley's definition as our foundation, coupled with the broader definition of magick as creative power and ability that we choose to use and master, or not, we move on to what it's for.

First a note about the distinction between MAGICK and MAGIC.

Magick with a 'k' is a spiritual path (per Aleister Crowley), versus magic, which is done on stage in Las Vegas. I don't doubt that some of what goes on in Las Vegas involves magick, but to make a clear distinction, ***magick*** is the spiritual path while ***magic*** is tricks, sleight of hand and optical illusions.

What's the purpose of magick? For me, it's two-fold. First, I use magick for transcendence, as a means of soul evolution and ascension. It's my way of accomplishing the Great Work, alchemy of the soul. Second, I use magick to make my life on planet earth as wonderfully close to the dream life I hold in my 3rd eye as I imaginably can.

We can use magick BOTH to **CREATE** something new, and/or to **TRANSFORM**.

Mind you, I'm not seeking to control the universal processes, nor am I seeking to control outcomes. There's a beautiful balance to strike when practicing magick.

There's the magick, and then there's the release.

Magick is stating how you'd like it to go, as specifically as possible, while **BEING** and **EMBODYING** what you're asking for, to help the magick do its job.

Then there's the release aspect of the process, where we 'let go and let God.' I'm not speaking here of a big man in the sky. I gave up belief in sky gods long ago, as we've discussed. When I speak of God, I'm referring to the Cosmic Mind accessed **WITHIN**. It's accessed within because it's my **TRUE MIND**. If I take my tiny little mind and pit it against the Cosmic

Mind, it's likely I'll lose, and painfully.

If I align my little mind with Cosmic Mind accessed within, it's likely I'll win, and win big.

Herein lies a secret I discovered long ago: the secret of 'sympathy' which is the essence of the magick I LOVE to practice: sympathetic magick.

Sympathetic Magick

Example: it won't work for me to be a mean-ass as I spell for — and fully expect to receive — a loving, kind and compassionate partner.

It would only make sense for me to make myself as sympathetic to the thing I desire so that it comes straight to me. Sympathetic magick is powerful. While people say "opposites attract" the Law says "like attracts like." Sympathetic magick exploits this law to the fullest.

Let me be clear, sympathetic magick is not about artificially altering self to manifest a desire or to 'get' someone.

It means that I get to **BECOME** the very **ESSENCE** of what I'm spelling for. Let's let this sink in: ***I GET TO BECOME IT.*** If I'm spelling for wealth, I get to **BECOME WEALTH**. If I'm spelling to get over a condition in the body temple, **I BECOME HEALTH**. If I'm spelling for a better career or an amazing business, **I BECOME THAT BILLIONAIRE CEO NOW**.

YES, this type of magick requires transformation! Indeed, it makes an inner transformation a non-negotiable aspect of the process. I like that. I have no desire to be the same person I was yesterday because I've chosen to use magick as a crutch or a shortcut.

Side note: I make transforming myself a major aspect of my magick because I'm primarily using magick as a means of accomplishing the Great Work, and secondarily to make my life on planet earth really scrumptious. If I were not practicing magick as a means of ascension, I would probably do things differently, and I would spell differently.

This is why all of this is personal. You're the only one who knows why you're practicing magick. What's your true intention? Only you know.

To summarize this chapter, my magick is simple and fluid. I craft spells from the deepest core of me, which is what I advocate and recommend for every magickal being, regardless of intention. No book, no matter how good, can teach you how to exactly spell craft specifically for yourself. You are the only one who can do that.

I have countless magick books. None of them have the power to replace the act of doing magick. Only practice will catalyze the development of spells and rituals that work **FOR YOU**. You're the only one who can synthesize all your learning and study into a bespoke magickal practice.

Ancestral Magick

It's my contention that the most powerful magick is the magick that runs in our bloodline. This contention doesn't preclude anyone from working with magick, because as far as I can tell, everyone has Witches somewhere in their blood line, whether they know it or not.

Witches are in EVERY CULTURE, in EVERY PERIOD OF TIME. There is not one race of people on the planet or corner of the globe that does not have Witches.

If you're aware of your ancestral magick and are working it, HALLELUJAH!

If you're not yet aware of the ancestral magick that runs in your veins, a good place to start is with the traditions and 'old wives tales' passed down in your family. I'm sure you'll find clues to your family's magick. Magick is everywhere.

Magick Misfires and Backfires

Magick is a powerful force that brings unanticipated consequences. We don't ever really know everything that will happen as a result of any particular spell.

Any number of strange occurrences could happen. The universe 'got jokes.' Having an insurance payout of $3,000 for your car being wrecked may not have been the precise result you were looking for when you spelled for and extra $3,000 to take care of a pressing financial issue. I've heard of Witches giving clear command to the universe for new items, then the old items burned. The new items arrived as requested, it's just that the fulfilled request didn't show up in a way that could have ben anticipated.

For me, the important thing to know is that the results did come. The universe ALWAYS hears us and responds. We'll get some kind of result doing our magick, of this we can be sure.

These magickal misfires and backfires are not reasons to not practice magick.

For me, they represent an impetus to climb higher with my magick... to become more intentional, to be a MASTER ALCHEMIST.

Newbies make blunders. We can't help it. It's the nature of the beast.

The hope is that if magick is that important to you, you will do WHATEVER IT TAKES to master your craft. Mastery does NOT imply that there will be no unintended consequences. After all, a Master Alchemist knows well that they do not control the entire cosmos.

A Master Alchemist routinely engages these 4 in a harmonious balance:

- LEARNS: studies the craft.
- PRACTICES: does the craft.
- OBSERVES: watches and records results of the craft.
- OPTIMIZES: makes the next spell and/or ritual better based on results.

I've had more magickal misfires and backfires than I care to list out here (plus I don't want to depress you).

I pray this word is sufficient: **BE CAREFUL** and **READY** to accept the consequences of any particular magickal working. You'll find out more about this the longer you practice. If you've been practicing for a while, you know this well.

Now that we've covered a brief definition of magick, why I use magick and what I use it for, let's take a look at the methodology I use in Christian Witchcraft, as well as magickal practices that support my craft.

What is a Spell?

A spell can be defined as, but is not limited to:

- A state of enchantment
- A definition (spelling out specifically what one desires)
- Bewitchment
- Charm
- Incantation
- Magickal words or the effects of magickal words
- A magickal process or operation designed to create and manifest a specific desired result.

A positive spell could be referred to as a blessing or creation or expansion. A negative spell could be referred to as hexing, banishing or cursing.

Dispensing with good and evil, we could say the universe has 2 powerful and potent energies available to us in spell work: creation (expansion/birth) and destruction (banishing/getting rid of). I use both. Not on people, but on ENERGIES. Once again, I'm sharing with you my path as a Witch. Yours may differ.

I don't seek to over simplify a complex eons old idea that is expressed as the word spell. A spell, I believe, is far beyond anything we could put into words, as is true of most of magick and spirituality as a whole.

With that said, let's take a look at 'spell' as defined for our purposes here:

Definition of Spell in This Context

Spell: a magickal operation designed to effect a desired result/outcome consisting of a specific incantation or set of words in a prescribed manner, order and/or cadence, in a consecrated or magickally prepared space (a circle cast in your temple, or in a cave, or along a riverside, etc.), along with prescribed physical actions (hand movements, body posture etc.), powered by focused and directed energy (the most important part), and projected or launched with a powerful intention (for the outcome and why) while BEING the very essence of the thing desired, and SEEING CLEARLY the desired outcome/result in the third eye.

That's a mouthful.

Let's dissect it.

Crafting and Casting

Crafting the spell is designing it from beginning to end and recording it in a grimoire. We could say that Spellcrafting is drawing up or designing the architectural blueprint. It's creating and writing out the recipe.

Casting the spell is performing it. This is the actual construction of the edifice one has architected. This is the act of making the dish from the recipe.

For Christian Witches, this follows the manifest and creation design of Genesis chapters 1 and 2, which appear to say the same thing twice. In reality, chapter 1 speaks of the design (creation of the world in Divine Mind) while chapter 2 refers to its manifestation (the world taking form in the physical dimension).

Spellcrafting is invisible and is an inner design.

Spell casting is visible and is an outward act.

For me, both Spellcrafting and spell casting are sacred acts.

Desired Result/Outcome

There's always a reason why we're Spellcrafting and casting. There's something we desire, or there's something we desire to change. Without a desire, there can be no spell. (More on desire is in the chapter on "Formula for Crafting a Spell or Ritual.")

Spell Uses

Spells can be employed to:

- Get rid of a negative experience/effect (i.e. get rid of poverty or a generational curse).
- To create and manifest a positive experience/effect (i.e. gain wealth).
- Elicit or induce healing.
- Make objects magickally potent (i.e. wands, swords, chalices, etc.).
- Consecrate items for magickal and spiritual purposes (i.e. vestments, crystals, Tarot decks, etc.).
- Create and charge amulets as symbols which are worn or carried for magickal purposes (i.e. protection, repulsion, attraction).
- Create and charge sigils as symbols of the essence of one's desires or as a means to make contact with spirits.
- Contact, commune with and/or command spirits (i.e. angels, demons, fairies, sprites, etc.)
- Command the weather.
- Create magickal servitors.
- Raise the dead.
- Create a golem.

Magick is a vast territory, as wide as the universe itself, so these examples are a representative list. There are more reasons to cast a spell than can be listed in any book.

Incantation

What is an incantation?

From Wikipedia under Incantation:

> *"An* ***incantation****, a* ***spell****, a* ***charm****, an* ***enchantment*** *or a* ***beWitchery****, is a magical formula intended to trigger a magical effect on a person or objects. The formula can be spoken, sung or chanted. An incantation can also be performed during ceremonial rituals or prayers. In the world of magic, incantations are said to be performed by wizards, Witches and fairies."*

I pretty much agree with this definition. An incantation is an ESSENTIAL aspect of magickal rites, spells and rituals. The **INCANTATION** is the **SPOKEN WORD**, a critical operative component of effectual magick.

One of the most famed of all magickal incantations is **ABRACADABRA** (the energetic equivalent to **I AM THAT I AM**).

For our purposes, we will use the word Incantation to refer to the part of our spell that are the **WORDS OF POWER** and **WORDING** (order of the words). I do not craft a spell without an incantation.

Words

The words are high on the list of priorities when it comes to spells. The words are an integral, critical ingredient that must be crafted as best one can. Great wordsmiths are great change makers, within the magickal field and outside of magick.

Being a wordsmith means that one understands not only the words themselves, but the energetic impact the words are having on consciousness (in this case, one's own consciousness) and especially the subconscious levels of mind (the non-local part of the mind that will cause the desired results to appear in one's world). In addition, the words are entering the cosmos as a whole, in order to reverberate and change something.

Everything is energy, and energy is affected, shaped and molded by sound. Sound is our words.

This is all scientific and magickal.

Words are of high importance to me because I'm a Keeper of the Word (you may be as well). This is a person who has a divine assignment relating to the word (either writing, or speaking or somehow advancing and ascending humanity by using the Word/words).

Words used in Spellcrafting and casting ought not to be common, ordinary words. Why? Because we're accustomed to every day words. They do not have maximum impact on the subconscious mind because they are the norm. Therefore, maximum results are not likely to be achieved.

Words that cause the subconscious mind to sit up and take note are:

- Unusual
- Formal
- Arcane
- Barbarous
- Hard to pronounce
- Used widely by many people in a reverent fashion (such as the Lord's Prayer or the 23rd Psalm).

These are the kinds of words we will use to craft our spells and rituals.

Hand and Body Motions

It goes without saying that every sphere of human endeavor has its associated hand and body movements, from sports to dentistry to cooking to magick.

Mastering our body motions as a Master Alchemist is part and parcel of magick. Hand gestures —with and without wands and magickal implements — must be practiced and mastered.

Even a basic ritual of casting a circle requires hand and body movements we get to master.

Envision

An aspect of potent magick is **SEEING THE OUTCOME** in the 3rd eye before it lands in the 3rd dimension.

The reason we're doing magick is to create or transform. We must have in our minds a **CLEAR PROTOTYPE** of what we desire the outcome to be like, look like, feel like. The richer and more vivid the images are in the 3rd eye, the better.

If you're a person who doesn't visualize well, fret not. Everyone's mind works differently. There are people who do not visualize well, yet can cast magick and get results like you wouldn't believe. How? Because they're able to cast themselves into the result in a **REAL, PALPABLE** way. They can **FEEL** their way there, or they can **SMELL** their results (yes, I know Witches who have the gift of Olfactory Magick who can literally smell spirits), or they can **BE** the result.

The bottom line is, for your magick to work like gangbusters, find ways to **PUT YOURSELF IN THE OUTCOME** more than you live in the current situation.

The easiest way to do that would be to see it vividly as a movie in the 3rd eye. If that's not working, meditation can help. If that's just not how your mind is wired, use your other senses (inner and outer) to make the **DESIRED RESULT VIVID** in your consciousness as a **RIGHT NOW REALITY**.

Part Art, Part Science

By their very nature, spells are not repetitive, if they work as desired.

However, if the results achieved are not optimal, one can uplevel the spell and give it a go again. I don't cast the exact same spell for the exact same issue more than once. I have certainty the universe heard me the first time. Intuition and awareness reveal to me when and how I'm receiving the results of the working. If the results are not optimal, I will adjust the spell work for a more precise outcome.

This is part art, part science.

Example: you craft and cast a spell to manifest the perfect love partner on the New Moon in Libra. You chose to petition Haniel, the archangel of Venus during the spell to ascertain information, influences and hidden factors related to receiving this great love you know is yours by divine birthright.

You receive information from Haniel that you have a broken heart.

It's now your responsibility to release broken-heartedness. You do this spiritual work over the next 90 days, in earnest, and voila! A love interest appears. It may have been someone you've known all along. You engage the love relationship and over time, it deepens into the love relationship you've imagined and dreamed of.

This would be a successful working.

For me, magick isn't linear. The results could appear in any number of ways.

If you feel the spell is not working, I wouldn't call the archangel Haniel every month on the New Moon to ask why I don't receive the love of my life yet.

A **HUGE** aspect of magick is **CERTAINTY**.

BE CERTAIN YOUR SPELL WORKED. At the same time, **BE PATIENT**. You don't own your results. The universe returns results based on YOU... who you are BEING and what you are DOING, almost like a computer program. Information in, and out spits a result. To change the result, the inputs must be changed. The computer of the universe is **ALWAYS** functioning **PERFECTLY**, even when we don't agree with the computations. The system is fool-proof, based on law. We can be certain the results are **ALWAYS** precise, based on **INPUTS**.

This certainty in the perfect workings of the universe elicits effective magick at the highest levels. If I desire a change, I will **ALWAYS** be able to create and manifest that desired change by changing **WHO I AM BEING** and **WHAT I AM DOING**.

Once you crack this code of the universe, it will be a fun adventure to create desired results magickally for you and in service to others if you're called and led to do so. What a gift!

Remember, results with any given spell will vary based on **WHO YOU ARE** and **WHAT YOU ARE DOING**. Bottom line: **BE YOUR BEST** as you **DO YOUR BEST**.

Spell vs. Magick

Some people are doing a spell, and not magick. Others are doing magick, without the use of any spells. Others are doing both.

There's no right or wrong, only distinctions to understand, so we choose wisely.

Spell WITHOUT Magick

Here's an example of a spell, sans magick:

- I take all the steps to craft a spell.
- I cast the spell at the perfect cosmic time.
- I release the spell to the universe and forget about it.
- I have no feelings, intentions, visualization, WILL or ENERGY infused into the spell.

Though I took all the steps in the prescribed fashion — crossing all the proverbial t's and dotting all the proverbial i's — without the energetic component, I have NOT PRACTICED MAGICK even though I've cast a spell.

Spell WITH Magick

Here's an example of a spell WITH magick:

- I take all the steps to craft a spell.
- I cast the spell at the perfect cosmic time.
- I release the spell to the universe and forget about it.
- I've infused my energy, WILL, love, visualizations of outcome and power into every aspect of the Spellcrafting and casting, as well as the tools and implements used.
- I've aligned my consciousness with the essence of what I'm spelling. I literally BECOME the thing I am desirous of manifesting. This is a requisite transformation in consciousness so that I not only manifest that which is desired, I SUSTAIN THE NEW RESULT.
- I change my life to be in alignment with the spell work.

I've literally HURLED MYSELF into the spell work.

Example:

I spell for a beautiful new love partnership.

In the first instance (spell WITHOUT magick) I cast a spell and keep on going about my business.

In the second instance (spell WITH magick) I cast the spell AND:

- Change my thoughts from mostly SOLO thoughts to COUPLE thoughts. **I ASSUME THE PARTNERSHIP NOW**, even though I haven't seen it yet.
- Feng Shui my bedroom for 2 rather than one.
- Set a place setting at meals for 2 rather than one.
- Walk the beach with my love energetically, rather than walking absent mindedly by myself while looking at all the couples and being sad or frustrated that my love hasn't shown up yet.
- All the other inspirations that will land in my consciousness to

potentize the **MAGICK** I'm to be engaging in for this area of my life.

Lusting After Results

You may think that doing all the 'extras' to align with the spell work is a form of lusting after results (a killer in magick). Being too 'thirsty' in magick — or too anxious for results — represents a spirit of fear, not confidence that the result is **ALREADY DONE**.

There's a fine line between lusting after results and **ALIGNING** with the spell work. Here's the major distinction:

Lusting for a result is fear that it may not happen. ALIGNMENT is the full body knowing that it has ALREADY happened.

If you can put yourself in the **ALREADY DONE** space energetically, there's no way that what you've spelled for would not come to you, with ease, grace and swiftness, regardless if you got all the elements 'perfect' for the spell or not.

Everything is ENERGY.

If you were already in a love relationship, wouldn't you have 2 place settings at the dinner table rather than 1? Wouldn't your bedroom configuration be different for you in a relationship than it would be for you as a single person? Wouldn't your closet(s) be different if you were in a relationship versus you as a single person?

Whatever changes are required — mentally, emotionally, physically, spiritually, financially — in order to **ALIGN** with what we've spelled for are what we get to **DO NOW**.

THIS IS MAGICK.

Anyone can do a spell. Not everyone is a Master Alchemist.

What is a Ritual?

The definition of the word ritual is:

"a religious or solemn ceremony consisting of a series of actions performed according to a prescribed order."

or

"the established form for a ceremony specifically *: the order of words prescribed for a religious ceremony."*

or

"ritual observance specifically *: a system of rites; a ceremonial act or action; an act or series of acts regularly repeated in a set precise manner."*

Ritual in this context is used to refer to a formal recurring spiritual practice containing steps designed to take the mind out of ordinary waking consciousness in order to activate the vast resources of Divine Mind within.

Let's unravel this.

Ritual is sacred. Ritual connects us with the Divine. Ritual is a portal to the otherworldly through which we gladly enter to perform our spell work. This is why ritual surrounds and underpins Spellcrafting and casting.

One of the other most potent aspects of ritual is memorability. We do not forget deeply meaningful rituals performed in a sacred and devout manner. They are etched in consciousness, thus forming a perfect pathway in consciousness for the manifestation of desires. This pathway is an energetic river upon which our desires can be continually conveyed to us.

Examples of Magickal Rituals

- A Tarot reading each Full Moon - you create sacred space in your Temple, cast a circle, and engage a full blown Tarot reading. Record the reading in detail, including drawing the cards, in a Tarot Grimoire. I practiced this ritual for several Full Moons in a row (needless to say, LIFE CHANGING).
- The steps you engage before, during or after you cast a spell - prayer, calling in the Spirit Team (see the chapter titled "Your Spirit Team"), lighting candles, casting a circle, etc.
- Daily morning or evening spiritual practices - ritual bathing, entering your Temple, lighting incense, prayer, meditation, journaling, breath-work, etc.

All of the above can elicit expanded states of awareness. This is the purpose of ritual... to disconnect from the ordinary and enter altered states of consciousness where there is no distinction or differentiation between self and God.

Ye are gods. Ritual reminds us of this truth before, during and after our spell work.

Christian Witchcraft

In this chapter we define and put forth the "7 & 9" methodology for Christian Witchcraft, should you choose to integrate or practice it. This is completely up to you, as there are no rules, dogma or doctrine in this spiritual path. This is simply me sharing with you what I do, and not a recommendation on what you should do. You know what you are to do. I honor this.

Christian Witchcraft Methodology

Every magickal system has a methodology, from Wicca to Solomonic Magic to Hoodoo and beyond.

The methodology consists of a set of underlying and defining principles upon which the magickal tradition stands. It could also be expressed as a framework of protocols. There are practices, rituals, rites, initiations, spells, and more for every magickal tradition. The specifics of these protocols are unique to each system, though the magickal underpinning of all the systems is universal.

I cannot triumphantly proclaim that I have the methodology for Christian Witchcraft figured out. I do not. I'm probably a lot like you, making it up as I go.

Again, the beauty of this path is its fluidity. There are no rules, no dogma, no doctrine in any Witchcraft tradition that I know of. The same applies to Christian Witchcraft.

There are, however, principles and universal laws.

Beyond the specific protocols of each magickal system, there are universal laws of magick we all have access to, just as the Law of Gravity applies to everyone on planet earth, and not just to people of a certain religion.

The varied and beautiful tapestry made up of the magickal systems of the world has an undergirding, a foundation upon which they stand. I find tremendous happiness and reassurance that there's a powerful foundation upon which we all practice magick, no matter what kind of magick we practice. There's something we can count on to work.

When establishing your methodology as a Christian Witch, ***be ruthless in your questioning and examination***. Not of others. Of Self. Ask your Self (Higher Self) hard questions. Continually question Self. The Divine Self has never been threatened or irritated by my unending and sometimes pressing questions. Truth can withstand my incessant inquiry.

This is how you work out what's true and right and good for YOU.

Here I'll share with you my methodology for Christian Witchcraft and how I arrived at it.

My Methodology

The foundation I stand upon and rest my magick on is **LAW, NATURE** and **PRINCIPLES**.

In addition, addressed here will be a mindset to inhabit in order to be at peace in the face of one's own staggering ignorance (the more I discover, the more I'm humbled in wondering if I know a damned thing at all).

This methodology is shared with you as inspiration and nothing more. It's not the Bible of methodologies, nor is it a methodology you ought to follow. Only you get to form your methodology, from **PRACTICE** and **EXPERIENCE**.

Three books have been pivotal in forming and shaping my methodology:

the Bible (including the Apocrypha, the Pseudepigrapha, the Lost Books of the Bible and the Gnostic Gospels), ***A Course In Miracles*** and the ***Kybalion.***

With that said, let's dive in.

Law

The LAW I'm referring to here is the collection of the 7 Hermetic Principles of ancient Kemet (Egypt) as expressed in the book the ***Kybalion***. I refer to these 7 principles as a composite LAW. Without going into an exhaustive explanation of all 7, I'll briefly state them here, paraphrased from **Sacred Texts** online:

1. **Principle of Mentalism** - THE ALL IS MIND; the universe is mental.
2. **Principle of Correspondence** - as above, so below; as below, so above.
3. **Principle of Vibration** - nothing rests; everything moves; everything vibrates.
4. **Principle of Polarity** - everything is dual; everything has poles. Like and unlike are the same, differing only in degree.
5. **Principle of Rhythm** - everything flows out and in; everything has tides.
6. **Principle of Cause & Effect** - every Cause has its Effect; every Effect has a Cause.
7. **Principle of Gender** - Gender is in everything; everything has its Masculine and Feminine principles.

I do not put stock in these laws because they're supposedly written by Hermes Thrice Great. Nor do I put stock in them because we're told they're from Kemet, or because they're deemed ancient.

The **ONLY** reason I put stock in any of these laws is because **I MADE THEM SCIENTIFIC**. I used them. I hammered them. I questioned them. I practiced them. I put them to work. I observed the outcomes. I course corrected. I applied them to very specific issues and received feedback in the form of results. I worked these laws and found them to be efficacious.

In short, I don't BELIEVE in these laws. I'm doing the best I can to rid myself of ALL belief. BELIEVE NOTHING. Belief is not helpful.

I stand on these laws because they're tested and proven in the scientific laboratory that is my life experience.

The Scientific Method

MAKE EVERYTHING SCIENTIFIC.

Making it scientific means WORKING with the laws by practical application to life and magick and carefully observing and recording results. From there, course corrections are made and the laws are applied yet again. Please know this is a years long process. Nothing about it is fast. Don't ask for fast. Ask for effective.

You'll know what works for you when using the scientific method. Not only will you know what works for you, you'll become a NINJA. **A MASTER ALCHEMIST.**

That's what I'm going for... **MASTERY**. My aspiration is to be a badass at whatever I choose to pour myself into. And since magick is deeply important to me, I aspire to be a badass at magick.

On the other hand, you WON'T know what works for other people when using the scientific method, which is the ultimate beauty of the scientific method. Each person is receiving personalized results. To tell someone else what will work for them because it worked for you is both irrelevant and irresponsible.

YES! Share what works for you, IF you desire and are inspired. YES! Reveal what you choose to share about your own scientific method and the results it yielded for you.

However, the second we declare our method as a useful method for someone else is the exact second religion is born.

I AM NOT FOR RELIGION. I do not espouse or practice organized religion. Religion teaches you what to think, not how to think.

At the heart of what I teach and practice is **SOVEREIGNTY** and **DIVINITY**. Everyone is a sovereign being. Everyone and everything is Divine, which means everyone and everything has **GNOSIS** of what it's to be and do.

This is also why I don't offer advice. I don't know what will work for you. I can only offer my experience, including what I've found to work for me, with an intention to inspire you to seek and find what works for you. It's out there. It's up to you to find it. If you've already found it, congratulations on doing the work!

On Being a Mystic

The essence of the spiritual path is that it's **EXPERIENTIAL** with no one-size-fits-all answers, solutions or methods. I love that.

This is the path of the mystic, the one who does not know, yet is filled with grace. The mystic is not frustrated because she does not know. When met with one's own ignorance, the mystic is filled with wonder and awe at how much there's yet to discover.

Never concern yourself when you don't know. Never regard ignorance or inexperience as frustrating.

Humbly accepting the massiveness of what I do not know is a beautiful sign that there's so much more to learn. Intentionally create spaciousness within as acknowledgment that there's much to discover. People who are too full and cluttered on the inside with what they think they know have little room to receive new or updated information.

Being a mystic is essentially an emptying.

Nature

Though Christian Witchcraft is not a religion, and we hold no dogma or doctrine, there are certain constants we can count on. I don't hold the view of a random universe (though everyone gets to decide for themselves what the nature of the universe might be).

The constants we can count on are akin to mathematics. The whole universe is made up of numbers and mathematical equations. Rather than holding this fact as cold and calculating, I heart-fully appreciate that I can count on certain unfailing aspects of the cosmos. For me, these unfailing aspects are expressed in and as **NATURE**.

Nature cannot lie. It's the forever, unfailing truth.

When I seek answers to questions that confound me, I go to nature. It's not hard to find the answer. Most of the time, the answers are stark in their simplicity.

Nature is dynamic, evolving and ever changing, yet the underlying laws and principles of nature DO NOT CHANGE because **TRUTH DOES NOT CHANGE**.

As an example, an acorn contains the potential to become only an oak tree. It cannot turn itself into corn. I find reassurance in this simple yet potent law of nature: potential is encoded in the seed.

An imaginative soul could work all kinds of magick with this one simple law. You could have an entire magickal practice consisting solely of sympathy using seeds.

Let's be clear, our discovery of nature yields information that's constantly changing. We're always discovering more. When we learn more, we displace old ideas and paradigms that no longer fit. The teaching ascribed to Christ is that one cannot put new wine into old wine skins.

Humility reminds us that there's always more to learn; we don't have it all figured out. We may never have it all figured out, an idea I find scrumptious. It gives us more to go for, more to discover. It elicits awe, and for me, an awe-filled existence is a happy existence.

This is an exhilarating process. I'm an adventurer at heart, so the idea of discovering more and more in our magnificent cosmos is a big fat hell yeah!

We get to understand the powerful distinction between NATURE'S LAWS and what we KNOW of nature's laws. The former is unchanging. The latter changes moment by moment the more we discover.

Principles of Magick

Lastly, let's address a few guiding principles I use in magick. These principles are expounded upon in greater detail in my book *Christian Witches Manifesto* (which is now a gift to members on my YouTube channel and can no longer be purchased for reasons I write about in a blog post at www.ChristianWitches.com), so I won't repeat here what's already been stated.

In short, my guiding principles are expressed in Galatians 5:22-23 as the Fruit of the Spirit along with a collection of energies that have served me well, both of which I'll share now. Once again, I don't use these as guiding principles because they're written in an old book supposedly by Paul. I don't know or care who wrote them. I care that they work.

The ***Fruit of the Spirit*** comprise 9 qualities or divine attributes:

1. **Love** (as the creative principle of the universe, not an emotion)
2. **Joy** (spontaneous bliss)
3. **Peace** (for me, this encompasses harmony and balance, or the essence of Ma'at, a way of being we will explore in my upcoming book ***Egyptian Magick for the Christian Witch***)
4. **Patience/Forbearance/Endurance** (nothing great can be accomplished without these because creating greatness takes a long ass time)
5. **Kindness/Compassion** (My grandma used to say "you can catch more flies with honey than you can with vinegar." For me, that's the essence of being kind.)
6. **Goodness/Benevolence/Generosity/Heroism** (taking the always harder, longer and more arduous HIGH ROAD; being a truly benevolent being on the planet as a force for GOOD and POSITIVE CHANGE in the human condition; being solidly on the hero's journey/hero's quest)
7. **Faithfulness** (we can count on you; certainty things are always working out perfectly)

8. **Gentleness** (not being a mean-ass or a hard-ass or exacting or oppressive, especially when it comes to self; I don't know about you, but I've been mean to me)
9. **Self-control/Self Mastery** (being a **MASTER ALCHEMIST**)

I haven't found any of these to be off the mark. They're all beneficial and useful in my life and magick, proven by **EXPERIENCE**. I haven't mastered any of these. They form a collective ***aspiration***.

A few more guiding principles that serve me well in life and magick, and that I have a deep inner commitment to, are:

- Acceptance
- Accountability
- Authenticity
- Awareness (especially self-awareness)
- Commitment
- Discipline
- Divinity
- Excellence
- Forgiveness
- Freedom
- Grace
- Honesty
- Humility
- Integrity
- Power
- Responsibility
- Sovereignty
- Trust
- Truth
- Wisdom

It would be a monumental task to put into writing here every principle that's served me in this life and on the path of Christian Witchcraft. I'm offering a sampling here so that the point is conveyed on the methodology I'm working with and how I came to it.

I chose to build my magick on a firm foundation of truth, which is a protection from my own mind. Fickle thoughts and emotional flights of fancy do little for the development and expansion of **MASTERY**.

Now that you know this about me, what's your methodology?

What are your guiding principles?

What foundation does your magick rest upon?

What do you know for sure?

These are valid questions for us as practicing Christian Witches. These deserve our reverent regard and prayerful attention until we arrive at answers that fill our soul with peace.

Magick I Personally Don't Do

Now is as good a time as any to explore the kinds of magick that I don't participate in, due to personal choice. You get to choose for yourself.

Considering the foregoing, I do not practice:

- **Magick on other people.** In my world, not required. Everyone gets to do as they damn well please. I have no desire to change what other people are doing. I've found peace in acceptance. Acceptance does NOT mean agreement or acquiescence. It also doesn't mean to stay in dangerous or unhealthy conditions without actively and immediately seeking and creating change. It simply means that the pursuit of control of other people is a fruitless endeavor. This does not mean that we do not influence those around us. We absolutely freakin' do. And they influence us as well. At the end of the day, we get to CHOOSE and we must live with ALL that comes with what we chose.
- **Hexes.** Not necessary. I'd rather bless than hex. ***There is no one and nothing other than myself that is more powerful than me in my world. This is the Divine power Source has gifted to each of us as***

Divine Beings. Nothing other than my own consciousness exists as the creative force and power of my life experience. I must therefore, take 100% ownership and responsibility for all I experience and choose what I'll do.

- **Removal of Hexes**. According to the Law of Mentalism and the principles of responsibility and creativity, I ALONE have creative power in my world. No one else creates my life. No one has the power to. This is why I'm unconcerned with hexes anyone else may attempt, or with what other people do or say. Everyone can do as they please, as can I. The effects of any hex exactly corresponds to what I think (consciously and unconsciously). I would rather relentlessly work with my own consciousness to be in a space of **ABSOLUTE SAFETY** and **PEACE** at all times that NOTHING can disturb. ***"Nothing outside yourself can hurt you, or disturb your peace or upset you in any way. Today's idea places you in charge of the universe, where you belong because of what you are."*** (*A Course In Miracles* Lesson 70). I AM is the ultimate power in my world, and I AM is not 'throwing hands.' **"Ye are gods."** (Psalm 82:6). A god is not subject to what other people do. A god is self-initiating. I know there are a lot of magickal people who may argue this point, and that's all well and good. I'm sharing with you my take on it. Only you get to choose where you stand.
- **Love spells for a specific person.** I don't do love spells on particular people (i.e. make this person fall in love with me, or get this person to notice me, or I want that person and that person only) because I'm not smart enough. I don't mean to be funny. I'm being as honest as I can. I've spelled for a certain person to be in my world, and it turned out disastrous. I've also found that there's a mystery to love that **ALWAYS** bought the perfect person in my life at the **PERFECT** time for the **PERFECT** reasons and we all grew and ascended from the experience. I also acknowledge I had little to no conscious control of that process. Higher Self is at work. Though I may think I know the exact person or the exact thing that would make me feel good in the love department, I've found that ultimately, my tiny egoic mind does not. What I

DO know is the quality and essence of the relationships in which I choose to engage. I KNOW MY INTENTION and I spell for this, irregardless of a specific person. I have a non-negotiable standard on what I CHOOSE to experience in my intimate partnerships: love, joy, peace, appreciation, honor, beauty and bliss. To keep my relationships in this space as much as I can, I seek to **EMBODY** love, joy, peace, appreciation, honor, beauty and bliss. As I walk about energetically embodying these, the appropriate people are always drawn to me and I LOVE how it turns out! I'm either receiving exactly what I asked for, or I'm receiving the necessary CONTRAST to what I asked for for the purpose of clearing in me whatever is creating the contrast so that I can have exactly what I asked for, energetically. Either way, the system is helping me. I've never been able to improve on the natural laws of love energy in the universe so I go along with them. Please understand, I am NOT advocating leaving it all up to chance. I DO NOT do that. I **INTENTIONALLY PRACTICE BEING** what I **CHOOSE** to experience. When I'm NOT experiencing what I would delightfully choose, I do what's required to lovingly change, shift, transform or grow into the ME that creates something different. This is in alignment with the Law of Cause & Effect.

The energetic underpinning of my magick is simple: **BECOME WHAT I DESIRE**. There's a beautiful **MATCHING** system that's always at work. Call it the Law of Attraction. I BECOME PEACE and there becomes greater peace all around me, and in the entire world. I am not claiming that if I become peace I will never be presented with a situation that is not peaceful. This would not be the truth. I'm offering that if I choose to **BECOME PEACE** my entire world will take on a peaceful FLAVOR, rather than chaos. My world will be in essence more harmonious, rather than filled with drama. My magick and experiences will be created from a peaceful mind, and my circumstances, whatever they may be, will be met with a peaceful countenance. I'll receive mostly peaceful results. YES!

Again, my confession… I'm not the master of peace. I'm choosing and intending to become peace as best I can.

A Sacred Promise

This methodology holds a sacred promise from the Divine: if you become it, you will see it.

This is law. Universal law, like the Divine, is no respecter of persons.

"Then Peter opened his mouth, and said, Of a truth I perceive that God is no respecter of persons:"
Acts 10:34 (KJV)

Magickal Practices

If you make your entire life "highly enchantable" as the amazing sorcerer Jason Miller describes, the magick could happen even more speedily and perfectly. He offers examples of this principle in his books ***The Elements of Spellcrafting*** and ***Financial Sorcery*** (both of which I LOVE and enthusiastically recommend).

He describes the principle in terms of a simple example I'll try not to botch too much here… making your life highly enchantable could mean being an entrepreneur rather than being a government employee (or in addition to being a government employee). If you're spelling for money as a government employee, with no other ways of large amounts of money to suddenly flow in, it's not going to manifest as easily as it would if you're an entrepreneur with pipelines already in place to receive large amounts of money at any time.

This doesn't mean you couldn't receive a large amount of money suddenly just because you're a government employee. To me, the principle means fishing with a net rather than with one fishing hook. I'm bound to come up with more fish.

In addition to the principle of making my life highly enchantable (or tipping the odds way in favor of what I'm spelling for) I also think of the holistic nature of magick.

The whole universe is magick! Even when you're not formally practicing magick, magick is still happening for you and all around you. You're a magickal being.

I rely on this principle such that I expect my entire life to be magickal in every respect. I don't expect magick to start when I enter the circle. I expect magickal outcomes and enchanting experiences that utterly awe me as a normal course of my existence on planet earth.

How does one cause magick to happen all the time?

Magickal Practices

By integrating magickal practices that become the very essence of one's life and way of being. These include:

- Spellcrafting (creating and preparing spells)
- Spell casting (DOING THE MAGICK... the most important part!)
- Meditation
- Prayer
- Visualization
- Invocation: calling up a spirit that expresses within self in order to commune.
- Evocation: calling forth the visceral, palpable presence of a spirit before self in a magickal operation.
- Utilizing Sound: Chanting/Words of Power/Song
- Drum circles
- Tarot Reading (especially pulling a card of the day and recording it)
- Dream recordation & interpretation
- Studying magickal texts
- Summoning Spirits
- Spirit Communication (including angels, fairies, house spirits, ascended masters, spirit guides, enlightened ancestors, etc.)
- New Moon/Full Moon Rituals
- Rites of Passage (including initiations)
- Ritual Baths

- Yoga (defined as 'union' so in essence we're referring to any bodily activity which inspires and/or induces a sense of union with the ALL)
- Tantra
- Trance Work
- Breath Work
- Dance
- Healing with crystals
- Growing plants, flowers and food
- Engaging plant medicines
- Darkness & sensory deprivation experiences
- Any act/practice that's magickal to you

Basically, it's the commitment to living a magickal life. ***Being*** a Witch. Doing everything in a magickal way, from a magickal consciousness. The more you **BECOME** magick, the more magick is happening all the time. It's almost as if there's a cosmic bank that observes and matches magickal energy. The more magickal energy you put out, the wealthier you become, magickally speaking.

From this consciousness, you'll practice the most wickedly effective magick imaginable.

Source of Power

Different magickal systems draw power from different sources. Some draw power from the earth, while others draw power from the ancestors.

In my Christian Witchcraft practice, I draw power from Source within. This may not be the case for all Christian Witches (as you know well by now, I don't speak for any Christian Witch save myself). You know from where you draw your power.

As a Christian Witch, I can see many perspectives. Some may draw power from Christ, while others may draw power from the Trinity, while still others may draw their power from their personal concept of God.

Each soul's spiritual walk is so unique that we cannot offer meaningful commentary on another's journey. We can only know our own, and walk it with integrity.

Source is the power accessed through the heart. The heart, for me, is the inner adytum, the soul sanctuary, the holy of holies, where I and the Father are One.

When I work magick, the power surges and flows from my heart center. Though it's powered by the will (housed in the solar plexus chakra), it emanates from the heart. The foundation and flavor of my magick is Divine Love (not the sappy emotion, but the pure creative, infinitely giving energy of the universe).

It's almost as if magick is pouring out (or at times shooting out) from the heart. The intention, direction and the endurance (staying power to successfully and effectively complete) derive from the solar plexus. The connection and cooperation between the solar plexus chakra and the heart chakra cannot be overemphasized in Spellcrafting and spell casting. They are intricately and intimately harmonious.

The intention emanates from the will (I WILL DO THIS...). Love is centered in the heart. If I channel my intentions through the heart, I have a greater likelihood of success, and a greater chance of doing holistic magick: magick that is good for the **ALL**.

This is the highest magick I can effect.

While it's good for me to have wealth and abundance, it's not good for the trees and the Earth Mother if I cut down every tree I find in the Amazon to sell to paper companies to increase my wealth. I could do a spell to be wealthy in this way, yet for me, this is not the highest use of magick. It takes into consideration only me and those who will profit with me, while effectively destroying the lungs of our planet, which will only wreak havoc later.

Or course the magick would work, if I'm an excellent spell crafter and caster. Yet, my personal considerations in doing magick go far beyond whether it will work or not.

The magick must be in integrity and alignment with me, who I am, and what I stand for. I stand for nature. I stand for Life. I stand for the whole of life, and not just what the little 'me' can grab or gain.

I don't want to sound like all my magick is transcendent and altruistic. It's not. Sometimes I may do magick to purely acquire something I desire. Yet, I channel it through the heart so that I have the best chances of it bringing no harm to Life as it returns to me my desire.

It's a fine line, and sometimes I do better than others. The key is **INTENTION**.

I took a vow of harmlessness many years back. I **INTEND** to be a beneficial force on the planet and in the cosmos. While that's all well and good, I'm sure I step on millions of ants and critters just walking around in a given day. This is an unavoidable aspect of living. Driving a car from New Orleans to Miami killed all the bugs that went splat on my windshield. The difference is I didn't wake up that morning and set out to kill thousands of bugs.

My **INTENTION** is to be **TRULY HELPFUL.**

"I am here only to be truly helpful."
A Course In Miracles

With this in mind, I make mistakes along the way. The more robust I play at life (and I love choosing the robust options!) the more mistakes I make. An intention for benevolence means unintended destructive acts weren't committed on purpose. Maybe you had a car accident. Maybe someone was hurt. That was far from your intention. Yet, things happen for reasons beyond our current knowing. When things ago awry, the beauty of the universe is **FORGIVENESS**. You get unlimited do-overs.

Only you know, in your heart of hearts, what your **TRUE INTENTION** is when crafting and casting spells.

EXAMNE YOUR INTENTIONS RUTHLESSLY. Why? Because our true intention is what's returned to us. The universe is uncanny in its ability to read and return our REAL intentions, whether we're aware of them or not. Rather than unwanted effects showing up, let's clean up our intentions as best we can. We'll do that work throughout this book.

Purifying the heart with love and channeling magick through this Divine Power has been a game changer and life saver for me.

Now let's give attention to your Spirit Team.

Your Spirit Team

Every soul has a vast Spirit Team at its disposal consisting of Higher Self, Enlightened Ancestors, Spirit Guides, Angels, Archangels, Ascended Masters and many more spirits than we can identify and name. This is an immense spiritual world, of which our physical dimension is but 1%. The other 99% of existence is imperceptible to the 5 senses. It is this 99% we will discuss here.

Also part of your Spirit Team are Gods/Goddesses and entities who have been communing with you for your entire incarnation, and who have been with you before this incarnation. If you're connected with them, wonderful. This chapter offers the invitation to go deeper. If you're not connected with them as you'd like to be, this chapter can help.

Let's start with a map of the cosmos that may be helpful. I'm not asking for agreement on this map, nor am I stating that this is the only map. This is a map as I see it, simplified so that the human mind can comprehend enough so that magickal action is taken.

3-Tiered Map of the Cosmos

For me, the cosmos is triple layered with spirits inhabiting each layer, or realm:

1. Celestial
2. Terrestrial
3. Infernal

I know this may sound like an oversimplification; I like to keep things simple for myself.

You may subscribe to a different cosmic map. All good. No rules. Go with your Inner Knowing.

Each layer mentioned above contains countless dimensions of consciousness, from the lowest to the highest and everything in between, as is the case in the world of humans. There are no inherently good or evil spirits. There are no useless spirits. If a spirit exists, it exists for a reason. Purpose is encoded in existence. The two are inseparable.

Since there are no inherently good or evil spirits, and every spirit has a purpose, then we must not be in fear when meeting ANY spirit. Fear is a killer and a liar and is never the appropriate reaction for the Master Alchemist.

We're explorers in this great cosmos, free to explore ALL realms and dimensions of consciousness, for no other reason than that they exist. GO FOR IT. Explore spirit realms, yet do so with ***protocols in place that form natural protection***.

Let's explore these 3 layers.

Celestial Realm

The celestial realm consists of spirits that are high in vibration:

- Holy Guardian Angel or Higher Self (see below)
- Archangels (see the chapter on "Angels")
- Angels (see the chapter on "Angels")
- Enlightened Ancestors (see below)
- Ascended Masters (see below)
- Goddesses and gods (Isis for me)

- Spirit Guides (see below)

More exists in this realm that I don't yet know about. It's above my pay grade, so we'll stick with these 7 as they'll prove more than ample for any and every magickal act a Christian Witch cares to perform.

Your personal Spirit Team

Terrestrial Realm

Terrestrial spirits are those closest to us in spirit realms:

Elemental and Nature Spirits:

- Earth: gnomes, elves, trolls, dwarfs
- Air: fairies, sylphs, pixies, sprites (although some sprites are water sprites)
- Fire: phoenix, salamanders, dragons
- Water: merpeople, undines/nymphs, sirens

It is important to understand that these nature spirits have been acknowledged and worked with (or against) in every culture of humanity, in every age. There is no denying their existence, without denying the experience of all cultures in nature. I can say for myself that there are a myriad of inexplicable things that have happened in nature that I can only credit to nature spirits. You may have had the same kinds of experiences.

Our ancestors were immersed in nature, without the distractions we're inundated with. They were completely enveloped in the river and its sounds, smells and spray. They could intuit, much more easily than we can — the spirits BACK OF what they experienced in the natural. They experienced all of nature as divine and had deemed this truth so imperative to our daily mode of operation that they invented a mythological language for it.

From the periodical Theosophical Siftings Volume 1:

> *"The creatures evolved in the four kingdoms of earth, air, fire, and water, and called by the Kabalists gnomes, sylphs, salamanders, and undines. They may be termed the forces of nature, and will either operate effects as the servile agents of general law, or may be employed by the disembodied spirits — whether pure or impure — and by living adepts of magic and sorcery, to produce desired phenomenal results. Such beings never become men."*

House and Land Spirits

- Spirits who dwell on the land where your house is situated.
- Spirits of those who may have lived and died in your home prior to you living there, or while you lived there, or long ago and have not crossed over.
- Spirits who rule the 91 parts of the earth as outlined by John Dee in Enochian Magic.

Territorial spirits are mentioned in the Bible, most notably in Daniel chapter 10, where the angel who appears to Daniel was detained by the Prince of Persia, whom the angel stated would be joined later by the Prince of Greece. This chapter can be understood in many ways. For me, it's a confirming statement by an angel that there are indeed territorial spirits who rule over particular regions, or who give areas, kingdoms and/or territories their qualities and/or culture.

Infernal Realm

The infernal realm is the habitation of fallen spirits and demons, also known as jinn.

This infernal realm is not literally situated beneath the earth, yet we refer to it as down because of its lower vibration.

Some would call hell the infernal realm.

Some call the underworld, where the mythological Hades rules, the infernal realm.

What we know is that energetically, this is a realm where lower vibration entities reside. Many of these entities are and have been quite useful to humanity.

Fallen angels have wisdom that they were able to pass on to humans:

- Gardening and knowledge of plants, trees and flowers
- Cooking and the culinary arts
- Pottery
- Iron working, smithing and knowledge of all metals
- Sculpture
- Music and composition
- Song and dance
- Art
- Makeup and applying paints to the face and body

This higher knowledge comes to humans telepathically as a result of choice. I believe it comes to us in 2 ways:

1. We love what we're doing so much that we open a portal.
2. We consciously contact a spirit in a magickal working to gain specifics.

In the first instance, we gain supernatural understanding of something because we love it so much. Anything we love will tell us its secrets.

Because the chef relishes cooking, secrets of the culinary arts are laid bare before her, almost as if a genius of that realm were communicating directly with the unconscious of the chef. This person understands secrets of food magick the rest of us are not privy to, making what they do seem otherworldly. That's because it is.

I believe many humans do this all the time without being aware that they are in connection with spirits and supernatural forces that are aiding them in their endeavor.

In the second instance, these spirits are consciously contacted by magicians seeking specialized knowledge. A comprehensive list of these spirits along with their spheres of influence is in Franz Bardon's book *The Practice of Magical Evocation* (well worth examination).

As with all spirits, those inhabiting the infernal realm can be contacted and communicated with for purposes deemed worthy by the Witch or magician. Be well warned and informed about these spirits. Keep in mind:

- Their nature is NOT the nature of angels, nor of terrestrial spirits. All spirits are different, and within the category of spirits there is further differentiation.
- They are not friendly. Spirits who are not friendly to one's aims are handled differently than spirits who are (such as angels who are more concerned with the cosmic order, or Enlightened Ancestors who have a vested interest in the bloodline's ascension).
- They require pacts with payment. If you're performing a magickal operation to commune with an infernal spirit or demonic entity for the purposes of gaining a specific benefit (i.e. find and access lost treasure), getting this entity to do your bidding will require a pact with payment. If the pact has a loophole, watch out. These denizens are tricky and old. They've been around for a long time and are used to humans calling them up at intervals to demand this or that. Proceed with caution. Because this is not the magick I do, I won't dive into it here.
- They're beguiling. They may trick, connive or outright deceive. Be aware.
- They require compelling, whereas angels do not. Infernal spirits are the type you must put on a short leash. If not, they'll turn you and your world upside down.

A peek into the internal realms as stated in the Testament of Solomon reveals that each infernal spirit (or demon) Solomon calls forth is ruled by an angel.

In Kabbalah, as far as I know, there are no evil spirits. All spirits work for God, including Satan. This is an important concept to meditate on in order to melt away any and all judgments, especially because Christianity teaches a deep good/evil paradigm that must be dispelled to become a Master Alchemist.

My ministry, calling and anointing is such that I exorcise demonic entities and untoward spirits, not call them. Each person decides for self what their relationship with other dimensions will be. Only you can decide and define your relationship with these aspects of the spirit world.

The magick I practice is Theurgic in nature, not Goetic. Once again, only you can decide on the magick of your soul.

I call to mind an aspect of Witches that I deeply adore: we put and keep things in cosmic order, including spirits. We tend to the order of the dimensions, seen and unseen. We can detect spirits, and if these spirits are not where they're supposed to be in the grand scheme of cosmic order, we're empowered to do something about it because we are Divine.

As Witches, we are emissaries who travel between the dimensions at will. We are the midwife and the death doula. At the crossroads you will find us. It's this aspect of our nature that makes us different from ceremonial magicians who call infernal spirits to commune. I'm not saying that Witches don't call infernal spirits to commune. I'm saying that some Witches may feel they don't have to. It's your choice. The most liberating aspect of magick is that there's no right or wrong.

Holy Guardian Angel or Higher Self

In my book Christian Witches Manifesto I write about this subject in more detail, so I'll give only the pertinent aspects of it here.

For me, the Holy Guardian Angel and the Higher Self are one and the same. This God as me is with me always, and has always been conveyed to my mind by upper realms as a giant angel over me in prayer. This angel is Head Honcho of the Spirit Team and is personal to each Witch.

This, to me, is the same as an Orisha, or one who rules the head in the Yoruba tradition. The Divine knew our life here would be full of absurdities, so it sent us here 'packing.' We walk with a Magickal Mafia. There's a head person, and there's the bodyguards and everyone else in the pack. This Spirit Team is around and with everyone, though how much we know about them and how much we work with them is completely up to each soul.

As a Witch, I desire full knowing and access of my Spirit Team. So I asked, and asked, and asked, and prayed and prayed and prayed until heaven got sick of my incessant pleas and revealed it to me. That's the best way I can describe this.

I realize this may fly in the face of the mandate not to pray for the same things over and over again as if heaven didn't hear us the first time.

There's yet another important distinction.

The aim of the Abramelin Operation (a rigorous, months long magickal operation detailed in *The Book of the Sacred Magick of Abramelin the Mage*) is to gain Knowledge and Conversation (K&C) of one's Holy Guardian Angel (HGA). The HGA serves manifold magickal purposes:

- Teaches us. Communes with us. Guides us. Leads us. Protects us. Heals us.
- Fills us with the love of God.
- Keeps us from toxic people, situations and entities.
- Keeps us safe in alternate dimensions.
- Keeps entities away from us that are not supposed to be in our sphere.
- Keeps us balanced, harmonious and is our own personal God.
- Everything else it does that I may not know about.

The idea is to FIRST get in contact with the HGA before proceeding to contact with other spirits.

The way I came into contact and stay in communion with Higher Self is through the practices I outline in this book.

Enlightened Ancestors

Our first ancestor is Source, from which all our forebears flow. We cannot reach Source without our ancestors. They form a long line issuing forth from Source all the way to me and through me to my offspring and theirs and so on, endlessly.

There are different types of ancestors. I don't call on all of them. I ONLY call on the Enlightened Ancestors.

I learned this many years ago as I was praying and asking for help. I noticed that there were a vast array of entities and spirits on the other side of the veil who were interested in me, yet not all of them had my absolute best interests at the forefront of their consciousness.

I intuitively prayed about the distinction and learned, in that moment, of the difference between ancestors who are FOR you and those who are not.

From that day forth, I've only asked for help and communed with Enlightened Ancestors, those who are here to be of the most benefit to me in this incarnation and desire ONLY my highest and best.

The reason these ancestors are FOR you is because they themselves are committed to their ascension and know that just as you cannot reach God without them, they cannot reach God without you.

We all go up together, as if linked by soul cords.

All the other ancestors can kick rocks as far as I'm concerned. If Uncle Joe was mean to me in this life, what makes him not mean to me just because he crossed over? If he hasn't had a change in consciousness, catalyzed by his own awareness, Uncle Joe still don't mean me good. Bye Uncle Joe. That is an ancestor I will NOT be calling on.

We ought to be discriminating with **EVERYTHING** in the spirit world. Ancestors are no different. Just because an entity was in your bloodline in another incarnation does not mean they are your friend.

Crossed over spirits are of a vast variety. Some are lost. Some are reluctant to return to Source. Some are caught up in the astral plane. Some have unfinished business here and continue to roam, seeking to gain closure. Some don't know they're dead yet.

All this makes for an interesting mix when it comes to calling on entities to help with magick.

Ascended Masters

Ascended Masters, as I experience them, are souls who have ascended by reaching the highest levels of initiation and are now committed to helping us do the same. Similar to Spirit Guides, yet more universal in scope and power and who take on cosmic duties for the ascension of humanity. These are a few of the Ascended Masters I've been in touch with over the years:

- Lord Christ (the preeminent Ascended Master for Christians and Christian Witches and keeper of the Piscean Age)
- Lord Arcturus (who appeared to me on several occasions during an intense spiritual practice I had each morning for several months)
- St. Germain (keeper of the Age of Aquarius)
- Kuan Yin (Mistress of Undying Compassion)

I don't know how many Ascended Masters there are, although I've heard the number 60.

In Christian Witchcraft, we have have access to Christ, especially if baptism has taken place, since this assumes you've given yourself to Christ on some level.

Spirit Guides

I view Spirit Guides as helpful people are are not yet done with their own ascension, yet are willing to help us with ours. They're in spirit form and may have been teachers in the 3rd dimension. They may have had a personal connection with you, and love you so much that they're willing to help you from the other side.

Some of the beings that I view as Spirit Guides who are helping us all are:

- Dr. Wayne Dyer - in this life he helped me and millions of others, I get the sense he's doing the same now.
- Louise Hay - her life and work left an indelible mark on humanity and I also sense she's continuing her work in another form.

If you're intuitive, you could be in touch with many Spirit Guides.

Intimate Visceral Connection

As a way of life and being, stay **DEEPLY** and **INTIMATELY IN TOUCH** and **VISCERALLY CONNECTED** with your ENTIRE Spirit Team headed by Higher Self.

How? 3 simple ways:

1. **INTENTION**. Set an intention that you will know intimately and connect deeply with your ENTIRE Spirit Team.
2. **PRACTICE**. Add to your spiritual practice time to commune with and hear from your Spirit Team. Do this daily. It doesn't have to be formal. I have never used a formal ritual to speak with my mother who left this life many years ago and who walks with me every day as a powerful ally. Talk to them. Listen. Have lunch with them. Set a plate for them at dinner. Buy gifts and offerings for them and put these on your altar. Create an ancestral altar. Make this commune a practice and **WAY OF BEING**. If you're already doing it, GO DEEPER. Relationships can always be sweetened and deepened for greater fulfillment.
3. **RITUALIZE**. Ritualize your work with them by conducting a Feast of the Dead each year on 10/31, or on their date of birth in their most recent incarnation, or create other rituals to connect. My daughter's grandmother (my former husband's mother) just crossed over as I'm writing this book. My daughter always received a sweet potato pie

> from her grandmother every Thanksgiving. We'll continue the sweet potato pie ritual every Thanksgiving with an intention to keep the spirit of grandma burning brightly in the kitchen, hearth, home and our hearts.

It's plausible that a Witch talks to and interacts with more spirit beings than with human beings in the course of a day. This spirit world communication is natural for all of us. Everyone is a spiritual being. Spirit communication is to be intentionally pursued and pulled to the forefront of our awareness for the practice of Christian Witchcraft.

Your Spirit Team in Spellcrafting

This conscious visceral connection with your Spirit Team is a must for Spellcrafting.

First, they'll let you know if you should be casting a spell at all, or if some other means is called for to address the issue at hand. Not everything is supposed to have magick thrown at it. There are many times when my Witchy self turned to magick, only to be redirected by the Spirit Team to prayer, or forgiveness.

They'll also reveal to you the inner workings of the issue at hand, so you can take a multi-disciplinary approach. If I choose to spell for greater abundance, they may also reveal to me prayers for abundance that I'll say as an embedded ritual in my daily spiritual practice, or they may show me an app that helps track spending. The Spirit Team is wise beyond imagination. We can always count on them to uplevel the spell work.

The Spirit Team goes before you into spaces you are consecrating so that they can prepare a space for you, or redirect you. You can ask your angels about a cave or a riverside where you intend to conduct your spell. You may receive a clear YES or NO. They know what's going on in those spaces. The human mind does not. They may know that there are a bunch of kids up to no good hanging out in the exact part of the woods you would love to do a magickal working, in which case they will redirect you.

I have learned, albeit at times the hard way, to gently go with redirection from above and never be too married to what I had in mind. There's a greater Mind I desire to access for the best path, process and results. The Spirit Team will reveal all this and more.

How They Communicate

The Spirit Team is communing with us energetically. They transmit messages into our consciousness awareness. The messages can come in endless forms:

- A sense of HELL YEAH!
- A sense of foreboding.
- Tingling.
- Symbols.
- Mental images.
- Bodily temperature fluctuations: cold/heat.
- Body functions: sweating, faster heartbeat, etc.
- Sense that some is standing behind you, or next to you, or seated on the bed (my grandmother does this all the time).
- Feeling someone move the covers in the night, or hands on you in the night (be mindful that this is distinct from a succubus or incubus).
- Jittery tummy.
- An unusual sense of calm.
- Super clear-headedness.
- Instantaneous knowing: knowing things without knowing how you know them; knowing information without a thought process or deduction.
- Visions and dreams.
- Sparkles above one's head or in one's line of sight.
- Books falling off the shelf at you.
- Items appearing and/or disappearing.
- Hummingbird(s) at your window.

- Dragonflies and butterflies landing on you or coming unusually close.
- Voices, sounds (be mindful that this is distinct from a mental health issue).

Remember, your Spirit Team doesn't speak English. They speak the language of **ENERGY** in a way **ONLY YOU** will understand.

Our job is to be present and connected such that we are able to intuit the meaning and application of any given message for success in life and magick.

Calling the Spirit Team

The Spellcrafting formula in this book assumes you are conducting your life and magick in the **CONTEXT** of a Master Alchemist in touch with the Spirit Team, thus there's no specific step to call in your Spirit Team. It's assumed they are with you always. The Spirit Team is integral in **EVERYTHING** we do in magick. (A Spirit Team invocation is below for inspiration.)

How to Be Clear

There's a way to be clear about the entities you're dealing with in other realms, just as you're clear about humans you deal with in this realm.

Ask Higher Self. LISTEN.

To access and keep in lockstep with Higher Self, we have intuition and divination.

With these two, a Christian Witch cannot go wrong.

INTUITION is honed over time through devout, unwavering, committed spiritual practice (see the chapter on "Magickal Practices"). If something feels 'off' or not quite right, pay close attention.

DIVINATION can be used as a magickal super power to know who you're dealing with, in this realm or another, at any given time and what to do about it.

Spirit Team Invocation

Call in the spirit team with the following invocations if they suit you, or tweak them to make them personally resonant. Or, use these as inspiration to create your own.

When you sense the presence of the beings you've called upon, such as the archangels, move on to the next invocation. If you don't sense a presence, continue calling to the entity/entities until you have a sense that their presence is with you.

This is an INVOCATION, so you are not calling forth the palpable presence of the being as is so with EVOCATION. Invocation means that you are inviting the being IN to unite in your consciousness with you, lending you their power and wisdom, as you undertake the ritual. We are one with all that is. The invocation is a simple acknowledgement that you have access to every being in the entire cosmos. It's almost as if you're joining minds with these beings for the working at hand.

- **Your Head Spirit/Holy Guardian Angel/Higher Self (looking UP):** "Higher Self I AM, I ask for your loving presence as I dive deep within the depths of my deepest, darkest interior so that I may know myself. I desire to understand what makes me tick, and what ticks me off. I desire to know and understand all aspects of my being and integrate these into a tapestry that is the whole of my being. THANK YOU. AMEN."
- **Enlightened Ancestors (looking at your heart):** "To the enlightened ancestors who attend me, including (**NAME** your matrilineal and patrilineal ancestral line as far back as you know it). I ask your power and presence be with me now. I humbly ask for your wisdom and guidance to attend me in all my affairs and in this undertaking so that I may fulfill the highest calling upon my life. I **COMMIT TO KNOW THYSELF AND MASTER THYSELF. THANK YOU!"**
- **4 archangels starting with Raphael (facing East)**: "To the divine keeper of the East and Holy Guardian of the element of AIR, the healing

power of our God known as Raphael, the one who taught Tobias how to defeat that evil demon Asmodeus whom took to flight before you, I invoke thy presence now in my working, so that I may perceive aright and have a clear mind for the work before me and so that I may conquer and vanquish all that is opposed to the light. **THANK YOU!**"

- **Michael**: "To the divine keeper of the South and Holy Guardian of the element of FIRE, the first of your kind created by our Mother/Father God, Ruler of the 4th Heaven, and instructor to Adam and Eve upon their exit from the Garden, I beseech your presence now, to awaken in me the fire to passionately persist in all that is mine to do upon this earth plane, to discover the fire within my soul, and to bring the great fire and light of Ra to the bedarkened aspects of my consciousness. **THANK YOU!**"
- **Gabriel**: "To the divine keeper of the West and Holy Guardian of the element of WATER, the holy one who visited upon our Blessed Mother Mary to announce the birth of the Christ, you whom visited upon Zechariah in the temple with the announcement "I'm Gabriel. I stand in God's presence." We now invite your holy and precious presence, knowing you bring forth the healing waters of the soul, purifying emotions, and causing all divine goodness to flow through all like a river. **THANK YOU!**"
- **Uriel (facing North)**: "To the archangels of the divine presence of our Mother/Father God: to Uriel, keeper of the North and Holy Guardian of the element of EARTH, teacher to Esdras, I beseech your presence here now for this ritual of understanding the light in my soul and approaching the shadow within me so that I may be made new. **THANK YOU!**"
- **Animal Totems:** "To the power animals who guide and protect me in this incarnation, I call upon you for your strength, guidance, wisdom and power now, for this undertaking of self-gnosis. **THANK YOU!**"
- **Christ:** "Ascended Master and Way Shower Christ our Lord, I beseech your presence here, knowing you are the Keeper of the Age of Pisces, the Lord of Hosts and King of Kings. I ask your presence and power

always be with me, filling me with the divine healing power of our Mother Father God, lifting self and all. I pray your bright light of truth sear through any thicket in consciousness revealing only that which is pure, true and worthy! I pray to be in all aspects of my consciousness and on all dimensions **ONE WITH THE ONE. THANK YOU!**"

- Call in any other members of your Spirit Team you desire.

Now let's prepare our reliquary.

Materia Magicka

In this chapter, a starter list of magickal supplies, tools, implements, essential oils and herbs are provided for those starting out. If you're experienced at Spellcrafting and casting, many of these may already be in your reliquary or apothecary.

Note: This is by no means an exhaustive list. As with all magick, follow the Inner Voice and trust that all the magickal implements, supplies and tools you require will come to you at the perfect time, in the perfect way.

FYI, this list is designed for those practicing Christian Witchcraft.

Books

- The Holy Bible with Apocrypha
- The Gnostic Gospels
- The Lost Books of the Bible
- The **Pseudepigrapha**
- The Kybalion
- A Course In Miracles
- List of books here on Amazon

Magickal Implements

- Crystal collection (all crystals that speak to you).
- Censor - to place charcoal in for burning incense. A piece of wood under the censor works as a handy heat conductor to protect furniture.
- Wand(s) - especially an acacia wood wand.
- Knife, sword, athame
- Water vessels/vases
- Chalice/goblet
- Copper vessel
- Bells/Chimes
- Glass Bottles - I'm in love with beautiful bottles and save them for Witch's bottles or storing herbs or other magickal purposes. Ok, I confess I have too many bottles!

Candles

- White
- Red
- Green
- Black
- Purple
- All planetary colors, elemental colors and angel colors for the angels you work with. ANY and ALL colors you're guided to by Higher Self.

Tarot decks

- Rider Waite Smith
- Morgan Greer
- More Tarot decks are here for your convenience at our Amazon Storefront.
- Any decks which speak to you.

Tarot Books

- ***Tarot for Your Self*** by Mary K. Greer - arguably one of the best books on Tarot I've EVER read (and that's a lot of Tarot books). A complete workbook with correspondences. If you have no Tarot books as of yet, start with this one. If you're an experienced Tarot reader, you may consider adding this one to your magickal library. WELL WORTH IT!
- *Tarot Celebrations* by Geraldine Amaral - my first Tarot teacher! Love her work. You can read the story of me taking yet another step out of the broom closet with my Baptist family after attending my first Tarot workshop with Geraldine in my book ***How to Be a Christian Witch***.
- ***Around the Tarot in 78 Days*** - a very unusual Tarot book with a novel approach to integrating Tarot. I love it! See my review of the book on my YouTube channel and how I used it to map my consciousness on the Kabbalistic Tree of Life with a Tarot deck and this book. (The vid is here.)
- ***78 Degrees of Wisdom*** by Rachel Pollack - the Tarot teacher extraordinaire offers us a timeless tome on Tarot.
- ***Learning the Tarot*** by Joan Bunning - I have used this book DAILY for long stretches of time to deep dive into Tarot. Excellent resource!
- Any books you're led to by Higher Self.

Note about books: I recommend acquiring BOTH the Kindle version (if available) and the paperback version of any and all magickal books that you're working with consistently. This is because the Kindle version provides easy, quick access to embedded links, whereas the paperback version is great for marking and making notes in and having in the sanctuary or Temple (or where ever you practice magick). I HIGHLY DISCOURAGE having technology in your magickal space. These energies are not always compatible and/or harmonious with the energies we work with in magick.

Altar Cloths & Tapestries

- Black
- White
- All Chakra Colors
- Patterned with sacred symbols, sacred geometry and that speak deeply to your soul.

Altar Items

- Feathers - I find feathers on the ground in the most bizarre places (definitely signs from angels). Pick them up if they speak to you.
- Bird Feathers and Animal Bones - I've been tempted on more than one occasion to pull over when I've seen road kill to harvest what I could of furry or feathered friends who have passed over... I just haven't had the nerve yet to whip out my blade and carve from a dead carcass what would work for me in magick, though I know Witches that have no problem with it and have harvested all manner of feathers and more from road kill.
- Animal totem representations
- Cords, ropes and ribbons
- Stones - especially from spiritually charged hotspots like Sedona (my healing stone is from there).
- Angel representations
- God/Goddess representations
- Crosses
- Ankhs
- Pennies/Coins
- Pentacles & Pentagrams (wearable & for the altar).
- Items from nature - I'm always finding sticks and stones and treasures in nature that are great for magick.
- Reliquary - a large chest or set of chests in which to keep highly charged magickal items.

- Any items that speak to you that you're led to place on your altar(s) and, of course, any items required for the specific spell you're crafting and casting.

Magickal Supplies

- Anointing oil - prepare your own or use the simple and effective recipe found at Exodus 30:23-25.
- Florida Water - in as many varieties as possible. I have a field day when leading retreats in Peru... the varieties there are plentiful.
- Palo Stick
- White Sage
- Wine and or liquor for the deity you're dealing with.

Incense

- Nag Champa
- Indian Temple Incense
- Frankincense
- Myrrh
- Dragon's Blood
- Patchouli
- All incense/perfumes you require for the magickal operation you're performing.

Essential Oils

- Anise Myrtle
- Basil
- Bergamot
- Blue Cypress
- Cassia
- Cedarwood

- Cinnamon Bark
- Clary Sage
- Clove
- Copaiba
- Cypress
- Davana
- Eucalyptus
- Frankincense
- Geranium
- Grapefruit
- Juniper Berry
- Kunzea
- Lavender
- Lemon
- Lemongrass
- Lemon Myrtle
- Lime
- Marjoram
- Myrrh
- Orange
- Oregano
- Patchouli
- Peppermint
- Rose
- Rosemary
- Sandalwood
- Siberian Fir
- Spearmint
- Tea Tree
- Valerian
- Vetiver
- All/any incense required for the magickal operation you are performing. I like to keep 60-70 essential oils at my fingertips at all times.

Herbs, Roots, Seeds, Flowers & More

- Acacia leaves
- Aloe Vera - if my mother didn't use this for EVERYTHING on us growing up!
- Angelica
- Basil
- Bay leaves
- Bergamot
- Camphor
- Coriander/Parsley/Cilantro
- Chrysanthemum flower - the first time I saw chrysanthemum flowers thrown into boiling hot water for tea was when I first visited China. I tasted it and was HOOKED. Bought back the flowers with me for tea. A powerful healing potion.
- Echinacea
- Garlic - it's true… Vampires hate it.
- Ginger - a POTENT healer all around the world. Almost every country I've visited reveres this root as a powerful healer. I can't get enough.
- Golden Seal - nasty as all get-out, yet my mother swore by it, so we grew up drinking it, with all the bits in the bottom of the cup, for all manner of ailments.
- High John the Conqueror
- Mugwort
- Mustard seeds
- Onion
- Oregano
- Peppermint
- Pine cones (I pick them up from the park in copious amounts for altar work.)
- Rosemary
- Roses - this is the most magickal flower I know. It's true, a rose is forever. This is the only flower that I will dry and keep all petals

from for magickal purposes and sacred self-love and healing baths and potions. Rose petals emanate potent magickal energies.

- Star Anise
- St. John's Wort
- Thyme
- Tumeric
- Valerian
- White Sage
- And of course, look in your kitchen at the good old spice rack!

Oils

- **Almond Oil** - GREAT as an essential oil carrier and for massage. I also utilize it nightly for face yoga and for around my eyes in the mornings.
- **Black Castor Oil** - LOVE this for my hair and scalp.
- **Black Seed Oil** - literally for OPTIMAL health (taken daily, this is NOT medical advice… simply sharing my wellness habits).
- **Castor Oil**- of course, we know this will move the energy out of one's system like nobody's business! A comprehensive resource on this oil — also known as Palma Christi (palm of Christ) because of its almost incredible healing properties — is Edgar Cayce (aka the sleeping prophet) who used Castor Oil (topically) extensively with miraculous healing results. (See the Association for Research & Enlightenment at EdgarCayce.org.)
- **Coconut Oil** - AMAZING for oil pulling in the mornings along with essential oils. My fave essential oils to mix in with organic first cold pressed coconut oil are Tea Tree, Cassia, Peppermint and Copaiba, or a mix of 2 or 3 of these. I also love slathering coconut oil on me, it's rich and luxurious and I LOVE the smell.
- **Fractionated Coconut Oil** - this oil (with the fat removed) is GREAT for massage and as an essential oil carrier, though it is NOT the oil to use for oil pulling.
- **Grapeseed Oil** - VERY nice for massage and as an essential oil carrier.

- **Olive Oil** - organic, first cold pressing. Was used in the tabernacle for keeping the Fire of the Perpetual Flame. The name says it all: O LIVE.
- **Shea Butter** - though shea is not an oil, it's more of a butter, I figured I'd add it in here as well. EXCELLENT for skin! I know of no better skin ointment.
- Any other oils and ointments you're led to by Higher Self.

Note: I recommend **ORGANIC, SUSTAINABLY HARVESTED** and **FIRST COLD PRESSING** for all oils where such is appropriate and available.

More Must Haves

- **Apple Cider Vinegar** - this one is a MUST HAVE for EVERYTHING. Keep in the fridge and take a couple of teaspoons a day for EVERYTHING. I throw it on salads on other foods since the taste is not one that I particularly enjoy.
- **Black Strap Molasses** - my mother shoved this down our throats daily to get us safely through winter season in New York City.
- **Honey** - my mother kept a wicked mix of honey, lemon, onion and garlic in the fridge that she doled out to us liberally morning at night at the first sign of ANY bug, until said bug deemed it unwise to continue its course in any body related to my Witchy mother. Honey is also used in a host of spells to sweeten outcomes, and in magick to include Honey Jars.
- All the additional items Higher Self, your guides and ancestors guide you to acquire.

Note: A few of my fave online magick shops to procure magickal items are listed in the Resources section in the back of this book.

Note on Essential Oils

Be persnickety about where you acquire essential oils! Many oils online are synthetic (made in a lab rather than in nature), are full of toxins (not organically grown) and could contain fungus, mold, mildew or other unwanted contaminants. The natural products industry is not regulated. This leaves the door wide open for nefarious players to pawn off fake goods to the unsuspecting or unaware. Find an essential oils supplier you've researched and TRUST for high standards of purity proven through testing. Nothing short of this will do. I have a recommendation (where I procure ALL of my essential oils) in the Resources section at the back of this book.

Finally

Lastly, ANY items you're led to add as a magickal implement, by all means DO. Magick is in you and all around you. The implements themselves do not have any more power than the power you imbue them with. You can anoint just about anything as a magickal implement, even if it wasn't specifically designed for spiritual use (I know of Witches who can go into 7/11 or the Dollar Store and come out with a full spell kit... THAT'S practical magick).

Crafting your own magickal implements gives you the opportunity to charge them with magickal power at each step in the creation process, if you're a DIY kind of Witch.

Never press, stress, rush or worry. Have fun letting all you require for magick come to you by the most mysterious, synchronistic means.

Magickal Timing

There's a universal powerhouse that can be tapped that I refer to as **COSMIC WEATHER.**

This is the astrological element of magick. Mastering the craft requires the ability to access, harness and focus the vast energies and forces of heaven, at the right time, for our magickal purposes.

We're sovereign beings; we have all the energies of the cosmos at our disposal.

All that's required to utilize these is an unyielding desire to learn (let's call it hunger), open willingness to explore (let's call this non-resistance) and committed, consistent practical application of acquired knowledge to produce results.

Rinse and repeat to master.

For me, cosmic weather is all about perfect alignment with the cosmos for the best results. **ALIGNMENT** is an important word for me... the more **ALIGNED** I am with the cosmos, the more magickal life becomes on its own, even when I'm not formally practicing magick. I love the flow of divine energy rushing through me, energizing me and swirling around me when I'm **ALIGNED**, like being in a river and floating downstream, rather than fighting the current.

We can utilize the movement and energy of the planets to align with the cosmos. This is simple. Our forebears and ancestors knew this well. They looked at the sky and took note of what effects were being caused on earth and in daily life. They saw the connections, and they honored and aligned with them.

What Cosmic Weather is NOT

Cosmic weather is NOT being a victim to the planets and stars. As stated earlier, lightworkers and others allow themselves to succumb to the planets by touting that Mercury is retrograde and is therefore wreaking all kinds of havoc on their tech. They sort of throw their hands up energetically as if Mercury being retrograde was the ruler of their life and experience. Mercury is retrograde a LOT. While I honor Mercury, I'm not willing to be bummed out or inconvenienced every time it goes retrograde.

The Alchemical Master will **USE** the retrograde energy of Mercury to stifle, or turn backwards, that which she does not desire to persist or proceed. An Alchemical Master **USES THE ENERGY** of the planets and cosmos for their own purposes rather than being ***used by them***.

Source did not create us to be victims to anything. That includes planets. You have dominion over your consciousness and how you will align your consciousness with the planets and their dynamic activity in any given season (cosmic weather).

We simply take the energy of the planets as information. This information can be used to fulfill our intentions.

If it's raining outside today, it may not be a good day for a picnic, but we know it's a good day for the lawn. Every energy in the universe is useful for something, and there is no inherently 'good' or 'bad' energy. Intention is key: why you're doing what you're doing.

There are 2 ways I go about aligning with cosmic weather for the best magickal outcomes, both of which are mentioned here. The first method is to calculate magickal timing based on intuition, tables and divination. The latter method is to use the Christian Witchcraft Ritual Year (as outlined below) for your magickal operations.

Let's begin.

How to Calculate the Best Magickal Timing

I use **intuition, tables** and **divination**. Here's a brief explanation of all three, as well as pertinent resources.

Intuition for Magickal Timing

Intuition is the major compelling guide in our magick. It's Higher Self communing with the lower mind. Tuning in and ascertaining by way of **DIRECT KNOWING** what is right for self is **CRITICAL** for the practicing Christian Witch.

What's the best means to hone intuition? Meditation. Hands down.

Experienced Witches know well that the perfect timing for a particular spell or ritual comes to us naturally the more we practice magick. We trust this intuitive knowing. It is the Divine within speaking.

Tables for Magickal Timing

Magickal time tables are in the book the *Key of Solomon* (free for anyone to read on the Esoteric Archives website). You'll also find in the *Key of Solomon* a table with the angels of each hour, as well as a separate table with the archangels, angels, metals, days of the week and colours attributed to each planet.

Over time, the information required will synthesize into a workable system. At least that's what has unfolded for me. I have a huge spell book with the names of the planets, the angel correspondences, colors, metals, herbs and more. Of course, it took years to compile this treasury of magickal information. It takes practice to understand the magickal correspondences as they relate to you as a soul.

I'm not married to what's in books, no matter how ancient they may state they are. I'm married to ascension to be fully realized as a Divine Being. My process is exploratory, as is yours. There's no need marrying a system that doesn't completely mesh with your soul.

There are many other tables all over the web, of which you get to choose what works best for you. There are variations, so I would stick with one system until mastered rather than hopping from system to system with each ritual.

If I still have questions as to when to engage a particular ritual or cast a specific spell, I'll engage divination.

Divination for Magickal Timing

Divination for magickal timing can be as easy as 1-3 Tarot cards or a pendulum swing.

If you have in mind a date already (such as the New Moon) pull 1 Tarot card or pull out your pendulum to acquire a simple YES/NO answer. This is the easiest form of divination, straightforward in nature, with little to no room for ambiguity. If the first Tarot card you pulled is not a clear YES/NO, pull another. Repeat until you have a CLEAR YES or NO.

If you work with a pendulum, and your pendulum is charged and accurate, use it to determine a YES/NO answer.

If there are several dates you have in mind, write out the dates and pull a card on each date. Read the card and its meaning. You may find vital insights as to process and outcomes if the ritual were conducted on each of these different dates.

Lastly, if you have no idea whatsoever of when to do a specific ritual or spell, I would turn to a full blown Tarot reading, such as the Celtic Cross (an excellent blog post on how to read the Celtic Cross spread is on Biddy Tarot, a HIGHLY trusted source for all things Tarot). This reading gives in depth insight into multiple factors and people involved.

Not knowing the best timing to conduct a ritual may also signal that there is not a clear intention, or that greater insight into the issue is required before proceeding with precision. This will all be cured with the Celtic Cross Tarot spread.

Now let's move on to the second method I recommend for magickal timing:

utilizing a Ritual Year design.

Christian Witchcraft Ritual Year

Conscious attention to these significant and recurring cosmic events and ritual celebrations and aligning with these in you spell work can produce astounding results:

- **New Moon** - 12 per year/note the constellation for each New Moon and proceed accordingly. Example: a spell to enhance and fulfill your gifting as a public speaker (and all it entails) could be undertaken on New Moon in Leo (considering the qualities as Divine attributes of Leo).
- **Full Moon** - 12 per year/note the constellation for each Full Moon and proceed accordingly. Example: a spell to end being shy and reticent and instead boldly speak up could be performed on the Full Moon in Aries (considering the qualities as Divine attributes of Aries).
- **Equinoxes** - 2 per year/Spring and Fall. These events usher in an energy of **HARMONY** and **EQUANIMITY** since the light and dark are perfectly equal. Do spell working at this time to achieve equilibrium, balance and harmony.
- **Solstices** - 2 per year/Winter and Summer. The longest day of the year (the most light) is the Summer Solstice. What spell working could you do on the day with the **MOST LIGHT**? Shining your light as in living your destiny and spells with a YANG energy. Conversely, the longest night of the year is the Winter Solstice. What spell working could you do at the point in the year when we have the **MOST DARKNESS**? Shadow work comes to mind, as well as all things YIN.
- **Feast of the Dead on October 31** - the veil is thin, which presents the perfect opportunity for meaningful commune with the ancestors and spirits of those crossed over (see the chapter "Dumb Supper Christian Witch Style"). Akin to this festival is the Beautiful Feast of the Wadi, an annual event in ancient Egypt honoring the souls of the deceased.

- **Lions Gate Portal 8/8** - This is a time when we receive an activation from the light of the star Sirius, aligning with the great pyramid at Giza on 8/8 each year. Sirius is double the size of our sun and 20 times brighter. With that much light, what magick could be wrought? All manner, if you use your imagination!
- **Your Solar Return (birthday)** - your birthday marks another trip around the sun! This is the perfect time to determine what you desire to accomplish during this next trip around the sun and decide what role magick will play in realizing these dreams. Then get started mapping out your Spellcrafting for the year.
- **Your Initiatory Ritual of Remembrance** - once per year on the anniversary of your Initiation as a Christian Witch (see the book ***How to Be a Christian Witch***).

Note: Cosmic weather is sun and moon based, while also integrating planets, stars and constellations. We access, harness and focus the great energies of heaven for magick.

One idea of a ritual and Spellcrafting calendar could be:

1. January New Moon
2. January Full Moon
3. February New Moon
4. February Full Moon
5. March New Moon
6. March Full Moon
7. Spring Equinox (circa 3/20)
8. April New Moon
9. April Full Moon
10. May New Moon
11. May Full Moon
12. June New Moon
13. June Full Moon
14. Summer Solstice (circa 6/21)

15. July New Moon
16. July Full Moon
17. August New Moon
18. August Full Moon
19. Lion's Gate Portal (8/8)
20. September New Moon
21. September Full Moon
22. Fall Equinox (circa 9/22)
23. October New Moon
24. October Full Moon
25. Feast of the Dead (10/31)
26. November New Moon
27. November Full Moon
28. December New Moon
29. December Full Moon
30. Winter Solstice (circa 9/21)
31. Annual Ritual of Remembrance (Your Initiation Anniversary)
32. Solar Return (your birthday)

This is a simple ritual calendar that works. Anyone can follow it, even without reading complex tables. Just look up at the sky, or Google any date desired (such as the Spring Equinox or Summer Solstice) then proceed accordingly with the spell or ritual.

Final Note

If you're keen on astrology, you'll know exactly what to craft and cast for and when.

Growing up in the cult of Jehovah's Witnesses meant I was clueless about astrology. I didn't know my birth sign until I was in my 20's.

I had to remedy this issue.

I took on a study of each constellation as the New Moon and Full Moon occurred.

If you don't have time to take on a full blown study of astrology, this 'as-it's-happening' approach deepens wisdom and understanding of the **ENERGY CURRENTS** at your disposal in that particular moon phase. It's an in the moment study of the current cosmic weather, informing whether to pick a raincoat or sunscreen.

Using the above Ritual Year helps us sail through the year knowing what we'll do and when for our Spellcrafting. We can map out our magick rituals in advance.

Granted, there are times when you may desire to craft and cast a spell or create a ritual for a particular purpose now, rather than waiting for a cosmic event to happen. That's all good. Simply use the first method above.

The bottom line: you have access to vast heavenly bodies and energies. Use cosmic weather to your advantage.

Now let's get to the formula.

Formula for Crafting a Spell

How does one craft a spell that WORKS?

I like to keep magick as simple as possible and yet still be profoundly potent and effective. If the job can be done with a spell or ritual that requires 3 steps, no need to add 5 more. The universe is PRECISE. I like magick to be as PRECISE, with no added fillers just for drama or to make one feel more 'magickal.'

Before beginning, a word of caution: ***understand your basic tendencies***. They'll bleed into your magick, for ill or for good.

For example, I have a tendency to operate with a 'just-in-case' mentality. One way this expresses is with way too many items in my purse or luggage. Since I know this about myself, I can function with **AWARENESS**. I can be AWARE if I see myself throwing in extra steps in any magickal ritual or spell just-in-case. I can make the necessary adjustments.

Not to harp on already known wisdom, yet the maxim **KNOW THYSELF** is of a critical nature in Spellcrafting.

Ritual Creation & Spellcrafting Formula

A simple step-by-step formula for creating rituals and crafting spells:

1. Desire

2. Intention
3. Sorting
4. Divination
5. Correspondences & Sympathies
6. Magickal Timing
7. Incantation
8. Even Better Clause
9. Release
10. Observe & Catalog Results
11. Optimize & Repeat

If you're new at Spellcrafting, I would highly recommend divination using Tarot at every step of this process and especially when questions or uncertainties arise. Divination, done appropriately, is literally tapping into Divine Mind for guidance.

If you're an O.G. (Original Gangsta) and you've been at this for a while, dive right in. You know what to do.

Step 1 - Desire

What's the desired outcome?

For clarity, let's define desire as it's used in this context.

Desire, for me, is the delicious awareness and irresistible pull to something **GREATER**. We all have this innate calling **UPWARD**, to something bigger, better and more fulfilling.

In Buddhism, the word desire is used as a warning against longing. Desire and longing, for me, are two distinct energies.

Desire, as we'll use it here, is the upward calling. Expansion. Possibilities. Fulfilling the GREATNESS within. It's climbing one's own Everest with an unwavering intention to stand at the summit and breathe in the beauty and exhilaration of the moment, while knowing that all the real gold came from the process. It's that HELL YEAH experience Life is consistently calling us to. **STRETCH. GROW. GO FOR IT! BE BIGGER** Life says.

Not because Life thinks we're not big, but because Life knows we won't be happy and fulfilled until we **EXPRESS** the **GREATNESS WITHIN** or at least **GO FOR IT.**

SOUL MAGNIFICENCE has to **SHINE** for ultimate happiness and bliss to be our way of being rather than falling into fleeting pleasures that have to be chased and replaced.

Desire vs. Need

Longing, conversely, is the absence of something, the feeling or sense that something's missing or lacking. Lack is inherent in longing, causing us to attempt to fill a hole. This is a mistake in magick. This, I believe, is the energy our Buddhist friends are warning us against. Much of the human race feels this emptiness and seeks to fulfill it with varied means, most of which prove unsuccessful.

This is a good time to give a moment of our time and attention to need. One of the foremost issues to rid oneself of as a Master Alchemist is need. We may think we have endless needs, when in reality, we do not.

We do have requirements for life: food, water, shelter, warmth, love. When we consider these requirements for life, they've all been provided for by Source. We've been given everything we need for the best life on planet earth. We do well to start with this knowing and build from there.

This doesn't mean we're supposed to hunker down in a cave somewhere eating only nuts and seeds.

Far from it, you're here to live the most magnificent, full, adventurous, love soaked life of your own unique creation, full of bliss, joy and fulfillment! YEAH BABY!

As Master Alchemists, when we realize that all we truly require has already been given us, an enduring and ever present **THANKFULNESS** dawns and abides in the soul. I know it sounds corny, but it's true, an attitude of gratitude is an incredible ally in magick.

Need is a perception in the mind, not a reality. The perception of need in consciousness is a sucking, low vibration energy. It does not give or bestow, because it seeks only to take. It is vampirism; which is why it's dangerous to be around people who have perceived needs. They will seek to manipulate others to get their perceived needs met.

The solution? A story from the annals of my crazy life...

Many years ago, I had a deep desire to manifest a beautiful, brand new home. I was in the process somewhere between not yet finding the home, even though I'd been qualified to buy. I had imagined a brand new home and had been taking daily walks through a nearby neighborhood full of brand new mansions. I would breathe, walk and take in all the details of each home as I walked by, marking what I loved about each one. It was a sort of walking meditation.

One day, doubt crept in. Things had not gone well for me in the housing arena at previous low points in my life. Clearly the fear and trauma were still with me, even if on a low level. Would it work this time?

What we know of doubt is that it's an insidious, low level energy detrimental to our blissful creation and manifestation. It only takes an ounce of doubt to sink the whole ship.

That's when the angel stepped in.

One day when I was in my spiritual practices, praying fervently, an angel began communicating with me. It asked a series of questions...

Angel: for the home you desire, you'll need nails. Is the metal for the nails already here?

Me: Well... yes. Whatever they make nails of, steel or something else, yes, the metal is already here, somewhere on the planet.

Angel: is the wood that will be used for the home already here?

Me: Yes, there's plenty of wood in the world.

Angel: is the stone that you desire for the stone front of the house already here?

Me: I think I see where you're going with this...

After the angel was certain I got the point that Source had already provided everything for me, the conversation ended with a charge from the angel to swirl all the components together to create anything I desired.

WOW. Mind B.L.O.W.N.

My mind wasn't blown because I hadn't thought of those concepts before.

My mind was blown because I had not deeply, in my subconscious mind, come to the understanding, on a visceral level, that **EVERYTHING** I desire is **ALREADY HERE** and that my job is to hold in consciousness the **DIVINE PATTERN** for the desire, causing the spiritual and physical raw materials to take on that particular configuration.

Before that conversation, I was overly focused on the 3rd dimensional considerations:

- Will I qualify for a mortgage?
- What paperwork do I have to pull together?
- Are all my taxes in order?
- Will it be enough income on paper?
- What about the payments?
- Will it be close to my daughter's school, because I love my daughter's school…

On and on my mind went with an endless stream of nothingness.

I'm not saying that the considerations aren't valid. They are.

What I'm saying is that I was overly focused on the aspects of the creation and manifestation process where I was not as strong as I would have liked, and where I'd had issues before, which caused doubt to arise.

Unbeknownst to me, I was focused on lack and limitation: what I thought I did not have, may not have, or could not produce.

Meanwhile, I was not focused on the **MUCH BIGGER UNIVERSAL PICTURE: ABUNDANCE**. God already has a beautiful home waiting for you, whether you have paperwork or not Valerie. God got you. All your needs have ***already been supplied***.

It's our job as Witches to **KNOW THIS** and **EMANATE THE VIBRATION** of **ALREADY DONE. ALREADY HERE. ABUNDANCE.**

Because my focus was erroneous, my creation would have been erroneous. **ATTENTION** is **CREATION**.

Warning: the reverse won't work either. To be completely focused on the universal principle of ABUNDANCE and not at all focused on the 3rd dimension is a mistake as well.

WE ARE SPIRITUAL BEINGS having a **3RD DIMENSIONAL EXPERIENCE.**

We get to honor **BOTH**, with **SPIRIT FIRST** and **FOREMOST**.

So pray, and collect your paperwork. Do your magick, and save money. DO BOTH.

I don't think the angel was telling me all this because it cared about my house. Angels don't care about houses. The angel was using the house as a point of reference because that's where my attention was focused. Source sent a messenger to **TRANSFORM MY CONSCIOUSNESS** from lack (on subconscious levels of the mind) to **ABUNDANCE**.

The angel reminded me that I wasn't asking for something that didn't **ALREADY EXIST.**

I was making it harder for myself than it had to be. I was limiting myself without being aware.

On that day, I was relieved of that burden. As you can imagine, the joy and elation that came forward as a result of that angelic intervention made the manifestation of that house pretty rapid and not nearly as hard as it would have been. Doubt was GONE.

Not only was the process of that manifestation altered, my consciousness was permanently transformed by the encounter, which made all subsequent manifestations likewise altered to be bigger, better, more joyful and effortless.

That's what angels care about. The work of Source in our consciousness. Our character.

And now I pass this knowing on, praying it becomes an even greater and more **VISCERAL LIVED EXPERIENCE**:

Your desires are ALL ALREADY HERE for you.
ABUNDANCE.

The angel's message was clear and never left me: **EVERYTHING YOU DESIRE IS ALREADY HERE.**

You're simply swirling it into a configuration that works for you.

NO ONE IS MAKING ANYTHING. We're all taking the raw materials of the universe — that have already been gifted to us — to create anything we desire. You get to come up with the idea and the new configuration from the existing raw materials.

On the 3rd dimension, the raw materials we use for creation are wood, metals, plants, etc.

In magick, our raw materials are earth, air, fire, water and the 5th element: Ether.

All the raw materials — both physical and magickal — are available to everyone without prejudice.

There's no such thing as lack in the universe. There is, however, lack of imagination or work ethic on the part of people.

The Law of Correspondence reminds us that we cannot receive fulfillment from lack.

As within, so without. As above (in consciousness), so below (in the 3rd dimension).

There's no escaping the fact that magick practiced from need can only create more need. We rid ourselves of need, wants, empty holes on the inside, unsatisfaction and unfulfilment as best we can in our daily spiritual practices. ***Getting rid of all need energy in consciousness releases us of from any lack mentality we may be secretly and unknowingly harboring in the subconscious mind.***

We live in a ridiculously abundant universe. The earth mother is right now spitting out plums, peaches, apples, and all manner of delicacies whether we eat them or not. **LIFE DELIGHTS IN EXCESS CREATION.** More than what's necessary or even sensible. It's not sensible how many apple orchards are in the seeds of one apple. Life is excessive. It gives us way more than we could ever use.

Successfully making these shifts in consciousness sets us up to receive the **HIGHEST IDEAL** of the **DELICIOUS DIVINE POSSIBILITIES** that beckon. There's **ALWAYS** a greater possibility awaiting you in EVERY area of your life and in EVERY situation. **ANYTHING'S POSSIBLE. DREAM BIG.**

We get to discover and manifest these infinite possibilities by means of magick.

4 Categories of Desire

Now let's talk about categories of desires.

Most desires fall into the following 4 categories (derived from the work of Florence Scovil Shin in her book *The Game of Life and How to Play It*). She refers to the following 4 areas (in her own wording) as the 4-square of life:

- **Health** - vitality, longevity, youthfulness, energy, beauty, sexuality, sensuality, virility, fertility, healing, etc.
- **Wealth** - financial abundance, prosperity, investments, business profits, perfect business partners and customers/clients, real estate, etc.
- **Love** - love relationships, Twin Flame/Soul Mate issues, could also include familial relationships, and all the people we love, in the different ways we love. According to my upbringing as a Jehovah's Witness (and this could be totally off base... yet I mention it now as it's fitting for a deeper understanding of the ways we love), there are 4 kinds of love: eros (romantic, sexual love), storge (familial love), philia (brotherly love, or the love between good friends) and Agape (the highest form of love that is a principled love of ALL), which is said to be the impersonal, all-encompassing, great unconditional love of Source.
- **Destiny** - fulfillment of one's gifting, anointing, calling and soul mission, the true purpose of life.

I've found that all issues I've come across and addressed for myself and clients can be found within these 4 categories, and sometimes more than one as the 4 are interconnected aspects of life on the 3rd dimensional plane.

Clarity of Desire

A Master Alchemist knows self so well that desires are **CRYSTAL CLEAR**.

CLARITY OF DESIRE is a critical first step. Most people are mentally muddy and unclear on what they **TRULY DESIRE**. I've asked at least several hundred people over the past 15 years a simple question: what do you want? My intention for the question? To get to the core of the true desire, so as to be of service to them in acquiring, creating or manifesting it.

Mind you, this question has been posed to all sorts of people who are highly intelligent, very spiritual or religious, with demonstrated success in their lives. I say this because it's important to understand that being unclear about desires has nothing to do with intelligence, spirituality or socio-economic factors.

It has to do with **SELF GNOSIS**.

Most people's responses began with or included what they did NOT desire:

- I just know I want to stop feeling this way. I've had enough of this.
- This relationship cannot continue and I just want to end it amicably.
- This is making me crazy. Anything is better than this.
- I have to make more money. Money would solve the problems I'm having.

On and on we go, with what we do NOT desire. This is called CONTRAST: the undesirable outcomes or situations that may be painful, or at the very least, annoying and inconvenient. In other words, it's what we DO NOT WANT.

For the record: MONEY SOLVES NO PROBLEMS. (I learned this first hand when I dated, married and had a baby with a man who had won $17,000,000.00 in the Powerball Lottery. YES, we lived lavish. And YES, we **STILL HAD ISSUES. ISSUES THAT HAD TO BE RESOLVED** and not by throwing money at them.)

Tony Robbins says that having money means you can show up to your issues in a limousine. It doesn't mean you don't have issues to show up to, or that you get to NOT show up to your issues. No one gets a pass. Rich people have issues just like everyone else. The universe plays no favorites.

A Master Alchemist knows that all problems are created and perpetuated in the mind. Hence, they are **ONLY** solved in the **MIND**.

Remember our first law: **THE UNIVERSE IS MENTAL**. This means we must go into realms of our **CONSCIOUSNESS** to get to the core of and reveal our **TRUEST DESIRES**.

Consider this:

YOU ARE ALWAYS ONLY DESIROUS OF A FEELING/STATE OF BEING.

This is mind boggling when deeply considered, meditated upon and integrated.

Tell yourself: **I AM GOING EXCLUSIVELY FOR A FEELING/S-TATE OF BEING.**

Examples:

- I may think I desire a Mercedes Benz AMG when what I actually desire is the FEELING of luxury, success, independence, etc. that I have when I'm driving that hot baby.
- I may think I desire a new romantic partner when I actually desire the FEELING of being loved, adored, doted upon, paid attention to, experiencing companionship, being in partnership, etc.
- I may think I desire a big beautiful new home when I actually desire a FEELING of stability, groundedness, rootedness, ownership,

belonging, being one with the land, family togetherness, the experience of being solidly anchored on the earth mother, etc.

We can readily see that the more in touch we are with the **UNDERLYING FEELING** or **STATE OF BEING** we think the physical manifestation will give us, the more SPOT ON our magick will be. We are not referring to fleeting feelings. We are defining **HOW WE DESIRE TO BE**.

In some cases, the best magick is to **FEEL LOVED NOW**, or **FEEL SUCCESSFUL NOW**, or **FEEL ABUNDANT NOW**. This is simple and immediately actionable. At all times, you're in charge of your feelings.

I think if more of us were CRYSTAL CLEAR on the FEELINGS as STATES OF BEING we're truly desirous of, magickal results would be easier. We'd literally be walking around as **VISCERAL BALLS OF OUR TRUEST DESIRES** which could only lead to effortless manifestation.

Let's add a twist.

Before we create and manifest a physical desired outcome, we only have an idea in our minds that this particular outcome will give us a particular inner feeling. We only have a hypothesis, if you will. The hypothesis has yet to be proven. That's why we're doing the spell work. We're going to conjure what we desire, and try it on for ourselves. It's only in the having it, or the experiencing it, that we truly find out what that thing is. Before we have it, it's a guess.

In other words, we don't know if that new Mercedes AMG will have the desired effect or not. That's the beauty of magick. If it doesn't yield results that are **FULFILLNG**, even if the results are DESIRED, we can create something else.

You may have huge success with your magick, and still not ultimately want what you successfully created. I've done this more times than you can imagine.

So, I began to view magick as akin to trying on shoes in a huge shoe outlet. I see a pair of shoes on the shelf that are super cute. I try them on. They pinch my little toe. Though they're gorgeous, and I thought they might be the perfect accompaniment for my new dress, I'm not buying them because they didn't feel good when I tried them on.

There's an aspect of magick that's akin to trying on delicious ideas. I think of something I may love (an expanded business) and I spell for it. I receive exactly what I spelled for, an expanded business. Then I realize that this expanded business — though bringing in highly increased profits — keeps me away from my family more than I'd like.

I've tried on the shoes, and see that they pinch my toes.

There are several options available to me. I could hire people. I could create a scenario where my family works with me, if they want to. I could decide to become more of a minimalist and cut back. I've actually done all of these at different junctures, after successfully receiving the outcomes of spell work.

The good news: anything you can create with magick, you can change with magick.

We are multidimensional beings dwelling in a dynamic cosmos. Anything is possible.

Before proceeding with Spellcrafting, ask yourself: what do I ***really*** want? Then write out the answers. Ask your Self this question at least 7 times. Listen for answers. Write what you receive in your heart. Be patient. There's no need to rush. This is your life. It deserves all the care, time and loving attention you can heap upon yourself to arrive at what's ultimately best for YOU.

When you're crystal clear on your desire (including the FEELING/STATE OF BEING and it's PHYSICAL MANIFESTATION), proceed with the next step.

Step 2 - Intention

What's my intention with this spell? Intention is not so much what I desire as it is why I desire it. What's the driving force, or **MOTIVATION BEHIND** what I'm spelling for?

Desire is the WHAT. Intention is the WHY.

Example: I'd like to increase wealth by making my business more prosperous. I decide to spell for abundance and prosperity.

Why do I desire greater prosperity? This is the first question I'd ask myself. Many people would just proceed with an abundance or money spell of some sort, yet I've discovered there are several more layers to unpack before diving in to the magick.

Why do I desire greater prosperity?

Asking the question 7 times or more will begin to get to the heart of the matter and reveal layers of unconscious drivers that are surely present, awaiting our awareness.

Why do I desire greater prosperity?

Layer 1 - because I want more money! I shouldn't have to explain myself.

Why do I desire greater prosperity?

Layer 2 - because I don't have enough money! I need more ASAP!

Why do I desire greater prosperity?

Layer 3 - because I have a nagging feeling inside.

Why do I desire greater prosperity?

Layer 4 - because I feel like I should be so much further along than I am at this stage in my life when it comes to money. I'm kind of ashamed at being where I am financially. At the same time, I don't know if I can trust myself with larger sums of money if and when they do come.

Ah, now we're getting somewhere... ***we've uncovered shame and issues of not trusting self.***

Why do I desire greater prosperity?

Layer 5 - because I've been struggling for too long. I can't take it anymore. I'm exhausted. I have to have a better life now!

Now we're acutely aware that frustration is present as part of the intention.

Why do I desire greater prosperity?

Layer 6 - I know I can do so much better!

Ah! Now we're tapping into potential!

Why do I desire greater prosperity?

Layer 7 - I have so many people to serve. I'd love to open that spiritual homeless shelter I've been dreaming about for years, where all homeless people are treated with love and care like they've never seen before! Yes! I love this vision! And I'm ready to do something about it!

Ah! Now we're tapping into service to humanity and the greater upward call!

I take myself through these layers because I MUST get to the root of why I'm choosing to spell for what I'm spelling for. It's not enough for me to cast a spell. I must deeply understand my **TRUE INTENTION**. The Law of Cause and Effect says that I'll receive EFFECTS according to the TRUE CAUSE. I'm going to work this law in my favor by uncovering the TRUE CAUSE and setting a POWERFUL INTENTION that will more than likely return to me its kind.

Intentions are tricky. They don't live on the surface. They have to be coaxed out into the open. We may think our intention is one thing, when really, it's another.

The most potent aspect of an intention is that it will return the same. If my intention (or the driving force) behind the magick includes shame, mistrust and frustration, I'll receive a situation which will make me frustrated, feel more ashamed and likely not to trust. I'll wonder why the magick didn't work, when in actuality it worked perfectly. It gave me my true intention.

As practicing Witches, if we know intimately our true motives and intentions at all times, including the unconscious drivers swirling around far beneath the surface, our magick will be that much more informed and effective.

Step 3 - Sorting

Now that I've uncovered several drivers in my consciousness, including:

- Shame
- Not trusting myself
- Frustration (a form of anger)

- Desire to fulfill my potential
- Desire to serve humanity

I'm going to take steps to rid all the unwanted aspects of what I desire (so that they do not return to me in any way in the results of the spell work) and infuse the entire spell with the **ENERGY** of the **DESIRED OUTCOME ONLY**.

This step could be referred to as sorting.

How is sorting achieved?

In 2 ways:

1. **Daily spiritual practice:** a Master Alchemist practices daily rituals for expanding consciousness, ridding self of negative energies and becoming God.
2. **Write and Embody the opposite:** write the opposite of the undesirable elements as the wording of the spell, or magickal prayer (i.e. joy instead of sadness; holiness instead of shame), then **EMBODY** these. (In the back of this tome you'll find an excerpt from my forthcoming book that provides words of power for Christian Witchcraft that can be used in spell work.)

Step 4 - Divination

A full Tarot reading or simple pendulum swing can give either in depth answers or a clear YES or NO, depending upon the spell involved.

Example: if I'm crafting a New Moon ritual to create expansion in my business from 400+ customers to over 1,000 customers within 90 days, creating greater income and greater impact for greater numbers of people (an actual spell I'm crafting) I'll do a Tarot reading to gain insight into several aspects of the issue, including:

- **What may be standing in the way of me having the outcome.** This would be as important to know — if not more important —

than how to actually attract the customers. I may be attracting customers to my door, yet the door still won't open because I have an unworthiness issue blocking the additional customers from walking through the door. In this case, my attraction is working fine. The issue is my 'receiving' ability since the presence of unworthiness in consciousness (as it is currently, with regard to this issue) does not allow me to let in what's standing right outside my door. This knowledge will influence the direction of the ritual, along with the resulting correspondences. For instance, 'attraction' correspondences are different from 'receiving' correspondences. For 'attraction' I would use sweetness and magnetism. For 'receiving' I would use Yin energies of darkness, penetration and opening to let in. Just as important, I would slather myself with ridiculous amounts of self-appreciation to melt the unworthiness, which is at the core of the issue. Channeling this magick through the powerful love energies resident in the heart chakra will also melt unworthiness and any and all inability or hesitancy to receive deeply from the infinite fount of good the universe has ordained for each of us.

- **Who? Who's affecting the outcome? Who's involved?** I may be seeking to accomplish an outcome that involves many other people. While it's true that much of magick likely involves other people, I'd like to gain greater insights on who these people are, how they're involved and what, if anything, I need to do about it. Tarot reveals this well. (Be sure victim mentality doesn't creep in here, as no one else is ever needful for you to do what you are going to do.)
- **What actions are required of me?** This is a biggie, or where the proverbial rubber meets the road. Obviously, I don't have the outcome I desire yet because I haven't done the work (either inner or outer or both) to receive the outcome. This will change with the spell work. Therefore, I must be willing to do something (or many somethings) different than what I'm currently doing. Perhaps I require more marketing to gain those additional customers, or hire an assistant or install systems I wasn't willing to discipline myself to

previously. I must be willing to do something different in my business to **CORRESPOND** to and **SUSTAIN** the outcome I'm spelling for. It does me no good to attract and receive 1,000 customers if I don't have the business systems to sustain them. I wind up going backwards ultimately, which is can be an unwanted side effect of immense and quick growth. I'm going to avoid that, as best I can, with Tarot as my friend and trusty guide.

- **Unknowns.** There could be any number of unknowns, including future events that I have no idea of. As I write these words (in mid 2020), we are in the middle of massive change on planet earth which affects just about every area of life as we know it, including medical systems, nutrition, soil, environment, public health, technology and more, while at the same time humanity is being forced to reconcile its black/white issues in America and globally. Needless to say, 2020 held huge unknowns, all of which no one could have seen coming. Tarot is of immense help with this. You'll know what to do even if you don't know what's coming.

Divination is not limited to one step in a linear process but is to be employed throughout the Spellcrafting process at any juncture when one desires to receive clearer guidance. Heaven is ever available to us.

Step 5 - Correspondences & Sympathies

Next, I look at the correspondences for the specific outcome. Correspondences include magickal implements, items, tools, crystals, herbs and more that correspond or match the outcome. I do quite a bit of sympathetic magick (which is really just a game of matching) because it makes sense to me as well as being simple and accessible.

It's easy to intuit that using rose petals and honey for sweetening my relationship with my boo (or creating a new relationship) would be a no-brainer.

If the correspondences are known — such as Cassia for the archangel

Haniel — then I'll gather these.

Likewise, if the correspondences are spelled out in a grimoire, acquire the items. This process could turn into a more arduous affair than first anticipated. Acquiring rare items from a specific magickal operation in an ancient grimoire may take years. Proceed accordingly. (This is not to say you must wait years to practice magick. It may mean that you'll gather the items over years for that specific operation. Many other spells can be crafted and cast in the meantime.)

If the correspondences are NOT known, then I'll turn to my magickal experience or books from other Witches and Mages I trust. What do they use? If it resonates for me, I'll go with it.

Lastly, if I don't know the correspondences, and haven't found these in a book or other source, I'll turn to divination.

Step 6 - Magickal Timing

Follow the instructions in the preceding chapter for optimal timing of your magickal operations.

Step 7 - Incantation

This is where we get ninja with Spellcrafting: with our **WORDS**.

Words carry power beyond what's uttered. Words are energy patterns we send forth that the universe will match and return to us as the results of what we spelled for. Hence, precision is an imperative.

I don't want to convey the idea that one must be a surgeon with a scalpel, yet I am a proponent of giving all you can to the formulation of your incantation by making it as precise and powerful as it can be.

If you're not a wizard when it comes to writing incantations, there's a hack for Christian Witches: use the book of Psalms. The book ***Secrets of the Psalms*** (though it's a Hoodoo flavored work) can provide any incantations you may require.

In addition, another resource is the book written by yours truly:

Magickal Prayers for Christian Witches (which provides a prayer/words of power for a variety of magickal purposes, along with the essential oil, Tarot card and angel correspondences for each).

Step 8 - Even Better Clause

There's a clause I love adding to my magick called 'even better.'

The meaning of this clause is that I'm asking for 'even better' than I spelled for. An example... not long ago I was checking out of one long-term apartment rental and into another managed by the same firm. The check-out time was 11 AM for the unit I was in, and the check-in time for the unit I was going to was 4 PM. I didn't want that big break in the middle. My desire was to go directly from one unit to the next.

I asked the company for late check-out on one unit and early check-in for the other. I expressed to them my desire to go directly from one apartment to the next.

They called me and asked if I would be willing to entertain an alternate solution. I replied affirmatively. The customer service agent let me know that he was somewhat playing a game of Tetris, with many moving parts to keep guests in their accommodations happy, as well as manage cleaning staff. The solution he offered me was that he would extend my stay in my current unit (at no extra charge) and overlap it with my next unit. Effectively, he would make my check-in to the new unit on a Thursday at 4 PM and make my check-out at the existing unit at 11 AM on Friday.

YES! Was my answer! This turned out 'even better' than I anticipated or requested or even knew to request.

Everyone was happy, and the customer service agent told me that us reaching this agreement made his week. This is the essence of my 'even better' clause.

The 'even better' clause is stated at the end, or during, any magickal working. It's saying to the cosmos that I desire this to be 'even better' than I asked for, spelled for, or currently know is possible.

Why is this valuable?

Because I don't know all the moving parts of the situation. I don't know what I don't know. There could be multiple solutions to the issue I'm spelling for. I may only see one, asking for late check-out and early check-in, for instance. I didn't know the answer would be even better than that, nor could I have imagined that the solution would be so good, and everyone would be so happy. Everyone ended up smiling. This is the kind of magick I love.

There's so much we don't know in any given situation. Spelling 'too tightly' is the bane of magick. It reeks of control. Control is born of fear. We're not here to control the universe. We are here to wield and master immense and infinite power.

POWER rather than CONTROL.

In addition, the 'even better' clause **INVITES** the universe to swoop in and arrange things beautifully on my behalf… even better than I can spell for.

Though I didn't cast a spell for the above mentioned situation, I had set a firm intention: that I was going from one unit directly to the other, in peace and joy.

That's exactly what happened.

I just didn't know exactly 'how' that was going to happen.

We don't have to know the details of 'how' the results of our spell work will be returned to us. We simply have **FAITH** and **TRUST** that the results are **ALREADY DONE**.

I don't use the word **FAITH** here as blind belief. I take the scientific method in magick and do not condone flights of fancy.

The word **FAITH** in this context means **CERTAINTY**, **CONFIDENCE** and **SURETY**. I am certain, confident and sure that my magickal workings are in full effect and are returning me results, ***even better*** than what I spelled for.

Adding this clause to your spell work can take your magick to a whole new level, and your intentions as well, even without spell work. Try it and let me know your results.

Step 9 - Release

We've arrived at the point of the completion of the spell and we are ready to **RELEASE** our desires into the cosmos for delicious return to us.

This is the hardest step for most of us.

There's a scripture that comes to mind:

> *"Cast thy bread upon the running waters: for after a long time thou shalt find it again." Ecclesiastes 11:1 (Douay-Rheims 1899 American Edition)*

To me, this scripture means: **LET IT GO**.

Oprah also taught a truth I love: you cannot go out and get what you desire; what you desire must be delivered to you. We look at Oprah and think she's the ultimate go-getter. Yet, she has a secret. She understands that we put our BEST out into the universe, then release it and ALLOW the yumminess to be returned to us.

Fascinating. This truth does not negate the necessity of doing the work, or putting forth the requisite time and energy to manifest dreams and desires.

We are in a great cosmic restaurant. Everything in the universe is on the menu. You can have anything you like. You order your food, and the wait staff takes your order to the kitchen, where the chef cooks it up for you. It will be delivered in front of you shortly thereafter.

Spellcrafting and casting is a lot like this. We order something delicious. We make it very clear to the cosmic kitchen what we desire, including special orders and instructions... hold the mushrooms, extra cheese, substitute agave nectar for sugar, etc.

Then we **RELEASE** and **ALLOW**.

No one follows the wait staff into the kitchen and oversees the cooking of the entire meal. No one leaves the table with their wonderful friends to stand over the chef and instruct him on how to saute the onions.

You **TRUST**.

You **KNOW** this is a great restaurant. That's why you picked it in the first place. You **KNOW** the universe is a great place, because you decided that it is.

You know you are in a delicious co-creation with universal forces far beyond comprehension. You know that there is a give and receive, a cosmic dance. You know you are dancing with the perfect partner: Source.

There is no need to rush the chef. As a matter of fact, the better the food, the longer it will take to prepare. Fast food is not high quality food, by its very definition.

You have no problem with this system in a restaurant.

It seems we all have a little bit of a problem, to one degree or the other, with applying the exact same principles to the universe, especially when a deep desire is, so to speak, on the table.

This is not helpful in magick.

Unilaterally dismiss:

1. any and all need to see results instantaneously.
2. rushing.
3. doubt/wondering if the spell 'worked' or if you did it 'right.'
4. need for results to show up a specific way, or with a specific person.
5. any and all nagging questions.
6. how it's going to happen.
7. control.

LET IT GO. Do your **BEST**. Then **LET IT GO**.

This is the release step. Because our minds can be tricky, write the release statement in your grimoire, as well as a physical action or a visualization that will serve to signal your lower mind that we are not thinking about this any longer. Example: see your desire as a golden ball of potential energy on a dove whom you release into the beautiful blue sky.

Then, never think of it again. Even better, forget about it if you can. Some of the best accidental magick I've ever performed is when I've completely forgotten about the spell, only to find a sigil under a rock somewhere, or a written out desire in an old grimoire and realize that it all came true.

I used to struggle with the **LET GO/RELEASE** part of magick. I didn't like it. Why? Because I was a control freak. Why? Because deep down inside, I was in fear.

How did I turn it around? **SELF-LOVE**. I get to love my Self so completely and rapturously that I **KNOW** I am the **BELOVED** child of Source who has one aim: **TO DELIGHT ME.**

Because Source only seeks to delight me, I **KNOW** the delicious results of what I asked for are on the way.

Some may say, well God knows everything, and already knows what you want. So why do a spell in the first place?

Good question.

God gave each soul **FREEDOM OF CHOICE. YOU MUST CHOOSE**, not sit back and let the universe choose for you. **YOU DECIDE. YOU** are **SOVEREIGN. YOU ARE A CREATOR.**

This is you taking your seat on the throne of **DIVINITY.**

YE ARE GODS.

Step 10 - Observe & Catalog Results

By law, results will show up. The Law of Cause and Effect assures you will receive an effect, based upon the causative act of magick and the energy you set in motion.

Results will come around, just like a boomerang. If they're spot on, great! If not, hold these truths in mind:

- I don't get what I want. I get my vibratory match. This is a vibratory universe governed by universal laws, one of which has the sole responsibility of matching vibrations. Am I a vibrational match for my desire? Does my energy and the energy of the desire correspond? Example: I spell for increased wealth yet poverty thoughts continue to plague me (an actual experience I had to contend with). The answer wasn't to do more magick. The answer was to change my thoughts.

Then, I could approach it again with magick, if desired.

- I don't control the 'how.' Though I am a powerful being, I humbly realize there are countless factors at work in this magnificent universe, most of which are beyond my knowledge. The 'how' could take many forms. Next time, I'll dig deeper into my intention, and will be sure to include my **EXPERIENCE** as part of the spell (i.e. joy, bliss, elation) and not simply the result.
- I get unlimited do-overs!

This is why magick is so much more than wearing a cloak while saying a few really good sounding rhyming words, whirling a wand with herbs on one's head and releasing it all to the universe.

The most powerful and indeed irresistible magick comes from the core of **BEING**. If you're **BEING** the energetic essence of what's spelled for, the universe couldn't NOT deliver the desire to you, beautifully, swiftly and accurately.

Either way, catalog **ALL** results in your grimoire so as to learn, grow and approach the matter again from an elevated station in consciousness borne from wisdom.

Step 11 - Optimize & Repeat

Congratulations! You've achieved measurable results!

To optimize results and approach magick in future spells, ask yourself:

- Do I have the desired result?
- Do I have the desired result in a way that's pleasing to me?
- Did I enjoy the process?
- What did I enjoy most?
- What did I enjoy least?
- What aspects of my Spellcrafting can be optimized for even better results?
- What can I integrate next time in order to produce better results?

- What can I eliminate that was superfluous or extraneous to the essence of the desire?
- Did I detect negative energy within me or surrounding me that may be hindering me?
- Did I detect vaster reserves of power within myself than I've previously accessed?
- What would I do differently?
- What is the intuitive Voice whispering to me about this magickal operation?

Proceed on your course of magick with the wisdom garnered.

Now let's address sacred space.

How to Create Sacred Space

Before discussing how to create sacred space, let's discuss why we create sacred space.

Why We Create Sacred Space

Sacred space is created to dispel unwanted energies and invite and fill the space with the desired energies for the magickal operation at hand. The energy of a night club, the energy of a restaurant and the energy of a Church are vastly different. The commonality is that the space was created and prepared for whatever was to unfold in that space.

Sacred space is created in manifold ways, I'll share here with you what I do. You get to create your own methods of turning ANY space into a sacred space.

The subconscious mind pays deep attention to ritual. This is one of the reasons ritual is so moving and powerful, and why it's included in every magickal system, spiritual path and religion on the planet. One of the ways to IMMEDIATELY get your subconscious mind to pay attention is to transform the space around you.

Kitchen By Day - Temple By Night

If you have a dedicated space for magick in your home, such as a room or space completely dedicated to your spiritual work, it will be easier to create sacred space.

If you do not have a dedicated space for your rituals and magickal operations, all good. You'll create sacred space where ever you choose.

All important in magick is **YOU** and your **INTENTION** and **WILL**, so sacred space is created by **YOU** and not 4 walls.

If you do not have a dedicated space, and you'll be using a common area in the home, such as a living room, you'll simply take a few extra steps to prepare your space. A living room can have many people and thus many energies flowing through it, doing many different things. There could be television watching or eating or game playing going on. Because the space isn't dedicated to spiritual work or magickal practices, you'll clear out whatever energies were there, and adjust the space to the ritual you're about to conduct.

If you have dedicated space — such as a separate room — for your magick, that's great too, although I wouldn't say it's better than not having it. **ALL DEPENDS UPON THE Witch.** While one Witch could whip up and perform a spell to move heaven and earth at her kitchen table, another could have a completely outfitted, full blown magick room and still not be up to snuff with the magick.

We remember at **ALL TIMES** that the **POWER** is **WITHIN THE Witch.**

There's something to be said for the imagination and improvisation that goes into transforming a space from busy kitchen by day to ritual temple by night. With a powerful enough intention, any space can become a sacred space. I've transformed my fair share of hotel rooms!

Clean and Clear

While there's greater detail in my book ***How to Be a Christian Witch*** with regard to cleansing and clearing, we'll talk about it a bit here as well, so that this work is complete in and of itself.

CLEAN. CLEAN. CLEAN.

CLEAR. CLEAR. CLEAR.

That's my mantra when creating sacred space. The very **FIRST** thing I do is **CLEAN. EVERYTHING.**

Grandma was right: cleanliness is next to Godliness.

I love angel magick, and have done everything in my power to make my space as inviting and magnetically attractive — energetically — to angels. Angels do NOT abide dirt, stink, filth, clutter, messiness or anything of the sort.

I do, however, know quite a few low level infernal spirits who thrive on dirt, filth and stench.

These are not the energies I desire to attract.

To clean, I follow these steps:

- **Clean myself.** A sacred bath of herbs will do nicely. (Though I write extensively about this in my other book, I'll also offer a little more on the sacred bath later in this book.)
- **Take down the existing altar.** Clean the top of the altar with fresh water, holy water, or if water is not appropriate for the top of the altar (altars made of fine wood), a clean, white cloth will do.
- **Clean all implements being utilized in the ritual or magickal operation.**
- **Clean the garments you'll wear in the ritual.**
- **CLEAN EVERYTHING.**

While I'm not talking about being obsessive compulsive here, a good cleaning will immediately raise the vibration. Dust bunnies hold and emit energy too.

Next, it's time to **CLEAR**:

- **Clear out all the extra paraphernalia that will not be used in the ritual.** I have an aversion to clutter, preferring my space to be open and airy. Yet, I do realize that as Witches, we accumulate a LOT of magickal items over the years. It helps me to have these items in a Reliquary (sacred chest that holds magickal items) or stored neatly on shelves, bookcases or baskets. **ORDER IS THE FIRST LAW OF HEAVEN**, and thus the **FIRST LAW OF CREATION**.
- **Clear out all technology.** That's just my preference. If your sacred space is in a living room, and you're not able to move the television, for instance, throw a holy cloth (or clean white sheet) over it for rituals. Televisions — and anything with a black screen for that matter — are portals.
- **Clear the energy.** Burning sage and spraying copious amounts of Florida Water are my fave go-to's. I also create my own mists, as you may also, made with essential oils for this purpose. I love using Frankincense and Myrrh. These are heavenly essences mentioned often in the Bible in regard to spiritual work and connecting with supernal realms.
- **Sound**. Sound is frequency. Singing bowls, bells, Native American Flute and gospel music have all been used to set the stage for me in my sacred space and shift out of regular waking consciousness into altered states of consciousness. Higher frequencies will attune the space to high energy beings on your Spirit Team who will assist with the ritual and/or spell work.
- **Wind/air element**. I open the windows and/or doors, especially when burning sage. Opening a door or a window AS you're clearing is critical to let any untoward spirits and energies ESCAPE. I learned this from Native American practitioners and never forgot it.
- **Fill the space with light.** Depending upon the spell you're crafting and casting, the space will be filled with a particular color light (such as in certain angel evocations). If the spell does not call for a particular

color light, fill the space with white light. This is done in your third eye, or the imaginal realm. This realm is the ***real world***.

- **Suffumigation**. Certain rituals will call for a specific form of suffumigation (filling the air with fumes from incense) while others may not. Suffumigation changes the atmosphere immediately and facilitates potent results.
- Anything else you're led to do to clear the space.

The next most important thing I do after creating sacred space is to construct the altar. Let's do that now.

Temple, Shrine & Altar

In this chapter, we'll clarify 3 terms as they're used in this context: *temple, shrine* and *altar.* We'll also take a look at altars in the Bible, and how they relate to Christian Witchcraft.

Dedicated Temple

A **temple** is the entire **DEDICATED** and **CONSECRATED** space where **ONLY** magick and spiritual practices take place and where the reliquary (collection of holy relics and magickal implements) is stored.

A temple can be a room (my temple over the years has been a separate room in my home) or ANY dedicated space that's closed off to ANY other activity other than spiritual and magickal practice.

I like the temple to be as high up in the home as possible. I like plenty of light coming into my temple — including sunlight and moonlight — for New Moon and Full Moon rituals. It's nice to be able to look up and gaze at the moon through an open window in your temple if you're not outside. It's also nice to be able to put your crystals (the ones who love moon bathing) on a window ledge in the temple for bathing in the beautiful glow of the Full Moon.

It's my preference in the temple for there to be at least 9 feet by 9 feet of open space in the middle of the floor for casting circles. The less I have to move in order to practice magick is a great incentive to practice magick on a regular basis. A dedicated space with room for a circle to be cast in the middle is so delicious and conducive to magickal practice that it may astound you if you're not already operating this way.

I'm a bit of a minimalist and big on Feng Shui, so having fewer items out and about creates a Zen sense of peace and calm in my temple that I like. Others are more energized with many items in plain view. You get to choose for yourself and create the beautiful, functional, highly inspiring temple that suits your spiritual practice. This is so personal. Honor your Self.

Experienced Witches know that a separate room is NOT required for a temple. Source is right where you are. Where you stand is holy ground. ANY space — it could be a wall in a room as well — can be turned into a temple. Use your imagination! Witches I know are imaginative and can turn just about anything into just about anything. INTENTION and WILL are the drivers.

Shrine & Altar

A **shrine** is the meeting place for you and your Spirit Team. It's a permanent structure in the temple where devotion takes place and where spirits who are associated with the shrine (your Spirit Team) will commune with you and you with them. These spirits may include Enlightened Ancestors (like grandma who meets you at the shrine), angels you're working with or any spirits you may have pacts with. A shrine is a touch point between this world and the next and is permanently placed. It could be as large as an entire wall, or as small as a desk or dresser. Make it work!

The shrine may be erected in the east (land of the rising sun denoting enlightenment), or in any direction you're led by Higher Self. Though the shrine contains an altar, it is much more than an altar.

Altar

While a shrine is a more permanent meeting space for you and the Spirit Team, an ***altar*** is a spiritually charged, impermanent surface upon which holy and consecrated items are placed for spiritual and magickal purposes. An altar is also a sacred, holy, consecrated space, a symbolic representation of the holy presence of Source.

There may be many altars in a shrine and in a larger temple. In my temple, I have 4 or more altars going at any given time, for different purposes. Some practicing ceremonial magicians keep 7 altars for the 7 planetary spirits at all times. One could also keep 4 altars at all times, with each dedicated to an element, placed in the appropriate direction for that element.

You get to ascribe any meaning to an altar it will have for you. You get to determine the spiritual use for any altar you erect.

Just like a shrine, an altar is a touch point between this dimension and dimensions beyond.

An altar on earth forms the base of a ladder to heaven (think Jacob's ladder, where he beheld angels descending from and ascending to heaven… more on this below).

As soon as any altar is constructed, angels immediately arrive to tend it and stay until they are released or if the altar is ever destroyed or profaned.

I construct altars in ANY place I sleep, including hotel rooms. I do not lay my head in a space without an altar. I also keep my purse on the altar so my money stays VIBED UP.

Temple, Shrine and Altar

Let's pull it all together into a working magickal space that becomes a cocoon nourishing, restoring and fortifying your spirit.

Example: a spare bedroom may be your temple. On the east wall is a huge dresser with drawers that functions as a permanent shrine. On the dresser is a working altar for sacred communion with the Spirit Team. There may be offerings here for entities on your Spirit Team, as guided.

Above the dresser on the wall hangs a beautiful tapestry containing sacred symbols. To the right of the dresser is an altar for a spell you're crafting. To the left of the dresser is another altar for the purposes of the magickal ritual at hand (Full Moon, New Moon rituals, etc.). The drawers of the dresser form the reliquary, where magickal implements are kept.

If your temple is NOT in a dedicated room, you can seclude your temple with curtains or room dividers (I love the beautiful Asian room dividers) according to your magickal vibe.

If your temple IS in a dedicated room, closing the doors contains the energy, keeps sacred space pure and discourages people from wandering in.

To sum this up with an analogy (not sure how good it is, but I think it may work), if the temple is your house, then the kitchen is the shrine and the table and counters in the kitchen can be altars.

We could also think of a church. The entire church is the temple, the shrine is the pulpit at the front of the church, while throughout the church there may be several altars.

Tabernacle in the Bible

In the Bible, the tabernacle was the movable house of worship and sacrifice for the Israelites as they wandered through the wilderness. The specifications are laid out in Exodus chapter 27.

In this chapter, specifications for the altar are also laid out in pretty clear fashion, down to the exact measurements.

It's also fascinating to note that the directional elements are provided in the chapter as well, which is a direct correspondence to the 4 directional elements in Witchcraft.

The altar was to be made of acacia wood, which is considered a magickal tree in some circles. In ancient Kemet (Egypt) the acacia tree was considered sacred since it was said the gods were born under the branches of an acacia tree in Heliopolis. Acacia is sacred to the Goddess Isis. A part of Ra's celestial boat was made of the wood of the acacia tree. A cursory study of the acacia tree online will yield intriguing associations between the acacia tree and Isis and therefore all things magickal. (As a side note, the acacia tree produces DMT, which the Kemetic peoples may have ingested to elicit supernatural experiences, which would explain a lot.)

Numbers chapter 3 makes for fascinating reading regarding the charge of the Levites to be priests and caretakers of the tabernacle.

A most interesting verse to Christian Witches is verse 15:

"And their charge shall be the ark, and the table, and the candlestick, and the altars, and the vessels of the sanctuary wherewith they minister, and the hanging, and all the service thereof."

Sounds like a reliquary to me.

Altars in the Bible

Altars are prominent in the Bible. Since we're Christian Witches, we get to examine a few references for insight and inspiration in building our own general altars.

Reading the context of the instances cited below will provide background understanding, as we'll only focus on the actual altars in each instance we're examining.

After the examples, we'll look at a couple of practical applications.

Please remember that nothing mentioned below from the Bible is literal. The Bible, as has been stated earlier in this work, is anything BUT literal (or at least that's my take on it).

Now on to altars in the Bible as representations of the presence of God.

Adam & Eve's Blood Altar

Adam and Eve are a metaphor for the primordial man/woman (yin/yang or Divine masculine/feminine). We are not speaking of gender here. We are speaking of **ENERGY**.

The story of their ousting from the Garden of Eden is well known, yet there are many aspects of the story that are not as well known or spoken of. These are found in a book titled ***The Forgotten Books of Eden*** (viewable on **Sacred-Texts.com**) which contains ***The First Book of Adam and Eve*** (also called ***The Conflict of Adam and Eve With Satan***). Also available online is *The Books of Adam and Eve* (viewable online at **Pseudepigrapha.com**).

As the story's told in *The First Book of Adam and Eve*, after leaving the Garden, the pair construct an altar and offer up their own blood upon the altar, including the blood that has fallen to the ground. This fallen blood is mixed with the dust of the earth and placed on the altar (a powerful magickal rite if there ever was one).

Of particular interest is the inner knowing by the duo that an altar ought to be constructed as somewhat of a pathway to the Divine, and the knowing that blood would somehow appease or please God, and that praise and prayers were to be offered at the altar.

Noah's Altar

In Genesis 8:20-22 we read of Noah constructing an altar after exiting the ark in the legend of the global flood. According to the story, Noah sacrificed clean animals (vs. unclean animals) on the altar, which could have been a suffumigation of sorts (as done in magickal rites). The verses say that God smelled the pleasing aroma arising and made a decision to never destroy humanity again (even though supposedly humans are evil through and through. I don't believe that's quite what God said, but we get the point).

Abraham's Altars

The Bible attributes 4 altars to Abraham, with the most legendary being the altar spoken of at Genesis 22:9, one of the earliest mentions of an altar in the Bible. It's constructed for the purposes of a human sacrifice: Isaac.

For me, it can be surmised that the charge from God for Abraham to kill his son Isaac would have to mean something other than the literal meaning. (Kabbalah answered this for me; so I highly recommend its study.)

In the story, Abraham constructs an altar and puts wood on top of it, binds Isaac, and places Isaac on top of the wood.

It's highly suspect that a man as old as Abraham would have the physical agility and strength to bind a young, strapping man like Isaac, lift him up and place him on the altar, (another reason for me not to take this story literally, but to peer into the deeper meaning).

For me, the bottom line meaning here is that something of great value is being placed upon the altar, something that's dear to me, that I may have a hard time giving up, yet I'm willing to 'sacrifice' it.

This principle is akin to the idea of Lent, when Catholics are asked to put away something they love on the earth plane in order to draw closer to God. I love the idea. It teaches us to let go and let God. It teaches us the high order principle of **NON-ATTACHMENT**, a **MUST** for the Master Alchemist.

If we apply this concept to magick, we come to the conclusion that we are to place what matters most to us on the altar, and/or be willing to metaphorically sacrifice what's nearest and dearest to us.

It reminds me of a class of the Mystery School in which we were delving into the burning of 'ancestor money.' While fake money named 'ancestor money' is sold in magick shops to burn as a sort of incense that rises our ancestors, one of the students shared that she had spoken with her ancestor about it and received the message that real money is what moves heavens, because it's DEAR TO US. Let's be clear, ancestors don't need real money. There's no money where they are. **WE NEED TO BURN REAL MONEY** because that's what dear to us, versus fake money we buy in plentitude at the metaphysical shop. We hold real money and fake money differently, ENERGETICALLY.

In our ritual that night in Sedona, we burned real money to our ancestors, demonstrating the Abraham sacrifice principle.

Isaac's Altar

Genesis 26:25 speaks of Isaac building an altar and "calling upon the name of the Lord."

The context speaks of how Isaac's growing wealth drew the ire and jealousy of his neighbors. There was a famine in the land, and as always, water was precious. Finding wells was a big concern, and the only way Isaac could keep his household — including huge and growing herds — from dying of thirst in a desert.

After Isaac had experienced trouble, God appeared to him and reminded him that He was with Isaac, just as He had been with Abraham. God reminded Isaac that he was blessed, and not to be afraid.

Right there, Isaac builds an altar and calls upon the name of the Lord.

It's interesting to note that right after building the altar, the verse states Isaac pitched a tent and his servants dug a well.

The way I look at this is that there are wellsprings of life-giving waters that my soul must tap into, and I an do that by communing with Source and establishing altars as a way of marking a specific occasion and location when God talked me off the ledge.

Jacob's Altars

Jacob had a dream in which God appeared to him to reassure him of the promise made to his ancestors Abraham and Isaac and to transmit additional information directly to Jacob's consciousness (Genesis 28:12-15). The dream begins with the vision of a ladder from earth to heaven upon which angels are ascending and descending in which God communicates 9 very specific and crucial pieces of information:

1. God identifies Itself ("I am the Lord").
2. God connects with ancestry ("the God of your father Abraham and the God of Isaac").
3. The promise of an inheritance ("I will give you and your descendants

the land on which you are lying").

4. The promise of many children and children's children ("Your descendants will be like the dust of the earth").
5. His family will be a blessing to others ("All peoples on earth will be blessed through you and your offspring").
6. Promise of divine presence ("I am with you).
7. Promise of divine protection ("will watch over you where ever you go").
8. Promise of return ("I will bring you back to this land").
9. Promise of fulfillment ("I will not leave you until I have done what I have promised you").

This was not a random set of vows to a random person. This does not represent a one-time event. Source makes these exact promises to **EVERYONE**. **EVERYONE** is assured of the Creator's presence, protection and blessing.

The essence of this set of promises is to dwell on one's land (or home) in peace and abundance, thriving with one's children and children's children. This is the life EVERYONE can have as a divine inheritance, if desired. You get to choose what life you'll live. Maybe it doesn't include children or land. Whatever that life is, you get to create it with ZERO limitations.

When one is practicing magick or spell work for children, or children's children, or land, or a home, or protection or for the enrichment and blessing in any area of life, one is actually spelling for what's rightfully one's own.

If you don't see your desires manifest in your world, **GO FOR IT**, because you're SUPPOSED to have an amazing life. NO ONE was born to suffer or be unhappy. Spell away for that delicious life of your own design!

Jacob wakes up in awe, and exclaims to himself that he is indeed at the gate of heaven and decides to name the place Bethel (house of God). He then constructs a simple stone altar.

"Early the next morning Jacob took the stone he had placed under his

head and set it up as a pillar and poured oil on top of it."
Genesis 28:18 (KVJ)

Though the story doesn't specifically name the stone as an altar, we know Jacob constructs it with the **INTENTION** to honor and acknowledge the presence of God. He anoints the stone with oil.

We see more altars from Jacob:

"And Jacob came to Shalem, a city of Shechem, which is in the land of Canaan, when he came from Padanaram; and pitched his tent before the city.
19 And he bought a parcel of a field, where he had spread his tent, at the hand of the children of Hamor, Shechem's father, for an hundred pieces of money.
20 And he erected there an altar, and called it EleloheIsrael."
Genesis 33:18-20 (KJV)

Genesis chapter 35 has altar construction unfolding in 3 phases.

- **Phase 1** - God speaks to Jacob and instructs him to go to Bethel and build an altar:

"And God said unto Jacob, Arise, go up to Bethel, and dwell there: and make there an altar unto God, that appeared unto thee when thou fleddest from the face of Esau thy brother."
Genesis 35:1 (KJV)

- **Phase 2** - Jacob speaks to his household letting them in on the instructions from God:

"And let us arise, and go up to Bethel; and I will make there an altar unto God, who answered me in the day of my distress, and was with me in the way which I went."

Genesis 35:3 (KJV)

- **Phase 3** - He builds the altar:

> *"He built an altar there, and called the place El Beth El; because there God was revealed to him, when he fled from the face of his brother."*
> *Genesis 35:7 (KJV)*

This altar was constructed to acknowledge God for revealing Itself to Jacob, taking care of Jacob in difficult times with his brother, and being present with Jacob as he travelled in a precarious nomadic lifestyle.

In verse 9, God appears again to Jacob and blesses him. In the verses that follow, God changes Jacob's name to Israel and reiterates his promise to his ancestors and now to Jacob that the land is theirs and a mighty nation will come from him, as well as kings.

> *"And Jacob set up a pillar in the place where he talked with him, even a pillar of stone: and he poured a drink offering thereon, and he poured oil thereon."*
> *Genesis 35:14 (WEB)*

Altar Construction - Common Spiritual Practice

As many instances of constructing altars as there are in the Bible, it would seem to figure that as Christians, we'd be taught to construct altars. Not so. I was never taught the magickal art and science of altar construction, though it's been well documented for thousands of years among worshippers.

The point: construct altars. Lots of them.

Your Altars

From the foregoing we can gain revelations about altar construction in Christian Witchcraft, especially if the Bible (and Pseudepigrapha) is used as a reference tool.

Elements that come to mind for me:

- Altar as representation of the presence of God.
- Altar as the base of a stairway to heaven.
- Altar as a place of remembrance/marker of a specific moment when God appeared.
- Altar as a place of devotion and offering one's self as represented by one's blood.
- Altar as a meeting place for angels.
- Altar as a place of making offerings to God and to spirits in the form of wine and/or oil.
- Altar as a place of making offerings in the form of suffumigation.

What elements come to mind for you?

We have the opportunity to integrate these as we construct our temples, shrines and altars.

Vestments, Cloaks & Robes

There's a reason superheros wear capes. As the superhero **TRANSFORMS** from being an ordinary somebody to being a SUPERHERO, they take on a NEW PERSONA. This goes far beyond a wardrobe change. There's a shift in the psyche, self-concept and presence of the superhero, and in some cases, even their speech. They literally become another entity, a super powerful entity.

I still remember the first magickal cloak I purchased for myself after coming to the realization that I was Witch, and that this powerful being inside me deserved regard and expression. It was a floor length purple cloak with a hood.

The first ritual I ever wore the cloak to was a Samhain fire festival I attended several years ago at the home of a Druid who lived in a house set in the middle of vast acreage on which he had created an outdoor temple in the woods. The Druid conducted the ritual with 3 Witches each year on Samhain, just as his ancestor had carefully prescribed. I attended several of these rituals.

I realize this may sound like a fantasy novel, yet I assure you it is all real.

Since those who participated in the ritual were cloaked or wore some sort of magickal garb, the whole occasion took on an air of palpable magick. Donning my cloak with a clan of magickal beings prior to setting off into the woods led by a Druid and 3 Witches set the stage — in dramatic fashion

I might add — to shift the mind out of waking consciousness and into altered states.

It's how Witches become superheros.

Cloaks and vestments are critical in magick: they instantly shift consciousness. One minute you're a human, then you don your vestments and become a wand pointing Witch uttering barbarous words into the ethers that command spirits.

BAD-A.

All magickal and religious orders have vestments, so on this path, you're invited to acquire and don the very best vestments you can. Your vestments are a reflection of your commitment to magick.

When I invest in magick, it means investing my time, energy, attention, focus AND money. The saying is that where our heart is, there our treasure will be also.

Setting aside funds to invest in magickal attire — while being fiscally responsible — is a statement to the subconscious that you're **ALL IN**.

We've all experienced the change in a person's demeanor and bearing when they are suited up. A judge wears a black gown. We respect that gown, and even if we don't, we acknowledge it.

A priest is immediately recognizable by garb, as is a shaman or a monk.

You are no different. Your holy path is magick. Your adornment reflects this sacred path.

Ideas on Vestments

While there are no rules, I'll set forth a few ideas that I've implemented when it comes to magickal attire.

Of course, we wear different vestments for different types of rituals. Witches perform rituals sky-clad (nude) as well as with full vestments (cloak, boots and more).

This is a deeply personal matter which you'll settle within yourself from Inner Knowing.

Here are a few ideas I've explored:

- I wear white when I desire to expand energy, create, and remind myself of I AM as my identity.
- I wear black/dark colors when I'm containing the energy.
- I wear colors corresponding to the nature of the magickal operation at hand (i.e. chakra colors or elemental colors).
- When in the Mystery School (Covenant of Christian Witches Mystery School or CCW for short), I wear red, purple and black as these are our school colors. Red symbolizes blood (and our blood oath as Witches and the blood of all Witches who have died for the craft, and for the blood of those who died for the craft because they were accused, but were not Witches), purple is for royalty and divinity, and black is for mystery and the blackness from which all emerges. We feel aligned in community when we wear the school colors. Color has the power to galvanize groups and movements, as it does for us in the Christian Witches movement.
- I wear head wraps when I desire to contain the energy or keep my crown ritually pure after a sacred bath.
- I wear Witch hats to honor the Witches from whom I come and all Witches.

Choose your vestments accordingly and wear them with your head held high.

Sigils & Symbols

s of the publication of this book, I have 7 sacred symbol tattoos on my person:

1. **Ankh** - my first tattoo, placed high on my right arm.
2. **Heart** - on my left foot, which contains the word "Faith" in the center.
3. **Heart** - on my right foot, which contains "Trust." (These 2 hearts form a collective charge for how I AM to move forward.)
4. **Sankofa** - on my right ankle. Sankofa is an Adinkra symbol from Ghana which means 'go back and fetch it,' teaching us to go back and fetch the gold from each life experience (and NONE of the pain) and carry it with us so we **MOVE FORWARD WITH THE WISDOM OF THE PAST**.
5. **Incan Cross** - placed high on my left arm to symbolize my initiation into plant medicine with Mother Ayahuasca and acknowledging the wisdom of Peru and the Inca.
6. **Butterfly** - my totem, placed in the center of my chest.
7. **Vishudda** - the symbol for the throat chakra, placed on the front of my throat to honor my destiny and divine charge to **SPEAK** and **EXPRESS TRUTH** to acknowledge and appre-

ciate my travels in India and Bali and my induction into the temples in both these sacred lands, and my acknowledgement of the Hindu tradition. Vishudda means 'essentially pure.'

More are coming.

If one could tattoo their way to ascension, maybe all this pain is for a purpose.

Even though I experienced momentary pain with them all (especially the feet… ouch), each serves as a holy herald of deeper truths.

HUGE meaning is encoded in one tiny design. This is the magick of symbols.

A sigil is a calling card to represent a specific entity or even a desire, as in sigil magick.

The magick of sigils and symbols is they encapsulate and express 1,000 or more thoughts or ideas in one tiny set of dots and lines. It's as if we're taking these huge ideas and putting them in pill form.

Your Inner Sigil and Symbol Library

The Spirit Team communicates with us via symbols and sigils. We communicate with them in the same way.

Spirits don't speak English.

Since humans and spirits speak 2 different languages, we turn to a language we can can both agree on: symbolism.

A substantial inner sigil and symbol library is critical for the Master Alchemist.

Your inner sigil and symbol library will contain both PERSONALIZED and UNIVERSAL symbols.

Personalized symbols can be used to transmit information to our consciousness during the dream state. The dream world is full of symbolism. Our dreams are packed with personalized symbols, although they can also contain a healthy smattering of universal symbols.

An example is when my Spirit Team shows me a gray cloak. For me, this is a symbol of the Master Alchemist. They're telling me to power up and blow out some bad-a magick.

The best way to reveal and catalog the inner sigil and symbol library is to keep a dedicated dream journal by the bed for recording dreams. I record them in as much rich detail as I can before the dream material begins to fade. Unforgettable dreams won't slip away quite as quickly, but they do fade over time, hence a reason to write them out in full descriptive detail. The practice only takes a few minutes and is more than worth it to catalog the inner sigil and symbol library.

This will make communication with spirit realms easier and faster and dream decoding easier too.

As for the use of symbols and sigils in magick, collect as many meanings as you can, catalog them in your Grimoires. We'll be using these in our spellcrafting.

Candle Magick

I love doing candle magick though I was never formally trained in it. I instinctively knew to burn candles with intentions for people I loved, or for specific results I was seeking to manifest.

The extent of my candle magick — before I gained deeper understanding — was to buy candles with saints and angels on them from the grocery store that seemed to match my intention and burn them. They were 7 day candles, so I'd watch daily how they burned, and would notice that each candle burned differently.

It was then that I began to understand the magick of candles: they can be used as divination, just like almost anything you appoint for this purpose, because they tell a story.

Multidimensional Nature of Candles

If someone died and I'd feel inspired to burn a white candle for them, not only would the effects be felt in this plane, I knew the effects were being experienced on other planes as well, including the astral. Souls must travel through the astral plane when leaving earth, and though they're accompanied by angels, the astral is fraught with all manner of spirits (both toward and untoward) and unhelpful distractions. A soul could get caught up in this realm and not continue ascending directly to Source. To help, burning a white candle felt like providing more white light for the soul to follow on its ascension, and it felt comforting in my home and heart each time I gazed at the candle burning for the loved one, knowing they were rising well, high and direct.

Candles are working magick on multiple dimensions at the same time.

I would argue that almost everyone understands candle magick on some level, considering the success of companies like Yankee candle and others who make candles for mundane purposes. You can't go into a home design store without finding a plethora of candles in all colors, styles, scents and shapes, all with their specific vibe and mood-enhancing effects.

We're instinctively and intuitively drawn to candles, even if we don't know why. Before I began intentionally practicing magick, my home was always full of candles. I was unconsciously working candle magick long before I knew anything about it.

Maybe you've experienced similar. Maybe you've been practicing candle magick all along.

Let's start with the most obvious of candle magick rituals: the birthday cake.

Candle Magick for Birthday Celebrations

A cursory search on the web will yield information about the origins of birthday cakes, and will allude to the Egyptians, Greeks, Romans and Germans.

As far as I can tell, the Egyptians were the first (on record) to recognize birthdays, yet not in the way we do today. The day of a Pharaoh being crowned was actually the birth of that one as a God, since Pharaohs were considered divine. A celebration was had each year on this 'birth' day, which could have been an early iteration of the modern day birthday celebration. It's important to note that this practice did not apply to everyone in society.

Next, the Greeks were said to be the first to put candles on moon-shaped cakes and offer them to the Goddess Artemis, who rules the moon and the hunt. The ritual was carried out on the 6th day of each lunar month. The candles were lit to represent the glow of the moon. Smoke from the candles carried prayers and wishes to heaven. I find this a beautiful practice.

We build on practices from our forbears. Candle magick is one of the powerful practices we inherited.

Your Genius

I've been intrigued with the idea of a personal genius for decades, ever since I discovered that a genius is actually a living entity. It could be considered a 'head spirit' or a 'tutelary spirit' acting as a teacher and guide and even a protector in the form of an entity who warns us ahead of time of impending danger or disaster.

This tutelary spirit is actually a god, hence the connection to our head. There's an urge, or divine unction, moving through each human being. This divine unction, or force, or energy is could be one's genius, or head spirit.

The 'head spirit' principle is one I can resonate with. To me, it's Source in a form that's personal to me. Some could even call it the Higher Self or the Holy Guardian Angel. I don' know for sure. I only know that the idea of this tutelary spirit has been with me for ages and resonates as true.

Candle Magick & Divine Realms

It's easy to deduce from the foregoing and other sources that the ancients knew the magick of candles, and utilized the energy in sacred rites.

What we know about candles is this:

- The light of the candle represents light on many levels: lunar, solar and Divine.
- The smoke of the extinguished candle can be used to carry prayers and intentions heavenward for fulfillment by higher powers. It's almost like sending up a smoke signal.

- Reading how a candle burns is a form of divination concerning the matter you're burning the candle for. How fast the candle burns, the traces of the wax on the sides of the glass (if burning a candle in a glass container), the color of the smoke and more are all messages.
- Dressing a candle, or adding essential oils, anointing oils and herbs to our candles magnifies the power exponentially for the intention.
- Candles set the atmosphere for supernatural occurrences, including angel visitations.
- Candles are used in to hold the energy of the elements in our sacred space based on color correspondences (see below).
- Candles in corresponding colors are employed in planetary magick.

While this is by no means a comprehensive list, the above knowledge can be utilized in spellcrafting with candles. I can't think of any magickal operation that couldn't benefit from candles, even if not specifically called for. Keeping white candles burning on the altar is always a good idea.

If you're not comfortable with burning 7-day candles all day every day when you leave the home, place the candle in a bowl of water. The water can be holy water, or water you've anointed for the purpose and intention, and can become part of the magickal working.

Candle Color Correspondences

Candle colors speak to us intuitively, just like nature. Here are a few color correspondences to keep in mind when spellcrafting:

- White: a good stand in color for all things spiritual. Good for light, purity and unveiling shadow energies. Also used for helping loved ones who've crossed over to ascend.
- Red: passion, fire, flames, movement, action, spiritual self. Element of fire. Wands suit in Tarot.
- Blue: calming, cleansing, restorative, flowing, emotional self. Element of water. Cups suit in Tarot.

- Pink: heart, love, friendship, healing, hope, inspiration.
- Green: abundance, creativity (especially for authors and other creatives), healing, nature, wellness, wholeness, freshness, new birth, physical self. Element of earth. Pentacles suit in Tarot.
- Yellow: earthy, grounding, solidifying, mental self. Element of air. Swords suit in Tarot.
- Purple/Violet: royalty, ascension, Crown chakra, divinity, angelic communication.
- Orange: sensuality, sexuality, energizing, expansive.
- Black: cloaking, subduing, destroying, halting, hiding, reversing, containing.

This chapter on candle magick is designed to fan the flames (pardon the pun) of your candle magick for profound results. Of course, you'll have to work with candles yourself to discover all the mysteries these hold for you.

If you're new to candle magick, the best thing you could do is go to the magick shop and buy every candle that speaks to you. Bring them home and place them on your altar. Listen carefully. They'll begin to speak to you, teach you and let you know what each of them is for.

In the Rituals & Spells part of this book, you'll see the exact candles I employed for the example rituals and spells provided.

Exorcisms

The magick I practice includes exorcisms.

The word exorcism is flooded with connotations that may or may not ring true, ranging from scary movies to Catholic priests performing what looks like bizarre rites over the bodies and souls of the possessed.

My take on exorcism is a lot simpler. Let's address the definition of exorcism as its used here, and then how I myself practice an exorcism. I'm sure it will be vastly different for you, so I share my experience with the intention to inspire you to get out there and do the spiritual work for your community — and the world — that you're called to perform.

Now let's kick some negative entity butt.

Exorcism Definition

For our purposes here, we'll use the word exorcism to include:

- Detachment of 'unhelpful entities' from their host.
- Transmutation of the energy of 'unhelpful entities' so that they no longer exist and the energy is returned to the cosmos pure and available for creation.
- Removing demons from their host.

- Returning demons to the Infernal Realm after removal.
- Helping lost spirits go to the appropriate realm.

Everything is Energy

There's a clue in the Bible of how to view the issues we all have as humans. The Bible refers to many common human issues as 'spirits.' Jealousy is a spirit. Deception is a spirit. Hostility is a spirit.

This is accurate. Everything is energy. The energy around an angry person is palpable. We've had the experience of walking into a cold room after those in the room were arguing or disagreeing sharply, and we sense the energy immediately. Every human is first and foremost an energy being.

The weapons of our warfare are not carnal. Though I don't agree with everything attributed to Paul, there's a noteworthy passage that's helpful:

"For though we walk in the flesh, we do not war after the flesh:
4 (For the weapons of our warfare are not carnal, but mighty through God to the pulling down of strong holds;)
5 Casting down imaginations, and every high thing that exalteth itself against the knowledge of God, and bringing into captivity every thought to the obedience of Christ;"
2 Corinthians 10:3-5

To me, this is essentially saying the same thing magick books say: everything is energy, and we are more than flesh. We are dealing with supernatural forces, and we must understand this and go beyond the flesh if we are to be Master Alchemists.

The Bible speaks of supernatural forces more than natural phenomena, which makes sense, since we've already discussed that the Bible is a manual of **ENERGY**.

Let's go further.

Unconscious Creation of Unhelpful Entities

There's a teaching in Kabbalah that's also paralleled in religions and spiritual paths throughout the world, including magick. That teaching is that we make entities out of our own consciousness. Magick concurs. Servitors are created in this exact manner.

Kabbalah also teaches that we create angels and demons according to the energy and pattern of our thinking.

Energy patterns are created from our thoughts (a blueprint of sorts), and we breathe life into it with our being (as God breathed energy into Adam and he became a living soul). We are creators, so to create spirit entities is no more surprising than creating human beings, both of which we're doing all the time.

The part that we're missing is that we don't see all the spirit entities we've consciously and unconsciously created over a lifetime, or multiple lifetimes.

I'm not saying that every thought creates a demon or an angel. I'm saying that we're creating entities with our consciousness from patterns of thinking along with our deepest and most powerful and potent emotions, and we may not have always been aware of when we were doing so.

As servitors are sent out to do one's bidding, so too these entities created out of our consciousness are entities that can come and go.

Because a servitor is a conscious creation with a specific purpose bought about with intent, order, a means of upkeep and in a magickal system or ritual, its likely to be obedient to its creator, unless things somehow go awry. For all intents and purposes, a servitor is designed and created to be helpful to its maker. It gets things done.

Not so with all the unconscious entities we've created. They're not helpful because they've been created unintentionally, from HABITUAL energy patterns of rage, or fear, or jealousy, or any number of natural emotive expressions we have as humans. We're not always aware that our thoughts and emotions can take on a life of their own.

That's where it gets problematic.

This is an energy issue. It must be handled with weapons that are not carnal.

Effects of Unhelpful Entities

We'll refer to these entities who have been created unconsciously as 'unhelpful entities.' They're not good or bad. There's no good or bad in magick. For me, all energy is either constructive or destructive, both of which are needful. Is the energy that's present constructive to the ritual and its intention? Is it destructive?

An example. Mold is a perfect destructive energy. It just doesn't belong in my house, where enough of it could turn into a real problem. However, mold in the forest and in other useful places is essential for life on the planet.

Everything in existence has a purpose, or it wouldn't be. Maybe the purpose of these unhelpful entities that we've created is to make us aware that we get to clean up energetically, not just physically.

This is the purpose of sage, incense, bells, water, salt, fire and any and all means of energetically clearing a space. I call it getting the cooties out. Cooties are pockets of unmatched energy that don't belong in my ritual space. In the Temple, I desire to start off with a pristine, clean canvas upon which to create.

No painter starts off a masterpiece with dirty brushes and mud on the canvas, unless it's part of the art.

No chef starts preparation of a 7 course meal with dirty knives in a dirty kitchen.

As a self-respecting Witch, I do my best to start off rituals and/or spells without cooties and other unhelpful entities hanging around.

If I'm conducting the Life Partner Spell, there's no way I'd want anger entities hanging around, polluting the ritual space. Everything is energy. This is our mantra.

The effects of these unhelpful entities is that they are not a MATCH to what I'm creating. That's the biggest problem. THEY HAVE GOT TO GO.

Also, it's my job to do my best to destroy the pattern of the entities I've created. Energy itself cannot be destroyed or created. The pattern I've created can be destroyed, and the energy can be transmuted. I implore the angels for help with this.

For anything to be held together in a form, there must be INFORMATION. All the cells in the body are the particular cells they are because of the information they received. Quantum physics confirms that energy holds to a specific pattern (chair, banana, person) due to information.

The information we've given this energy pattern was to be angry.

We're creators, so we can destroy that energy pattern with a new intention and transmute the energy to create something else.

I believe prayer does this super effectively, as does forgiveness and many of our spiritual practices. We're transmuting energy we've previously put out, where ever it may be. We don't have to be in the presence of an unhelpful entity we've created in order to do something about it. We can destroy the energy pattern and transmute the energy no matter where we are physically in relation to the entity. Distance healing is just one example of the truth that we are all connected in consciousness.

Another effect of these unhelpful entities is that they're karmic in nature. They come home to roost. We must do something about that.

Unhelpful Entities vs. Demons

I view unhelpful entities and demons quite differently.

Demons are specific entities — according to the Biblical story — who were once angels. These angels rebelled and were cast out of heaven. I'm not sure if I'm all the way on board with that story, as I never quite understood how a perfect God could have such crazy kids, with one of them being an entity that could actually rival God Himself. I don't care how old my 3 kids get, none of them will ever be an equal to me or could possibly rival me.

I like the Chinese way of looking at it instead. There's no devil belief for them to overcome, so it's easier for them to get right to the magick.

They, according to a magician I love who teaches magick globally, Lon Milo Duquette, think that if your God has a rival, your God is not God enough. I concur.

Westerners are saddled with deeply held beliefs in good versus evil, which become an impediment to good magick.

Witches and magicians I know don't view the world from as limited a position as good versus evil. Everything in existence is here for a **PURPOSE**. I'm not concerned about whether demons are evil or not. What's their purpose?

For me, unhelpful entities are unconscious 'servitors' we've created unintentionally that must be dealt with.

Demons, on the other hand, can also be unhelpful, and it's my job as a Witch to help keep universal order. Therefore, if a demon is problematic to a person, I do have the authority and power to right the situation, as Christ did, and as you do. Humans, because of our divine nature, can command spirits. We just have to learn how.

It's wise to be aware of what we're dealing with in any given moment, so that we understand the appropriate action to take, if any.

How Spirits Present

I have the blessing of leading retreats all over the world, even though most of the work I do is creative, like writing books or making videos, which are solitary activities (except for the spirits who ritually hang around me).

When I'm with people at our retreats and events, I get clear reads on what's going on with them in the spirit realm. If you're reading this, you probably have the same kind of thing going on, you can see into spirit realms.

A short list of spirits I've seen that are attached to people:

- Spirits of laziness and sloth that keep people sleepy, or moving slow, or unspired with no fire in the belly. The people suffering from this kind of spirit sickness are unmotivated and don't know why. They usually have huge potential and are highly intelligent. Yet, they don't produce or create on par with their potential.

- Spirits of anger, rage and conflict that keep people fighting. You may know some of these people. The answer to everything is a fight or an argument. You can love them more if you know that they are under spirit attack.
- Spirits of jealousy and envy. Some people literally turn into another person when they're insecure or jealous. I've had this play out in my life on both ends of the polarity: I've been the jealous, insecure one, and I've been in partnership with a jealous, insecure one.
- Spirits of depression and feeling down. No, I am not saying that depression is caused by a spirit. I'm saying that there is spirit activity than can cause one to feel down. I've lived there. For years.
- Spirits of low self-worth, and a skewed self-concept, causing people not to view themselves as God.

While there are many more spirits than can be listed in a book, our task when it comes to supernatural realms is to **BE AWARE.**

My First 'Exorcism'

The first time I successfully displaced energy was for a client who couldn't sleep. She had bought her home brand new and had never slept well. There always seemed to be some low level disturbance going on, without anything looking out of place on the surface. Her home was beautifully decorated, clean and tidy. And because she's a magickal being, she was careful about who she let in the house.

This is textbook spirit activity, where everything in the physical looks normal, yet there's an energetic disturbance.

I came to her home with another spiritual practitioner. I wore white, my usual for spiritual work. My head was wrapped in white as well. I wore anointing oil made with essential oils and burned a stick of incense that I carried with me throughout the house along with my open Bible, while praying the 23rd Psalm.

There was nothing on the first level, and nothing on the upstairs level where the bedrooms were. I inquired about the basement.

She took us down, where we found the source of the issue: an entire family of slaves (in spirit form) still living on what had been their plantation. They didn't know they were free. There were 3 generations of them, living in a corner of her basement.

Up until that point, I had never seen such a thing in all my born days, but it was not to be the strangest thing I would encounter.

This did not call for anything other than a release of dead spirits. Talking to them worked. In spirit realms, I let them know what had transpired, and that they were free to ascend. They did. All of them.

My client slept like a baby in her home after that day.

I was filled with compassion when I saw this misplaced family. They weren't evil. They weren't trying to cause problems. They were out of place. This is the nature of spirit realms. Everything has its place. When things are out of place, disturbances occur.

I also learned the valuable lesson that all spirits aren't hostile. Some are lost. Others are suffering. Others are energetically imbalanced.

My Exorcism Method

My method to rid people and spaces of unwanted, unhelpful entities is crazy simple:

- **FAITH**
- **PRAYER**
- **FASTING.**

Many years ago I read in the Necronomicon that any demon could be expelled with the Lord's Prayer. I didn't know what to make of it at the time, as I had never tried it, though it seemed simple enough. Something about the passage spoke deeply to me. Inside I could feel a plant growing that was of a fearless variety. It was an intuitive knowing that I was always prepared and equipped for anything, no matter how crazy it may seem. The Lord's Prayer is a powerful non-carnal weapon.

The famous passages in the Bible in which the disciples could not cast out a particular entity even though Christ was easily able to do so reveal truisms for exorcisms. When asked why he could deftly accomplish what they could not, he replied:

"19 Then came the disciples to Jesus apart, and said, Why could not we cast him out?
20 And Jesus said unto them, Because of your unbelief: for verily I say unto you, If ye have faith as a grain of mustard seed, ye shall say unto this mountain, Remove hence to yonder place; and it shall remove; and nothing shall be impossible unto you.
21 Howbeit this kind goeth not out but by prayer and fasting."
Matthew 17:19-21 (KJV)

This passage reveals that faith, prayer and fasting are what's required to cast out any entity.

- Faith: **KNOWING WHO YOU ARE** and **WHAT YOU CAN DO. CERTAINTY**. This is NOT blind faith held simply because we've been asked to believe without evidence. This is a deep, visceral, **INNER KNOWING** of **SELF AS SOURCE** and that there is nothing Source cannot do.
- Prayer: the Lord's Prayer and the 23rd Psalm can make short work of any entities.
- Fasting: I could write a whole book on fasting, yet what we're essentially talking about here is the reliance more on spiritual sustanance and nourishment than on physical. It's an orientation, or a way of being. In fasting consciousness, Spirit is our go-to Source for life first and foremost, while physical food is secondary. This is a way of being that causes one to show up as a Spiritual Being most demons would

rather not bother with, and that will cause unhelpful entities to leave and transmute rapidly, on command.

While Hollywood is oh so dramatic, none of the exorcisms I've conducted over the years has been anything like what's been pictured on television. Most of the people who have received relief, in my experience, wanted to be healed. They wanted to release the entity and no longer play host to a vampiric spirit. By the time they landed at my doorstep, they were READY TO RELEASE.

I remember one person who I saw a demon literally leaving her auric field while we were in an Ayahuasca ceremony. In that instance, Mother Ayahuasca was cleaning house.

This is all happening by divine providence. God will never put anything in front of you that you cannot handle. I trust this with my life. Since I'm called to serve humanity in this regard — very much like Christ — it always works. I give thanks.

V

Angel Magick

Angelology for Christian Witchcraft.

The Nature of Angels

What is an angel? To understand the answer from a multi-dimensional perspective, it's important to rid our minds of false ideas we may hold about angels.

After that, we'll proceed with a working definition of angels, 6 angelic systems, Christian Witchcraft Angelology, the elemental angels and where to start. Let's roll.

Mistaken Notions About Angels

Flawed thinking in the general populace leads to a plethora of mistaken notions about angels. It seems that, generally speaking, people think of angels as:

- White. Most of the angel depictions I've seen are white people. They're portrayed with long hair and presented in a way deemed by societal standards to be 'beautiful.'
- Wearing long flowing robes. Angels are depicted as wearing long beautiful robes in corresponding colors.
- Helpful and gentle. Angels are generally thought of as helpful, gentle and overall good beings who help everyone.
- The opposite of demons. Angels are erroneously depicted as the

opposite of demons.
- Cut, fat and cuddly. Cherubs are often pictured as cute, fat babies that pierce people with arrows to make them fall in love.

What Angels Really Are

- Vast, unimaginable, incomprehensible and unfathomable **COSMIC FORCES**.
- Immense beings of such enormous power that it's said they strike terror in the hearts of humans they appear to, often having to say 'fear not' when approaching.
- Assassins. Yes, angels are the most prolific and swift assassins in the Bible, including a single angel who kills 185,000 people in the army of Sennacherib in one night. (2 Kings 19:35) Angels are depicted as bloody. Of course, this is metaphysical, not historical nor factual. This is an allegory that points to a greater truth about an aspect of angels: they can be swift and thorough assassins of the enemies we hold in consciousness (shadow beliefs that hold us back, hatred, fear, doubt, worry, etc.).
- Task-Specific. Angels are not ***generally*** helpful but are ***specifically*** oriented. If you ask the wrong angel for the wrong thing, the answer will range from non-effective to an angelic pimp slap. Angels do not do anything other than what they are created and charged to do. This is one of the most important elements to understand when dealing with angels and performing and mastering angel magick.
- Intolerant of foolishness. Angels, in my experience, are beings who do not tolerate or abide foolishness, ignorance, impetuousness or stupidity.
- Engines of the cosmos. Angels are vast energy currents that serve as the engines of the cosmos. Everything in creation is subject to its own angelic forces and/or influences, including humans, whether we know it or not. To illustrate this truth, the Kabbalists teach that not even a blade of grass grows until it receives its instructions from the angel

that governs it.

- Asexual, immaterial and above race. Angels aren't human, and though we humans anthropomorphize every entity we can get our hands on to make them more approachable and understandable to our tiny minds, angels are beyond sex, race, color, creed and billowy robes, even though they may appear to us in these guises so we can digest what's going on. However we think angels are is how they'll usually show up.

Definition of Angel

For our purposes, we'll define an angel as:

A vast cosmic force of the celestial realm created for a specific purpose in accord with the great order of the universe.

To distinguish an angel from a demon (who is also a vast force created for a specific purpose), we note that angels are of the celestial realm, while demons are of the infernal realm. Yes, the distinction between angels and demons goes far beyond where they live. We're keeping this simple so that we act and not analyze.

Legions of Angels

There are an uncountable number of legions of angels and archangels arranged in **DIVINE ORDER**.

There's no universal consensus on how many angels there are and the exact order all the angels are arranged in, which gives rise to sundry angelic systems (6 of which are mentioned in the next chapter and 1 of which is deeply explored in this work). The multiplicity of angelic systems gives us great variety. Humans aren't all the same. Our spiritual practices reflect our diversity, and shouldn't become cause for confusion.

The fact that we have an abundance of angelic systems can either be overwhelming or inviting. It all depends on how we look at it.

In the coming chapters, I offer a system of angel magick that's approachable (even for newbies) and yields astonishing results fast.

With all the angelic systems and their varied strata, correspondences, colors, herbs, planets and more, our job is to find what works for **SELF**.

There's no one system of angel magick that's right. They all have their benefits, characteristics, pros and cons. I do know this: selecting an angelic system to work with and being true to it over enough time to understand it well will yield better results than jumping around. I've learned from experience that a certain level of penetration into any given system yields secrets one would never have been privy to if that exact same system had been engaged only superficially. Select a system you love based on intuition, give yourself to it as a lover and watch the magick happen!

As you master one system, you may find you're led to move on to another, or you may stick with what's working. Either way, Source will lead you by **RESONANCE**.

I've read countless angel books which outlined — to greater or lesser degree — the 9 tiered hierarchy of angels, consisting of 3 triads. This take on angels never resonated with me. As I scanned my energetic system, nothing moved. My heart was not stirred. My soul didn't leap up.

Conversely, when I was divinely led to the Kabbalistic Tree of Life and the archangels and angels of that system, there was a **DING DING DING** in my soul. The lights flipped on!

This is an ongoing process in a great game of energetic connect the dots we're all playing with the universe. **GO WITH WHAT RESONATES DEEPLY IN YOUR SOUL.**

Angels Who May Not be Angels

When you look at your bloodline magick, angels may not be called angels. They may be referred to by other names, or described differently.

It's my intention to honor and respect all spiritual paths. To do so, we can intuit into the spaces where these systems are speaking of the same energy even though their physical presence may be described differently.

Everything is energy. If we are speaking of the great angel of the east, for example, the healing power of God known as Raphael, we understand that this energy conduit may appear in various forms to various people. Raphael may be white to white people, and Hispanic to Latin people. This cosmic force carries different names in different cultures.

Focusing on the exact likeness of an angel is tricky and can be misleading. As mentioned, angels are far beyond color or country or culture. This bears repeating. We've had decades of conditioning about what angels look like. When we think the word 'angel' an immediate mental picture comes to mind. This mental construct is the result of conditioning that may have nothing to do with the truth of angels.

In ancient Kemet (Egypt), winged entities were also present, which one could equate to angels (though I'm not stating this from a viewpoint based in fact… this is an intuitive hunch). I mention Kemet because it's in my bloodline and the most powerful magick is in the bloodline. Look at your bloodline and see if you find winged creatures. Even though there may be entities in the magick of your bloodline that do not seem to be angels in the Biblical sense, you may intuit that these entities could be the very same cosmic forces we know in the Christian sense as angels.

The most important aspect to focus on and align with is **ENERGY**.

Now let's take a brief look at 6 different angelic systems.

6 Angelic Systems

A powerful starting place for angel magick is selecting an angelic system and diving in.

Let's take a look at 6 different ways of looking at angels, which for our purposes here, we'll call 'angelic systems.'

6 Angelic Systems

Because these systems are simply ways of looking at or considering angels, we need not be dogmatic about any of it. This is simply a perspective. Many perspectives exist. Be at peace with your perspective while allowing others to have their own perspective without seeking to change them. If you have an angelic perspective that works beautifully for you, wonderful! If you're seeking to broaden your perspective, or see things from another perspective, wonderful!

As you consider each system, there will be 1 or more that will deeply resonate with you. We understand this resonance as the clarion call from the Divine it is.

There are more angel systems than we can possibly discuss in one chapter, let alone several books, so we'll do a brief overview followed by the system offered in this book:

1. **Christian Angelology** - 9 Types of Angels in 3 Triads (see below).
2. **Directional/Elemental** - 4 Archangels (the basis for the angel magick in this book; see the chapter titled "The 4 Directional/Elemental Archangels").
3. **Kabbalistic Tree of Life** - 10 Archangels (see below).
4. **The Book of Enoch** - 7 Archangels (see below).
5. **Planetary Angels** - Angels Corresponding to 7 Planetary Spheres (see below).
6. **Enochian Magick** - 200+ angels (see below for a brief note).

Add to this list ***Christian Witchcraft Angelology*** - the integrated, harmonized system offered in this book (see the following chapters).

I share these to illustrate the fact that there are an abundance of systems with vast differences between each system. Some systems feature the same angels.

There are brief notes on a few of these below. Detailed study and dedicated practice over time are the keys to mastering effective angelic rituals and angel magick as a whole.

Christian Angelology

Considering that this is a book of Christian Witchcraft, and is being written from the perspective of integration of Christ and the Craft, we'll first take a look at Christian Angelology.

A word about the following: some of the following saints hated Pagans. Some were Church 'Fathers' who were on a mission to destroy anything unlike their own narrow knowledge of God and the world. Understand that in looking at Christian Angelology, we must also consider the often hostile origins of the Christian faith. I honor all the Pagans, Witches, Wizards, Warlocks and Magickal Beings of all times who have been affected by hate, religious crimes and any other action and/or attitude that is not love. May God bless their souls.

With love and forgiveness, we have the power to purge and melt the effects of hate, injustice, murder and crimes against humanity perpetuated by religion. When we do, we free ourselves to practice magick from a liberated consciousness.

Let's proceed.

From Pseudo-Dionysus we receive the most widely accepted Christian Angelology map, which consists of 9 levels of angels in 3 orders:

First Order or Sphere:

- Seraphim
- Cherubim
- Thrones

Second Order or Sphere:

- Dominions or Dominations or Lordships
- Virtues or Strongholds
- Powers or Authorities

Third Order or Sphere:

- Principalities or Rulers
- Archangels
- Angels

From St. Ambrose we receive the following classifications of angels:

1. Seraphim
2. Cherubim
3. Dominations
4. Thrones
5. Principalities

6. Potentates or Powers
7. Virtues
8. Archangels
9. Angels

From St. Jerome we receive this angelic classification:

1. Seraphim
2. Cherubim
3. Powers
4. Dominions (Dominations)
5. Thrones
6. Archangels
7. Angels

The Apostolic Constitutions offers this classification:

1. Seraphim
2. Cherubim
3. Aeons
4. Hosts
5. Powers (Virtues)
6. Authorities
7. Principalities
8. Dominions
9. Thrones
10. Archangels
11. Angels

From St. Gregory we receive this list:

1. Seraphim
2. Cherubim

3. Thrones
4. Dominations
5. Principalities
6. Powers
7. Virtues
8. Archangels
9. Angels

The Middle Space

These angel classifications, in my mind, came from human beings, which may or may not be useful for our purposes as Christian Witches. I've never had proof that this is how it is in heaven, although some of the works I read early on in my magickal journey decades ago espoused the above as if they were law. I see things differently.

When I've had contact with angels, it was in times of:

- **Disaster** - something disastrous was happening and supernatural help came my way seemingly 'out of nowhere' and instantaneously
- **Hopelessness/Despair** - when I was depressed and couldn't string two days together without wanting to stay in the bed with the covers over my head and the shades drawn, some supernatural help kept appearing in my consciousness lifting me as if on invisible hands. In the Christian faith, we call these the everlasting arms.
- **Avid and Sincere Questioning** - when I've been in deep questioning of my life, the soul, my place in the cosmos and other questions that only God can answer, I've received inspiration that provided the satisfying answers my soul was thirsting for.
- **Problem Solving** - with persistent, aggravating issues and problems I've been able to call on supernatural help and it showed up, giving detailed and insightful information that I had never considered or had known previously.

I could go on and on, and I'm sure you quite the hefty list too. Countless masses have experienced unexplained supernatural help that came at the right time, miraculously, and solved whatever was present, or provided a grace-filled exit. I'm not purporting angels are here to save us from ourselves. I'm stating that we **ALWAYS HAVE ACCESS TO SUPERNATURAL HELP** beyond our human capability to understand or quantify.

When I've had these experiences, I've never asked the angelic presence what tier in heaven they came from. I didn't care. I just wanted to solve whatever was going on. The job got done, and I was happy and relieved.

The other polarity to the angelic presence showing up at the right time is the intentional ritual to call an angel for a specific purpose. This I love as well. This is the approach in the chapters to follow.

There's also a middle space where we intentionally court and cultivate communication with angels while going about the business of our every day lives while being open, ready and EXPECTANT for them to show up at any instant. I guess this is where I live most of the time. Not in the reactive space of having an angel to show up to save my butt, and not in continual angelic rituals to call specific angels, but in the in-between space of allowing and seeking. I like this space. This doesn't preclude angelic rituals, which are highly recommended and laid out here. In the resources section, you'll find the best of the best resources on angelic rituals, and I pray you engage them.

What we get to become aware of is that angels are present **AT ALL TIMES** and we would do well to make use of this ever present access to heaven.

Angels on the Kabbalistic Tree of Life

The 10 archangels of the Kabbalistic Tree of Life represent a complete system from earth to heaven, which means it's likely you'd find an angel on the tree for just about anything you would cast for.

The angels of the Kabbalistic Tree of Life deserve volumes, so we'll only lay out here the angels and the sphere they're associated with.

Kabbalah has been my bridge between Christianity and magick. It gave me the missing magickal insights on Moses and other great magicians of the Bible. And since I was familiar with the language and characters of the Bible, it made me feel right at home. The Kabbalists seem to have a handle on magick as well, and understanding of supernatural forces that I had not encountered before studying Kabbalah. (See the Resources section for my FAVE books on Kabbalah.)

Through deepened study over the years, I've come to see that there are elements in Kabbalah and Jewish spiritual practice that have its roots in Kemet (ancient Egypt), including the 10 Commandments. For me, this doesn't take anything away from Kabbalah, it simply broadens my scope of thinking, opening up new vistas and possibilities in magick.

The wisdom of Kabbalah teaches that the Tree of Life forms a map of creation and contains the code the Creator used to bring our world into physical manifestation — by energy traveling down the tree in a lightning bolt formation — and is therefore a key to the entire cosmos. By traveling up the tree, we reunite with our Creator, which is the true thrust and aspiration of every soul. While the Tree of Life is far more, this is a brief summary for the purposes of our discussion here.

Note: Sephiroth is plural, while sephirot is singular.

Each of the 10 sephiroth on the Tree of Life represents an **EMANATION OF GOD** and is ruled by an archangel who in turn rules, leads or commands a legion of angels or heavenly hosts. Here's a list of the sephiroth, along with the corresponding divine attributes, ruling archangels and heavenly hosts they command. There are variations in the archangels of the sephiroth, depending upon which source you choose. I've included these variations in parenthesis.

1. Keter - Crown - Metatron - Holy Living Creatures
2. Chokmah - Wisdom - Raziel (Ratziel)- Auphanim
3. Binah - Understanding - Tzaphkiel - Aralim
4. Chesed - Mercy/Loving-kindness - Tzadkiel - Chasmalim
5. Gevurah - Strength/Judgment - Chamuel (Khamuel) - Seraphim

6. Tifaret - Beauty - Michael (some sources say Michael, others say Raphael, others say both rule this sphere together) - Malachim
7. Netzach - Victory - Haniel - Elohim
8. Hod - Glory/Splendor - Raphael (some sources say Raphael and Michael rule this sphere together) - Ben Elohim
9. Yesod - Foundation - Gabriel - Kerubim
10. Malkuth - Kingdom - Sandalphon - Ashim

There's overlap in the Christian Angelology schema and the Kabbalistic approach.

When I began working with these angels, the first thing I did was draw out the Tree of Life in my Grimoire and add the angels to it with pertinent detailed information. I consult this resource for Spellcrafting and recommend you create your own sort of Angel Bible as well.

The Book of Enoch

According to the Book of Enoch, here are the 7 Watchers:

> *And these are the names of the holy angels who watch. 2. Uriel, one of the holy angels, who is over the world and over Tartarus. 3. Raphael, one of the holy angels, who is over the spirits of men. 4. Raguel, one of the holy angels who takes vengeance on the world of the luminaries. 5. Michael, one of the holy angels, to wit, he that is set over the best part of mankind and over chaos. 6. Saraqâêl, one of the holy angels, who is set over the spirits, who sin in the spirit. 7. Gabriel, one of the holy angels, who is over Paradise and the serpents and the Cherubim. 8. Remiel, one of the holy angels, whom God set over those who rise.*

It's easy to see the overlap of familiar angels we'll be working with in our angelic system for Christian Witchcraft so it may be helpful to read the Book of Enoch.

Planetary Angels

The only thing I can tell you about planetary magick with the angels of each planet is that I don't practice it, but I can refer you to a bad-a magician who does, and literally wrote the book on it: *Seven Spheres* by Rufus Opus.

If you want a simple, actionable, real initiation into the 7 spheres (the 7 planets visible to the naked eye that our ancestors worked with) and all it entails, this is THE book for you.

Note: the magick taught in the book is not so much about the archangels as it is about the planets themselves and the energy they express in the cosmos.

Here are the planets with their angelic correspondences, which are the Intelligences of each Sphere:

Jupiter - Sachiel
Mars - Sammael
The Sun - Michael
Venus - Anael
Mercury - Raphael
The Moon - Gabriel
Saturn - Anael

In the book you'll see everything required to take on this type of magick and WIN. After I dive in, which I will, I'll let you know how it went.

Enochian Magick

Many years ago, a strange and magickal set of occurrences ended with the book *Enochian Vision Magick* in my hands, by Lon Milo DuQuette, a mage I ADORE. I hadn't heard of Dr. John Dee or Edward Kelley at that juncture (who could be classified as the veritable Batman and Robin of Renaissance Magick).

After thoroughly studying the book, and working with the Enochian calls, I came to the conclusion that this is a field of magick I best give myself to if I'm to get anywhere.

With over 200 angels in the system and complex tables, this is not a system for the casual.

Plus, Enochian Angels bite. They're not nice. Sometimes they're really hard. Enochian Magick will knock any ideas our of your head about angels being these lovely, kind beings who wouldn't hurt a fly. I haven't found that to be the case.

Proceed at your own risk lol.

Now that we've had an overview of the angelic landscape as it exists in a few complementary paradigms, let's go into Christian Witchcraft Angelology and Magick.

Angels in Christian Witchcraft

As we've seen, angels figure prominently in quite a few systems of magick, AND they're central and key players in the Bible, which means they lend themselves exquisitely well to the practice of Christian Witchcraft.

Whether you find it easy to communicate with angels or not, they're here for our upliftment and can be invoked or evoked based on a set of parameters that once learned, can yield magnificent results. The conversations I've had with angels over the years have left indelible marks on my psyche, not to mention every aspect of my life.

Here are a few considerations for engaging in angel magick.

Relationship

Imagine you're the author of a new bestselling book. You're being contacted by podcasters and media outlets for interviews. You say yes to a major media outlet. When you arrive, they've taken care to have a well arranged green room for you before you go on the show. They've filled the green room with items you like, the kind of water you love to drink, and a decadent selection of your favorite snacks. When it's time to go on air, you're escorted to the stage and the interviewer greets you warmly. Lights, camera, action and the show has begun! The interviewer gives an impeccable introduction of you, your accomplishments and why the book you've written is so vital to humanity now. Each question the interviewer asks you seems to be perfectly matched for you to give perfect answers. You shine. The interviewer has done their research. The interview goes off flawlessly. After the show, everyone claps and celebrates! If this media outlet asks you to return for another show, you know your answer will be a resounding YES.

This is an analogy for working with angels. If you loved the experience of being interviewed, it's your turn to be the interviewer when it comes to angel magick.

Do this well and the results of your angel magick will be stunning.

First things first: **RELATIONSHIP**. Ask yourself:

- How well do I know the angels I'm calling on for help?
- How well do I know what they like/don't like, including fragrances, colors, etc.?
- Angels are beings of specificity; how well do I know the specific tasks in the cosmos this angel is in charge of and the purview of this angel?
- Heaven is ordered; how well do I know the ranking order of this angel, and who oversees this angel?
- How well do I understand my own intention as it relates to the specific angel I'm evoking or invoking?

Relationship is first and foremost, and must be addressed. I would even venture to say that relationship is even more powerful than getting all the exact details of the particular angel right. The angels will let you know when you're off base, trust me.

Dedicated Angel Grimoires

The portal to relationship building with the angels begins in the mind with a simple intention. Angels can hear everything, so the second you set your intention to attune your consciousness to angelic realms, it will start to happen in the most magickal and surprising ways.

After making up my mind to be in close contact with the angelic realm (and not just for emergencies or problems) I decided to acquire a beautiful journal for each angel I desired contact with. I started with the 4 in the next chapter, since they were the most accessible to me then.

Each journal I bought represented the colors, energy and essence of the angel I was dedicating the grimoire to. I asked them to fill the grimoire with their energy, giving me vital keys to connecting with them and learning from them, for the benefit of all humanity. The angels did not disappoint.

Before I knew it, beautiful journals were floating to me, effortlessly, for each of the angels I sought to court and commune with. Writing is a sacred and magickal act, so writing their names and attributes put my consciousness in immediate contact with these beings in an introductory sort of way. Nothing takes the place of a full-on angelic evocation in a magickal rite. My grimoires were a starting point, an introduction and opening of the portals to divine realms.

If you haven't started yet and have made up your mind to delve deeply into angel magick, acquiring a grimoire for each of the 4 archangels in the following chapter is ideal. It's not required. It will, however, give you ready access to the detailed information you'll require for each angelic ritual.

Angel Magick in Christian Witchcraft

Here's a somewhat different take on how to figure out which angel to work with, and for what purpose: study the angels and angel appearances in sacred books including the Bible, Apocrypha and Pseudepigrapha. The details in the stories of angelic appearances and acts in the Bible, other holy books and sacred texts reveal vital keys to angel magick.

If Gabriel appeared at least twice to announce a birth to a barren woman, maybe this is a clue that I can call on this angel for matters of fertility, pregnancy, midwifery and delivery of healthy babies.

Reading and studying the Bible and holy books will help with angel magick. I realize I may sound like your mom at this juncture, but your mom may have had a point when she told you to read your Bible.

This is the exact approach we'll take in the next chapter, bringing together and integrating what we know of the 4 great directional/elemental archangels and their Biblical lore to create a harmonic system of angel magick.

Let's proceed.

The 4 Directional/Elemental Archangels

I love the power and presence of these 4 so much that I feel anyone can practice effective angel magick for decades working exclusively with these archangels.

I call these 4 present in every ritual I conduct as keepers and guardians of the elements and directions.

In this chapter, we look at these archangels in light of their appearances in the Bible and the Pseudepigrapha to intuit how these mighty forces can best lend their aid.

The 4 Directional/Elemental Archangels

These archangels are the big 4 many practicing Witches and magicians are acutely aware of and intimately in communication with. For easy reference, they're listed here with the meaning of the name, corresponding direction, element, aspect of self and Tarot suit:

- Raphael (*God has Healed*) - east - air - mental self - Swords
- Michael (*Who is Like God*) - south - fire - spiritual self - Wands
- Gabriel (*God is My Strength/Might of God*) - west - water - emotional self - Cups
- Uriel (*God is My Light*) - north - earth - physical self - Pentacles

Raphael

My ALL TIME FAVE story about Raphael comes from the book of Tobit in the Apocrypha.

In the story, Raphael demonstrates how to heal blindness, reclaim riches and conquer a murderously problematic demon by the name of Asmodeus, while simultaneously pairing a young lad with his perfect betrothed. If you haven't read the story, it's well worth the investigation now, before continuing here, and can provide an underpinning and foundation to proceed with when working with this angel. It clearly outlines the angel's purview in allegory form.

From this fascinating story, one would surmise that Raphael can help with:

- **Healing** in all cases of dis-ease and/or illness, including blindness. Raphael's name means *God has healed*.
- **Reuniting one with treasures** (physically and metaphysically) that one had formerly earned and tucked away. This could also apply to accessing treasures in consciousness you've earned in prior lifetimes yet may not have conscious awareness of now.
- **Safety in travel**.
- **Mastery over dark forces**, as represented by Asmodeus.
- **Matters of betrothal, match-making and pairing** the appropriate people (though not specifically with love and matters of the heart, which I would tend to lean on Gabriel for if working exclusively with the 4 archangels here. If working with a broader system of angels, as in planetary angel magick, I would go to Anael, the archangel of Venus for matters of love.)
- **Shape-shifting**, which all angels are masters of.
- **Guidance and teaching in the healing arts**. In the story, Raphael teaches Tobias (Tobit's son) how to draw the heart, liver and gall from a fish and use them to cure both spiritual and physical issues. The heart and liver is used for repelling demonic entities and the gall was used

> to clear blindness. (Please do not take this passage to mean that you should go fishing and draw these items from a fish and practice the exact thing in the tale. This is a metaphor, or an allegory that points to a greater truth. We use the greater truth in magick.)

Raphael is possibly the angel mentioned at John 5:4 who 'troubled the waters' of the pool of Bethesda at ***appointed seasons***. Everyone who entered the pool when the waters were agitated by the angel would be instantaneously healed of anything and everything, no matter the infirmity (blindness, paralysis, etc.).

This has deep meaning for me because of my African ancestry. There's an old 'negro spiritual' (as it was called back in the day; now I think the term is politically incorrect but you get my drift) called *Wade in the Water*. The song was written about Harriet Tubman's guidance when leading slaves to freedom to walk in water rather than on land when possible, so that their scent could not be picked up by dogs employed by slave owners.

Harriet Tubman was divinely guided, having received dreams from God that ensured her she would never be caught and the whole group would always be safe as she fulfilled her divine destiny to free others from their shackles.

This very much aligns with Raphael for me. Safe travels. The angel who troubles the waters causing them to be healing currents and conduits of freedom for slaves.

You may associate other symbolism with Raphael. That's the beauty of angels. They're not picky about what we think of them. They simply get the job done.

Michael

Daniel is a book in the Bible we can explore for understanding more about this archangel.

I've always found Daniel fascinating, even as a little girl who read tales of his feats of being true to himself in a foreign land, where his spiritual practices differed from everyone around him. Because his integrity was beyond question, he rose to the highest levels in the reigns of 2 separate kings. As can be expected, he was repeatedly schemed against by those who were jealous of the foreigner who was able to gain special favor with kings, along with vast power. One of the schemes landed him in a lion's den. We know the story. He emerged unscathed.

In the other story we have of Daniel, his 3 Hebrew companions, Shadrach, Meshach, and Abednego (Hanania, Mishael, and Azariah in Hebrew) were thrown into a furnace that had been heated 7 times hotter than usual for their religious 'disobedience.' We know what happens. An angel of the Lord appears in the fire with them, and all 3 are miraculously delivered, without so much as 1 hair on their head being singed. They emerge from the fire with not even the smell of smoke on them or their clothing. (Some people say the Bible has no magick. To these people I say look again.)

Daniel chapter 12 describes a supernatural vision Daniel had after fasting for 3 weeks. He was disturbed by a premonition he'd received of a coming war.

Verses 11-14 have always intrigued me. I've read Daniel countless times over the years. He's by far one of the more 'magickal' beings in the Bible, someone I deeply connect with. In these verses, the 'man' who was sent to Daniel is clearly an angel, who says that as soon as Daniel began praying, God immediately dispatched him to answer Daniel's prayer, but this he was detained by the Prince of Persia (in spirit realms) for 21 days, until the archangel Michael came to his aid.

The Bible is better than the best epic fantasy. It has more magick and supernatural occurrences than anyone could wish for. That's why I love it so much, and why many may be confused by it.

I digress.

Back to archangel Michael. He's the only angel in the Bible referred to as an archangel, or commander, or one of the chief princes. Clearly, he's a head honcho of sorts from the Biblical perspective.

Digging deeper, we find more intriguing tidbits of information about Michael in *The Books of Adam and Eve* (as state previously, this can be read free online at Pseudepigrapha.com).

In the never mentioned in church saga of the life of Adam and Eve after expulsion from the Garden of Eden, Michael plays a pivotal role in teaching the couple life skills, including:

- **Midwifery**: how to appropriately birth a human baby: archangel Michael and 11 other angels and 2 'Virtues' attend the first human birth (Cain), effectively midwiving the delivery.
- **Farming**: how to plant seeds and turn the vast wilderness outside the Garden of Eden into farmland.
- **Walking on water**: Michael strikes a body of water with his rod, instantly freezing the surface. Michael and Adam walk across.
- **Burial rites**: archangels Michael and Uriel give instructions on how to wrap the dead bodies of Adam and Abel with byssus (fine linen also used in Egyptian burial rites to wrap Pharoahs) and how to bury the dead.
- **Mourning**: that it should take no longer than 6 days (on the 7th day is the resurrection).

When reading the saga, it occurs to me that Michael is somewhat of a caretaker of humanity, beginning with Adam and Eve and continuing down to this day. At points, it seemed they were clueless about life. Enter archangel Michael to instruct and guide, especially in earthly matters.

One can extrapolate from the Michael stories that this powerful entity could be called on for:

- Help to understand troubling visions and/or premonitions and dreams.
- Protection: spiritually and physically. The weapons of our warfare are not carnal. Michael is probably the best go-to entity for spiritual warfare. Remember, everything is energy, and every malady in the physical has its cause in the unseen.
- Questions that require supernatural answers.

- Midwifery and births to ensure a safe delivery.
- Consecration of the dead and burial rites.
- Farming.
- Help and support at moments when your life on planet earth is fraught with trial and tribulation and you have nowhere to turn.

Gabriel

Ah, we've arrived at the baby angel. I love Gabriel. Angels are androgynous, yet this vast entity always seemed to have a feminine essence about it.

Taking a look at the Biblical appearances of Gabriel, we find this angel is associated with significant births:

John the Baptist

Archangel Gabriel visits the the priest Zachariah whose wife Elizabeth was barren. They were both advanced in age, so hopes of an heir were nonexistent. The beauty of Zachariah and Elizabeth is that they loved God, followed God's commandments as they understood them, and found favor with the Lord.

On the day of incense burning, it was Zachariah's turn as part of his priestly duties to burn incense in the temple. While the throng of gathered worshippers prayed outside, Zachariah entered the temple only to discover — standing to the right of the altar of incense (just like we would expect an angel to do) — the angel Gabriel. Of course, Zachariah is seized with fear. The angel reassures him by saying 'fear not' (an oft repeated phrase in the Bible when angels appear to humans).

Gabriel delivers the message that a son will be born to Zachariah and Elizabeth. His name is to be John (God has favored) and he is to be a key figure in God's plan: in the spirit and power of Elijah, he prepares the way.

The angel also states that there will be great joy and exultation.

Gabriel reveals John's destiny as put forth in Luke 1:17:

- to turn back the hearts of parents to their children
- to turn those who are disobedient and insolent into people who are receptive and open to the knowledge, wisdom, will and love of God
- to prepare people spiritually and morally to receive the message and presence of the Messiah

As we can imagine, Zachariah is incredulous. He asks the angel for proof, especially considering that he and his wife are advanced in age.

What happens next is fascinating.

Gabriel states:

"I am Gabriel, that stand in the presence of God; and I was sent to speak unto thee, and to bring thee these good tidings."
Luke 1:19 ASV

It's almost as if the angel is setting Zachariah aright… 'let me get this straight, you're asking me for proof when you're looking at an angel standing in front of you, not just any angel, an angel who stands in the very presence of God who was sent by God to give you good news, and you wanna not believe? Ok boo, I got something for you…'

Next, Gabriel strikes Zachariah speechless and tells him he'll remain speechless until the baby comes.

WOW. Like shut up.

Angelic pimp slap.

Jesus the Christ

Next Gabriel appears to Mary with this salutation:

"Hail, full of grace, the Lord is with thee: blessed art thou among women."
Luke 1:28 (DRA)

Mary was not frightened by the angel, but she was troubled as to the meaning of the salutation:

"But she was greatly troubled at the saying, and cast in her mind what manner of salutation this might be. [30] And the angel said unto her, Fear not, Mary: for thou hast found favor with God."
Luke 1:29 & 30 (ASV)

I've pondered over the years on the fact that Mary was not in fear of the angel, but was troubled by what the angel said.

My answer came when I was in Barnes & Noble one day and the Spirit of God guided me to the *Lost Books of the Bible* on a table for only $6.95. I snapped it up quickly and began reading. I was drawn to the story of Mary and read it first.

Mary's Birth

Turns out, Mary's birth also has a supernatural story with it. You can read all about it in *The Gospel of the Birth of Mary* (available free online at Sacred Texts).

Note: I find it quite telling that the story of the miraculous birth of Mary is eliminated from the official Bible canon, as it's highly relevant. Yet, there are elements of the birth of Mary story that do not align with the Jesus story as it's been handed down to us, thus it makes sense why interested parties would be motivated to remove these.

Before Mary's birth, her mother Anna and father Joachim were likewise unable to bring forth children.

There's a bit of background information that could prove useful here. Earlier in the story we read that Joachim is a rich and that he and Anna had a sacred ritual of dividing all their income into 3 parts: part 1 went to the temple, part 2 went to poor people and they themselves lived on the remaining third. Clearly, these are devout, reverential people who not only profess their faith, they walk it out.

On a visit to the temple in Jerusalem to bring his offerings, Joachim was reprimanded by the High Priest (some accounts say Issachar while others say it was Reuben) for not having children, clear evidence — in the High Priest's mind — that Joachim had been cursed by God and thus had no business offering anything in the temple.

Insulted and ashamed, Joachim leaves the temple and doesn't go home, but instead goes out into the pastures with the shepherds in one account. In another account, he goes into the wilderness — and after pitching a tent, decides to fast for 40 days and 40 nights — where he has a supernatural experience:

> *"BUT when he had been there for some time, on a certain day when he was alone, the angel of the Lord stood by him with a prodigious light."*
> *The Gospel of the Birth of Mary 2:1*

Of course, Joachim loses it and the angel has to reassure him not to be afraid and that his prayers have been heard by God, his alms have ascended to God and ultimately, that he's not cursed. (Apparently, High Priests don't always know what they're talking about. Correction from God is a good thing.)

The angel gives several examples of barren women who went on to become great mothers, or of holy men born of barren women. Examples the angel cites for proof that Joachim and Anna are not cursed:

- Sarah (barren until 80)
- Rachel (barren and yet bore Joseph who became a Governor in Egypt and saved many from starvation during a famine)
- Samson & Samuel (both of whom were born to barren mothers)

The angel then delivers the message that his wife Anna will have a baby girl, and that her name is to be Mary. She will be filled with the Holy Spirit of God from her mother's womb. Sound familiar? Yes, long before John the Baptist, the angel spoke these exact words with regard to Mary.

The angel then prophesies about Joachim's grand child: Jesus will be his name, and he will be a savior to many people.

Before departing, the angel gives Joachim instructions to go to the Golden Gate of the temple where his wife Anna will meet him.

The next appearance recorded is a visit to Anna, Mary's mother-to-be.

When the angel visits Anna, it announces that it is the angel who presents Anna's prayers and alms before God.

The angel then shares with Anna that the baby will be full of the grace of God from birth and that she is to be with her parents for the first 3 years of life. When she's weaned, she is to be taken to the temple, where:

- she will live until her discretion (onset of menses)
- she will be devoted to God in the temple and not be in conversation with 'common people'
- she will be in fasting and prayer
- she will abstain from every unclean thing

Eventually, as a virgin not ever having known any man, she will bring forth a son ('know' in the Biblical sense refers to sex).

Anna promptly goes to the golden gate of the temple, meets up with her husband. The 2 share their vision with each other, greatly rejoice and go on their way KNOWING a child will be born.

They had no questions and no doubts.

When Mary was weaned and her parents took her to the temple, something miraculous occurred. They set Mary down on the first step approaching the altar and she was miraculously able to ascend all 15 stairs to the top completely unaided as if she were a grown person. Those who witnessed it knew it to be the work of God.

From that day forward, Mary enjoyed conversations with angels daily, and received every day 'visitors' from God who kept her safe from every manner of evil and taught her thoroughly. It was also said that she did not eat human food but received her food from the hand of an angel.

This provides key information that facilitates depth of understanding about why Mary was not at all afraid of any angel. She had been communing with angels daily since she was 3 years old.

When the angel visited her regarding the birth of Jesus, she wondered what the greeting may have meant, as it was peculiarly different from anything she had encountered in her many conversations with angels.

Gabriel Appears to Daniel

Gabriel appears to Daniel twice after having received a confounding vision. Gabriel states the purpose of the visit:

"Daniel, I have now come to give you wisdom and understanding."
Daniel 9:22 (WEB)

Daniel had been in prayer in an incessant quest to understand his visions. The angel taught Daniel with patience until he understood what he'd seen.

The bottom line for this section on Gabriel (and the baby messenger angels) is that we have clues as to types of services for humanity are under this angel's purview. I would call on Gabriel's help for:

- Infertility issues
- Clarity about why one may not be having a baby
- Clarity on what can be done to prevent miscarriages (it's consoling to speak to an angel about these deeply emotional issues. I've been there.)
- Midwifery
- Safe Births emotionally, spiritually and physically
- Baby blessings
- Baby naming
- Dream interpretation
- Vision quests
- Third eye opening
- Divine wisdom and understanding

- Teaching ability

As your spirit leads you, you'll know what to contact this angel for.

To contact angels you don't have a name for (there are many), name the angel's exploits in your rituals and you will make contact. Once contact is made, the angel will give you its name. (More on this in the chapter on Angel Magick Spells.)

Uriel

This archangel is not mentioned in the official Bible canon of 66 books, yet is spoken of extensively in the Book of Enoch and elsewhere in the Pseudepigrapha.

Uriel means *God is my Light* (u-ra-el) and is Regent of the Sun.

In the Testament of Solomon (read it at EsotericArchives.com), we find a fascinating account of the demon Ornias tormenting a young man who was a worker in the building of Solomon's temple. Solomon cared much for this young man, so was intensely interested in what was going on with him. When Solomon discovers that the issue is a supernatural problem, he prays to receive an answer. The archangel Michael appears to give Solomon a ring with a seal consisting of an engraved stone by which he could command any demon and constrain them into his service. The seal is a pentagram.

Solomon promptly lays hold of the demonand interrogates it. The demon states that his supernatural boss is the archangel Uriel. Even though constrained, the demon isn't cooperative (as one would expect). Solomon prays to ask for Uriel's help. Forthwith the angel appears, coming down out of heaven and gets the demon straight right away and issues marching orders.

Uriel is the angel who:

- Guarded the entrance to the Garden of Eden after the expulsion. He's spoken of as both a Cherub (NOT a chubby baby) and a Seraph.

Michael was sent by God on more than one occasion to enter the Garden for supplies. He had to first explain his mission from God to Uriel before being allowed to enter.

- Was present at the first burial. According to the *Books of Adam and Eve,* Uriel along with archangel Michael buried Adam in the Garden after his death and preparation for burial.
- Visited Noah to give warning of the coming flood along with instructions on creating the ark. In Jewish lore, there's another aspect to the story that's quite revealing for magickal purposes. The archangel gives Noah an engraved sapphire that Noah places in the ceiling of the ark. The stone provides continual light in the ark, representing Uriel, or the Light of God.
- Carried the baby John and his mother to Egypt during the massacre, thus saving John's life. The baby John and his mother Elizabeth are led to meet up with Mary, Joseph and Jesus, who were already safely in Egypt.

There are many more Uriel appearances. These are but a few from which we can intuit what types of spells are best suited to this angel. For me, Uriel is excellent to call on for:

- WISDOM. Uriel can be contacted and counted on for the wisdom of God, problem solving (especially hairy, recurring issues that are not easily solved), alternate ways of looking at complex issues so that they are easier to resolved (almost like a universal puzzle master).
- Protection of babies and children.
- Travel protection and safe journeys.
- Creating and manifesting a home and keeping it safe (being the archangel of the earth element). Angels are excellent watchers and can surround a home with an impenetrable shield that only allows love to enter. I warded my brand new home I bought several years ago with this type of spell and I could literally see certain people not being able to enter. I had forgotten to take down the wards when I left and was

reminded later supernaturally to do so, at which point I promptly did! (See the Home Wards Spell.)

- Burial rites.
- Light. Anywhere in your life (or shadow work) where you require the LIGHT OF GOD to enter and clear away the energetic darkness.

Now that we have a working understanding of how to determine who to call and for what purpose, we'll look at one of my accidental angel summonings.

But first, a confession.

My Angel Magick Journey

Being honest with you, I had challenges with angel magick. Not because I couldn't speak to angels. I've been speaking to spirits since I was 3. I was having challenges because of a conflict I was making up in my head.

The essence of the inner conflict: on one hand was me speaking to spirits and angels as naturally as washing my face, and on the other hand were the ever growing collection of grimoires I was reading:

- The Greater Key of Solomon the King
- The Lesser Key of Solomon the King containing the Goetia, Theurgia Goetia, Ars (or Art) Paulina, Ars Almadel, Ars Notoria
- The Testament of Solomon
- The Heptameron (or Magical Elements)
- The Picatrix
- Arbatel

Besides poring over countless grimoires trying to make heads or tails of it and pull forth enough accurate information (with the correct angelic seals) to practice and not have the whole thing blow up in my face, I was listening to all these amazing magicians on podcasts like Glitch Bottle and Rune Soup and on YouTube channels I love.

I struggled. I thought something was wrong. Why couldn't I practice magick like this incredible magicians who were clearly in another stratosphere than me. There was no way I could do what they were doing.

Which is precisely the point: I wasn't supposed to be doing what they were doing. They had found what worked for them, and it was up to me to work what works for me, and not compare. A great teacher taught me that comparison is a form of 'self-violence.'

What Fear Does to a Witch

My magick was simple, with connection to angelic realms and spirits natural and free flowing, even without magick circles, suffumigation, the right incense, the appropriate day and hour, the right altar, barbarous words and the best sigils.

There were a LOT of steps in the magick I was reading and hearing about, which was all good for the ones practicing that kind of magick.

Magick is unique and personal. Every Witch and magician has their own magick.

My magick had nowhere near that amount of steps or accoutrement, which caused me to unconsciously discount what I was doing. I thought my magick wasn't up to snuff because it wasn't as complex and exotic, even though the results were astounding.

It was a classic case of gazing longingly at the greener grass on the other side without looking down to realize that the greenest grass is under my feet.

I was getting hammered by unconscious resistance during the writing of this book. Part of me was saying: if I put my simple magick in a book, people will say ___________.

Who the fuck cares what people will say?

That's not why I write.

I write and speak because I can't NOT. It's my breath, the Divine unction and call of my soul... a space of pure and utter bliss and fulfilment in an alternate reality where I get to be a bad-a Witch, even if I do sometimes confuse myself with being a fearful human.

I do this because this is what I was born to do.

The inner conflict, fear and unconscious resistance are what I had to get over to even write this chapter.

I couldn't understand why so much resistance was coming up…

It was because I was afraid. Afraid to be seen. Afraid to let it all out there. Afraid to bare myself to the world and have people take jabs at me. Being totally honest, afraid of 1 star reviews on Amazon (confession is good for the soul, so I'm putting it all out there).

I'm grateful to Source for bringing me through every time I get lost in the thicket of my own thinking.

No matter what we're experiencing, we have access to Source. Heaven is always available, so that's where I went.

I did a Full Moon Ritual (see the chapter titled "Confession Water Release Ritual") on the beach in Puerto Rico where I'm putting the finishing touches on this book. It worked wonders to dissolve and release unconscious tar that was holding my feet in place.

The next morning, I went deep in a meditation to ask what was happening and why the book wasn't being completed. I felt the strong energy current of this book, and knew the material was Divinely ordained to be shared. This book is filled with what I love. It was clear I was on the right path, yet something was off.

It was my fearful mind. Making shit up.

The Answer

The clear answer from Source: *Write your heart and soul. Share your experience. Be authentic. You are priceless to me daughter. I am with you. Fear not. Give your Self. Then release the beauty to the universe with great gratitude.* The angels chimed in: *we'll take it from there.*

My answer: YES. I can do that God. You have me. All of me.

What You Have Here

Every book I write heals me of issues I didn't know were still getting me to the degree they are. Revelatory AND fun! The adventure continues!

Thank you for being here with me.

What you have in this book is exactly what I do when it comes to angel magick. If it works for you too, great. If it doesn't, I know your soul is on a path of discovery that will be rewarded. I'm with you Witch.

Let's get into it with my story of angel summoning for money.

Angel Magick for Wealth

When I was a novice at spellcrafting, I remember having an unforgettable experience with the angels.

A little background… at the time, I was suffering financially. I had just gone through a bitter divorce and child custody battle. I was emotionally spent. I'd moved out of my beautiful dream home due to foreclosure and had moved into a 2 bedroom apartment. Income was low and at times non-existent.

I had been battling lack consciousness for decades, even when I had money. When my net worth was high, I was still in fear, afraid of losing money. I spent money out of control when I had it. I was a good investor, yet still found a way to sabotage my way out of wealth.

This happened repeatedly, which meant a massive overhaul in the subconscious mind was in order.

One morning, I sat up in my bed completely frustrated and mad at God. I had done what I thought I was supposed to be doing with my life. I had sold my financial planning practice at American Express years ago to write books (my passion and calling) and speak (my passion and soul calling as well). I had done what I was led to do in my heart. At first it went well. Really well. I landed a 5-figure advance with a major publisher for a 2-book deal. My agent and I were elated. My first public workshop I offered in April of 2005 was attended by 80 people who came as a result of radio interviews. At the end of the workshop, I offered the opportunity for the women in the audience who desired to take their work further with me to a retreat named the Divine Life's Purpose Women's Retreat. Though I had prepared as best I could for the entire event that Saturday, I was NOT prepared to be bum-rushed by 20+ women at the end of the Saturday event ready to register for the retreat coming up 2 months later in June.

In addition, I had a side business teaching financial education and helping others invest in real estate that bought in huge chunks of change because it was related to financial services, a forte of mine from being in the financial services industry.

Yes, for a while, I was flying high.

Then came a crash.

When Everything Goes to Hell

Everything went to hell. Fast.

The businesses fell apart. The book royalties couldn't fully support my lifestyle and a divorce left me mentally, emotionally and financially spent, at the brink of being destitute.

I had run out of any and all answers, options and solutions. I was past the limit of what I thought I could tolerate, and there still seemed to be more pain and suffering in store for me, with no visible way out.

I couldn't take it any more.

One morning, with little other than a prayer, I sat up in my bed and, eyes closed, and called out to the Angels of Abundance, the Angels of Prosperity, the Angels of Wealth and the Angels of Money.

These are all different, I knew, so I called out to different sets of angels so I could cover all the bases.

IMMEDIATELY my bed was SURROUNDED with angelic presences, as if they were arranged in the exact order I had called out to them.

WOW. Finally, I'm about to get some answers around here!

I asked:

Angels, is there a money solution that works for everyone?

They responded in unison:

YES

WHAT?!?

Ok, let's back up for a moment to my question. Why did I ask the question in the way I did? Because I'm a teacher on spirituality with a special focus on wealth and magick. For my entire adult life, I've been irresistibly drawn to financial markets, investing, real estate, residual income creation, entrepreneurship and all things wealth creation.

I had to gain this knowledge and understanding for myself, and I HAD TO TEACH IT.

Back to the angels and the answer to my first question.

I was almost dumbfounded that there was an answer to money that works for everyone, since I had coached so many different kinds of people, and because each individual's finances are like a fingerprint, I didn't honestly believe, or let myself even consider the option of a blanket solution that could work for everyone.

My next question:

Well could you give me the answer please?!?! I promise I'll tell everyone I know!!!

The angels responded, again in unison:

LOVE.

What?!? Love?!?! What are you talking about? I have plenty of love and still NO MONEY!!! Would you please say more because I DON'T GET IT!!!

Then the lessons began. They taught me 7 elements of Love that make one wealthy. I have worked with these 7 principles from that day until this one and the results have been crazy good. I went from:

- Lack consciousness
- Couldn't pay rent
- Every dollar was spent before I received it
- Despair
- No savings
- Debt
- Disarray in finances

To

- **Wealth consciousness**
- **Higher and higher income** (it keeps going higher and higher without me doing much more work). I went from a low of $15 for a coaching session when I first began coaching to $25,000 in coaching fees per client in mastermind programs with several clients. The income continues to exponentially increase.
- **Savings**. I call it excess money or money that doesn't have a name on it that hangs around, calling its friends to the abundance party.
- **Debt payoff**. Because income exceeded expenses, I could use the discretionary income to start paying down debt.
- **Investments**. More discretionary income also means more investing in crypto, Angel Investing (ironically) and in business and creative ventures I love.
- **Order**. Order is the first Law of Heaven and the first Law of Creation. Order is the foundation without which nothing substantial can be built. Order comes forth out of chaos. It was my job to order myself,

my mind, my emotions, my actions, my words and my finances in such a way that was aligned with wealth, abundance, riches and prosperity. (I teach these principles in the '40 Money' series of books: *40 Money Mantras, 40 Money Spells* and *40 Money Scriptures.*)

There's so much more to this money journey that I will put it all in a book for you, I promise. For now, I'll share what I named the ***Ultimate Money Answer*** (it seemed fitting, even the angels didn't give it a name). Below is a summary, followed by fuller commentary. These 7 principles serve as a collective **INVITATION** for **ANYONE** who chooses to **MASTER** them:

The Ultimate Money Answer is LOVE:

1. **LOVE YOURSELF** – Love who you are, and who's you are, enough to remove and clear all money blocks and any and all blocks to your abundance, prosperity and wealth. Nothing amazing can be created without **SELF LOVE**. The angels were instructing me to start there. Loving yourself is not selfish, as we may have been conditioned to believe. Loving self is loving God.
2. **LOVE WHAT YOU DO** – Love what you do so much that you'd do it for free.
3. **LOVE HOW YOU DO WHAT YOU DO** – how you do what you love is almost as important as the thing itself.
4. **LOVE WHO YOU DO IT WITH** – Loving the ones you serve makes your job that much easier, even in the challenging places.
5. **LOVE THE RESULTS OF WHAT YOU DO** – Love the results of what you do as they appear, without attachment to HOW they appear.
6. **LOVE HOW YOU FEEL AS YOU DO WHAT YOU DO** – Become hyper aware of all the feelings rushing through you as you do what you do. Do you **LOVE** how you feel? Are you in a **HIGH VIBRATION**?
7. **LOVE WHO YOU ARE BECOMING AS YOU DO WHAT YOU DO** – You are becoming a new being the more you engage in your

loves. You will never be the same. Love this.

Love Yourself

Because the term 'love yourself' is a bit of a cliche, let's look at subtle forms of self-hate and self-loathing that I myself have engaged in. If any of these apply to you as well, great! If they don't, great! You've mastered self-love. Now, let's take the self-love EVEN DEEPER, WIDER, TALLER.

Here's a short list of the ways I engaged in self-loathing thoughts, feelings and behaviors:

- **Noticeable absence of pleasure**. My life was austere for no reason. I was reared on the 'modesty' found in the cult of Jehovah's Witnesses. The cult viewed wealth, riches and luxury with derision, teaching that these were traps designed to ensnare one and draw one away from God. While this is what the cult taught, this is not what the cult practiced. The organizers of the cult of Jehovah's Witnesses harbors billions of dollars. Very interesting. This was one of the cold hard facts that forced me to look at my life and ask PENETRATING QUESTIONS. Did I truly desire, in my heart of hearts, to live a modest life of normalcy, obedience, modesty and austerity? HELL TO THE NAH. That's when I began to give myself permission to experience pleasure (without being excessive, which has a cost on a soul level). I realized my life was void of pleasure. I changed that.
- **Overworking without giving myself breaks, vacations, restoration and appropriate relaxation**. Unworthiness caused me to keep working, produce more, work more and do more to be more. I was on a treadmill.
- **Not giving myself the best possible sleep I can enjoy including: linens, temperature, bedtime rituals, perfect sleep environment, and more**. I used to sleep on bad mattresses and cheap sheets. I used to fall into bed at night after rescuing people during the day, with no bedtime rituals to free my mind of fear and worry over what I

had to do the next day. I used to sleep in a crowded, messy bedroom. No more.

- **Too much social media.** This is a fairly recent issue that had to be tackled and tamed. While I'm not a hermit, I'm not a social media junky either. To stay in peak emotional states and peak creative mental clarity and receptivity to fulfill my divine potential and operate at my personal optimal, I had to learn to keep a tight leash on social media (like a well-trained dog).
- **Too much tech.** I can easily fall into this trap after I've been writing for hours, reading on my Kindle for a couple of hours, and creating a video for my YouTube channel. How many hours I stare at a blue screen during the day can increase without my conscious awareness, even though I'm doing what I love. It takes diligence to turn off the technology, sleep in a bedroom with no tech and no tv, and all around give myself plenty of time away from technology. I even started dictating my writing more, rather than sitting at a computer.
- **Not giving myself the most excellent food.** Food is fuel for the body and is to be the absolute best if the desire and intention is to have a body that performs at the absolute best. I love bio-hacking, so ingesting delicious, healthy and beautiful food each day is not a stretch. It's a must.
- **Not giving myself the most excellent clothing I can.** For me, cheap, fall apart clothes were revealing my low self-worth and unwillingness to put myself first. I learned that excellent, quality clothing doesn't always mean expensive. I'm an avid shopper who LOVES to find the most expensive outfit for a not expensive price. I'm worth it. This goes beyond vanity. What's next to your skin is touching your body all day, feeding information to your subconscious mind. Do you desire your subconscious mind to be fixated on 'cheap' or 'luxury?' You get to choose. Luxury has little to do with money and everything to do with a mindset. I had to change my mind from dollar store to Nordstrom and beyond. The money matched my mindset.
- **Thinking spa treatments, massages and other self-care rituals**

are luxuries rather than must-haves. I used to live in this camp, believing that massages were luxuries I got to plan every so often when I wanted to treat myself (maybe a couple of times a year or on my birthday). Even then, I would almost recoil at the prices on the spa menu, thinking of all the things I could buy with the money instead. There are a couple of ways of looking at this. On one hand, spas in the United States could be viewed as expensive, considering that I've gotten 90-minute massages on the beach in Bali under a palm tree for about $8 (U.S.). Expense is always in the eye of the beholder. What one person perceives as expensive another perceives as a value. Either way, the amount of money on massages is not the issue here. Deep self-love causes you to be able to attract the very highest quality care where ever you go and whatever the cost. You'll have it, no matter what. In China, massages are an essential part of life, with all kinds of people engaging in massages as a wise health ritual, not a high end spa treatment. My body thrives on frequent massages. Holistically, massages are critical to excellent health and bio-hacking.

- **Not flying first class.** I realize what I'm about to say may sound 'bougie' and smacks of what my mom meant when she issued the warning "Don't forget where you came from" I'll proceed anyway. I didn't fly first class until I was in my 50's, even though I'm an avid global traveler. If I'd known the wonders and beauties of first class —rather than scoffing at the people in the front of the plane who got to board first and always looked relaxed in those nice big comfy seats, drinks in hand — I would have flown first class a long time ago. First class is a mindset, and like all things related, has nothing to do with money. For me, it has to do with **SELF-CONCEPT**, the driving force of **EVERYTHING** I do for myself. I'm not saying that everyone who flies first class loves themselves and everyone who doesn't fly first class doesn't love themselves. I'm saying that for me, first class was a real eye opener on how much I'd let myself suffer over the years because deep down inside, I didn't really feel like I was worth it. First class, like everything else on the spiritual path, is a LESSON in an ever unfolding curriculum and has nothing to do with big, comfy seats on planes.

- **Not getting into nature**. Not absolutely making SURE I get into nature EVERY DAY to discharge the harmful effects of electro magnetic frequencies, charge my electric and auric field naturally, and ground myself on the Earth Mother.

I could add a whole lot more to this compilation of how I've subtly allowed and tolerated self-loathing over the years by inflicting needless suffering on myself or not **MAKING THE COMMITMENT TO GIVE MYSELF THE ABSOLUTE BEST.**

To sum it up: self love invites me to **RAISE MY STANDARDS** across the board, leaving no area of my life untouched.

A helpful exercise could be to take an inventory of all the ways you desire to love yourself more deeply and robustly, and then get to it. Throw in added accountability from another Witch or a Coven and you're on your way to making sustainable change in the signal you send out to the universe of non-negotiable love and tender care of **YOU**.

Love What You Do

It's near impossible to become wealthy, be fulfilled and experience joy doing what you hate.

I see people who hate their jobs or careers and wonder why they're not happy and satisfied. There are also people who, while they don't hate what they do, don't love it either. Both are problematic.

The angels clued me in on the direct correlation to doing what you love and wealth, abundance, riches and prosperity.

While doing what you love isn't the ONLY component of an expanded, more joy-filled financial world, it's indispensable.

Everyone who LOVES their work hurls themselves into it and relishes it so much they'd do it for free. Counterintuitively, if you could do it for free, you open a portal to being paid more than you ever imagined.

Love How You Do What You Do

By her own admission, Oprah is a teacher who loves teaching. Being a teacher in a 3rd grade classroom and being the teacher she is today are vastly different.

How you do what you love is as important as the thing you're doing.

A person who loves writing, like me, could find infinite ways to write. I recall a member of one of our healing circles who was also a writer. She worked for a company who was contracted by lawyers and insurance companies. She spent her days writing about car accidents and slip-and-falls. She admitted that every article she wrote was deflating.

On the other hand, I write exactly what I'm inspired to write, so it's feeding me. Prayerfully the writing is serving others as well, yet the joy was in writing it. There's a fulfillment in what I do that goes beyond money. This fulfillment, ironically, creates more money.

Love Who You Do It With

The angels were showing me the value in service. Who am I doing the work with or for?

Who do you do your most amazing work with or for? Children? Seniors? Single moms? Single dads? Who do you most LOVE being with?

This is another key to infinite abundance.

There are teachers who don't like kids. I'm not sure what that's about. I do know that no good can come from it on a cosmic level. It's out of alignment with the universe. We can distinguish in a second teachers who LOVE kids from those who don't.

Whoever you work with and serve, LOVE THEM through and through, a way of being reflective of your own self-love.

This is a good space to throw in a word about judgment. If we judge the people we work with or for, we cannot love them. Love and judgment cannot happen simultaneously. Pick one.

We only judge others if we haven't addressed the aspects of self we're judging. Love self and loving others will not be hard.

Love the Results of What You Do

If you love the results flowing from your work, they energize you to do even more. The world is filled with even more love. The cycle perpetuates!

I get energized by the results of what I do to the max. It's another driver to keep going, even when it's difficult.

Love How You Feel as You Do What You Do

Notice how you feel as you do what you're doing. Do you feel uplifted? Inspired? Happy? Intrigued? Fulfilled? Powerful? Adventurous?

The state you choose to operate from is entirely up to you. While it's possible to feel amazing states of being independent of what you're doing, what if what you were doing was aligned with these states? Who would you be? What would you accomplish?

Love What You Are Doing as You Do What You Do

This is the character building aspect of wealth creation the angels love to point out. There's no permanent transformation into a bigger, better financial world without YOU permanently transforming into a bigger, better, more prosperous YOU.

We want the results, yet we don't always want the work required.

The promise from the angels is clear and sure: we change and our world will HAVE to change.

The problem is that it's not easy to change.

Hence the practice of magick. Our intention to become a Master Alchemist means we've accepted the necessity of change.

No one can stay the same and receive something different.

How to Engage This Wisdom

The title of this chapter is Angel Magick for Wealth, not an angel spell or ritual. The magick is in you being different.

How?

By taking the following inventory and making the requisite changes.

Wealth Creation Inventory

This inventory is designed to bring AWARENESS of how well we're aligned with the angelic wisdom that **LOVE** is the ultimate money answer. Bring to mind what you currently do for income. Now assign a number between 0 and 10 to each of the 7 aspects of love (with 0 being a complete no and 10 being a HELL YEAH).

BE RUTHLESSLY HONEST. DO NOT FOOL YOURSELF. It's easy to do. It's a TRAP of the little mind to make us think we're good when we're NOT. The way OUT is to **TELL THE TRUTH**. Especially to yourself.

The intention of this inventory is **AWARENESS** and NOT judgment. The first step in any transformation is **AWARENESS**. We can change nothing we're unaware of. Once we have awareness, we're 80% of the way free.

Judgment blocks awareness. The power of self-love to the rescue! Loving self means we tell ourselves the truth about self in any given moment, **WITH ZERO JUDGMENT**. Judgment is the idea that we should be doing something other than what we're doing in the moment, or that things should be other than how they are.

Do not judge your answers. **SIMPLY BECOME AWARE:**

1. I love myself as robustly and deeply as I know I can. Score: _____
2. I love what I do so much I jump out of bed in the morning to run to it! Score: _____
3. I love every aspect of how I do what I do! Score: _____
4. I love everything about the people I work with and serve! Score:

_____

5. The results of what I do are so stunning and spectacular that I'm literally blown away! Score: _____
6. When I'm doing what I do, I'm pulsing with enthusiasm and inspiration! Score: _____
7. When I look at the person I'm becoming as a result of my great work in the world, I'm AMAZED! I'm transforming into the Master Alchemist I always knew myself to be! Score: _____

Your Total Score: _____

What To Do With Awareness

Now that you're aware of where you stand on the love/abundance scale, **DECIDE** to make a change. This is the challenging part. Deep down inside, we don't want to change. Something in us is receiving a charge out of what we're doing now, even if it's painful. This is why we keep creating the same undesirable situations over and over again.

CHANGE stops that cycle.

Pick your LOWEST score above to focus on for the next 40 days (40 is the number of transformation) and intend that you will change it. **COMMIT** to the change. Taking on ONE THING AT A TIME eliminates overwhelm and gives the opportunity for a DEEP DIVE into one aspect of wealth creation.

For instance, if your score on #4 is 3 because you find yourself surrounded by people you don't love and adore being with, select this as a starting point. It will be a KEY to unlock the other 6.

MOVEMENT IN ONE AREA CREATES MOVEMENT IN ALL AREAS.

This is why you don't have to take on everything at once, which could prove ineffective and counterproductive because you may start to actively resist massive changes. Plus, I've found that these upheavals in consciousness are not pleasant, nor are they required.

A back door hack is in order. Here's one that's worked like a freakin' charm...

Kaizen

Years ago, I came across the principle of Kaizen and have used it **CONSISTENTLY** to catalyze **MASSIVE CHANGES** with **TINY EFFORTS**.

The wisdom is Japanese in origin and is the idea of making tiny, incremental and continuous changes to perfect a thing. Kaizen is an ongoing process of continuous improvement. If 1,000 tiny, yet beneficial changes are made to any process or operation, a massive difference in results is achieved. While this process is usually applied to businesses, we can adapt the principle to magick.

Before we address how to utilize Kaizen to make massive changes with minimal effort, let's first consider why Kaizen works.

The reason Kaizen works is because the changes being made are so tiny and seemingly inconsequential that your subconscious mind will not put forth any active resistance to said change.

I've used Kaizen to make all kinds of changes (that I did not initially want to make) because the changes were so tiny my mind didn't bother to put up resistance.

An example: I hate unpacking after returning home from a trip. My suitcase would just sit there for weeks, with dirty laundry and all, and me swearing to myself every day that I would unpack that day. Of course, I didn't do it and another day went by of procrastination and not being my absolute BEST.

Kaizen to the rescue!

This may sound silly, but it worked. I made a commitment to remove 1-2 items from my suitcase every day until the entire suitcase was cleared out. It was such a tiny little commitment that any inner resistance that would have reared its head didn't even bother to pay attention. My inner resistance almost laughed at me.

Day 1: I take 2 items of clothing out of the suitcase and put them away.

I feel good, but it feels like I'm not really getting anywhere (that's how Kaizen feels at first, which causes people to give up before the magick kicks in).

Day 2: I take 2 items of clothing out of the suitcase and put them away. I don't see a dent in the work that still has to be done. My mind lied to me: *this is not working*.

Day 3: I take 2 items of clothing out of the suitcase and put them away. Hmmm. No comment from my mind.

Day 4: I take 2 items of clothing out of the suitcase and put them away. The pile of work is going down.

Day 10: I take 2 items of clothing out of the suitcase and put them away. I notice I'm close to be done. I go ahead and knock it out and put the suitcase away.

Bad-a Witch: 1

Procrastination: 0

I use Kaizen to transform myself from procrastination queen to Bad-a Witch who gets shit DONE.

Your Turn

Create a 4-Day ritual around getting DONE one of the above 7, starting with the lowest scored area first. Use the Formula for Spellcrafting for a blueprint if required.

Then let me know on social media or on the blog or in your book review (if you choose to write one) how it all turned out.

The angels have your back.

VI

Rituals & Spells

Here's a sampling of rituals and spells from my practice that have caused seismic shifts in consciousness and soared my soul and my magick.

From my heart to yours,

Enjoy!

Cooking Spells vs. Instant Spells

This is a good place to make a distinction between what I call 'cooking' spells and 'instant' spells.

Cooking spells are those that cook over time, like a stew in a crock pot. Throw in the ingredients and they cook for hours. Every so often, you stir the pot, but for the most part, it's cooking on its own once you assemble the ingredients. For example, I initiate the spell work, and keep it on the altar (or other appropriate location) and it continues to work over time. I call this 'cooking.'

Instant spells are accomplished in one ritual. An instant spell takes no more time than one magickal operation. For instance, a New Moon spell to increase abundance during the current moon cycle. I call this 'instant.'

Though there may be other names for these two types of rituals, a clarification of terms for purposes of our discussion here seems pertinent and helpful.

In the outline of each of the following spells, I will denote if the spell is a 'cooking' spell or an 'instant' spell.

Let's begin.

Christian Witch Integration Spell

This is the exact spell, step by step, I used to integrate two warring factions inside myself: Christian on one side, Witch on the other. There was no compromise between the two and no giving in. Just a serious face-off.

This is a recipe for inner conflict, struggle and uncertainty about one's path, none of which incites peace.

For me, INNER PEACE is PARAMOUNT.

I choose bliss, joy, love, peace and the high vibration states of being that produce the very best results I'm divinely capable of.

Because I was in so much inner turmoil, peace was a distant longing.

SOMETHING HAD TO BE DONE.

This is the spell I cast, born partly out of desperation. I followed my intuition and it all came together. The results were astonishing. The magick, as I practiced it back then, was simple. One would argue that it was too simple to have had such a dramatic result. Yet I cannot argue with results. Upper realms delivered... BIG TIME. I felt more integrated than ever, as if an inner marriage had happened.

I'll share a little background as to where I was on the spiritual journey at the time I undertook this magickal working. I was in school at Inner Visions Institute for Spiritual Development, studying, engaging in healing and applying myself as best I could to the rigorous curriculum and requirements to become ordained as a Minister of Spiritual Consciousness. Altogether the process was 4 years, though it could have easily taken longer.

In this particular year of my studies, we were at the point where we were to write out sermons and ceremonies for major life milestones, such as marriages and baby blessings. I chose to write out a complete wedding for a couple, with one partner being a Christian, and the other a Pagan. It was a beautiful ceremony, written out from start to finish, that I'd love to perform one day for a couple who has this particular spiritual need.

I know that writing that ceremony, from start to finish, including all the steps in the wedding for how I would conduct a ceremony between a Christian and a Pagan, while honoring both, was a vital key working in the background of the spell that's laid out here.

You won't have to write out a full wedding ceremony to do the spell here effectively. I'm letting you in on what was happening for me at the time, and giving you privy to elements that were not directly related, yet were highly influential.

This is a deeply personal spell, so following it precisely is not the aspiration here. You'll have to make the spell personal to yourself. This is a spell that you will intentionally retrofit for your personal use, where ever you may be in your journey of integrating Christ and the Craft.

Though it's deeply personal, I'm led to share it with an intention to inspire anyone who may be having a struggle similar to mine. When we share with each other, we shorten the time any of us spends in uncertainty, suffering or anything other than bliss.

Adapt the spell to your spiritual requirements. Remember, the spell starts the moment you **DECIDE** you're doing the spell. Be mindful.

FYI, this is a 'cooking' spell.

Acquire & Assemble Materials

Acquire and assemble any materials you'll use, including the ones below that fit you, and any others you're led and inspired to add. These are the materials I used:

- Holy Bible - one that's meaningful for you. Soft cover is recommended (due to the nature of the spell work).
- A white altar cloth.
- A second beautiful cloth that's meaningful for you. I used a gorgeous butterfly covered glittery swath of cloth I absolutely love. Remember, you're infusing the spell with love, peace and harmony.
- Your favorite Tarot deck. I used ***Rider Waite Smith.***
- A cord. My cord was blue in color (a blend of the blue of the throat chakra and the deep indigo color of the 3rd eye chakra).
- An index card. Choose an index card in a color that most speaks to you. Mine was white.
- A writing instrument. A purple pen is great.
- Ink of your choice. Dragon's blood is a nice option. (There's a great article on Dragon's Blood Ink here.)
- A chosen principle. My principle was **TRUST**. Choose a principle most closely aligns with the results you desire (i.e. PEACE, CLARITY, FAITH).

Preparation

Here are the ideal prep steps, which I share with the benefit of my current understanding. I conducted this spell many years ago, and did not have access to the wisdom born of experience that would inform how I would conduct this spell now. There are subtle variations in what I would choose to do differently, so I'll share elements of both versions with you: what I actually did then, and what I would do now. The essence of the spell remains the same. The current variations would likely 'super-charge' the spell so that it works more swiftly, or render it more immediately efficacious.

- Select the appropriate day, date and time for the spell according to planetary, angelic, astrological influences or any other timing influences you work with in your magick. If you do not have a frame of reference for any of these, I would go with the New Moon (for planting seeds of a new experience of inner peace and harmony). Write the timing elements out in your grimoire. FYI, I didn't choose the magically appropriate timing for the spell, and it still worked. However, we have access to vaster influences if we utilize magickal timing.

- Formulate and write your intention in your grimoire while in a meditative state. You will read your intention aloud in the magickal working. FYI, I didn't write out an intention, though I was VERY clear on what I desired to experience. I desired to **TRUST** my Inner Knowing, and that it was leading me in the perfect direction at all times. Why was I so drawn to the Witchy side of life? Why was I super intrigued by magick? Why was I sucked straight in by the occult? I had to trust these inner urgings enough to **GO BOLDLY WITH THEM**, no matter what, if I was to experience inner peace and harmony. (I've included a sample intention statement below for inspiration.)
- Write your name — in your chosen ink — on one side of the index card.
- Flip the index card over and write your principle. Decorate the index card if desired. My index card had a butterfly on it to signal that I'm seeking wisdom and support from one of my totems.
- Erect an altar for this working, using the white altar cloth (see the chapter "Temple, Shrine & Altar").

Spell Steps

Here are the steps I followed (adjust for your requirements):

- **Prepare Sacred Space** - this spell will take place in your sacred space. Choose your sacred space according to what most aligns with your outcome. I conducted the spell in the sacred space in my home, before my altar. It can also be performed in nature. Once you've selected sacred space, prepare your space according to the steps outlined earlier in this book (and in the book *How to Be a Christian Witch*).

- **Prepare Yourself** - cleanse yourself. Clear your energy. Come into a meditative state.
- **Intention** - read the intention aloud.
- **Pray** - in the way that works for you. If a prayer doesn't come naturally to you, you can always find a suitable passage in the book of Psalms.
- **Bring Forward Your Bible & Your Tarot Deck** - open your Bible, with one hand, to a 'random' page. Take your Tarot deck, face down, into your other hand. (The idea behind the 'sides' is that on one side of me was the Christian, represented by the Bible. On the other side was the Witch, represented by the Tarot deck. I needed to bring these sides together into one integrated WHOLE.) Place 1 Tarot card in your Bible at the opened page. Open to another 'random' page, insert another Tarot card. Continue placing Tarot cards into your Bible at 'random' pages until the entire 78-card deck is integrated into your Bible. The Bible may be bulging and/or much larger, depending on the type of Bible used. I used a soft cover, which made expansion easier. The Bible will grow quite a bit with all 78 Tarot cards placed lovingly on different pages. *Helpful note: I didn't think through the process. I didn't intentionally select certain scripture pages in which to place a Tarot card. I was in a meditative state and went completely with the FLOW.*
- **Place Your Principle** - place the index card on the outside front of the Bible.
- **Cord Your Integrated Bible** - bring forward the cord you selected. Lovingly and gently wrap the Bible around it's mid-section with the cord as you pray your integration prayer, which is essentially a collection of words of power. When you've wrapped the Bible completely with the integration cord, tie it off in a meaningful way, perhaps with a bow.
- **Wrap Your Integrated Bible** - bring forward the beautiful cloth you selected. Lovingly and gently wrap the entire integrated, corded Bible in the beautiful cloth.
- **Place Your Integrated Bible** - place your spelled Bible under the altar, out of sight. Mine was on the floor under my altar. Leave it there for

40 days or longer, or until you feel a noticeable shift in response to what you spelled for.

- **Release**. After you've placed your integrated, corded, wrapped Bible under the altar, RELEASE. Let go of what you think should happen, and forget completely about the integrated Bible under your altar. When the spell is done 'cooking,' it will call you.

Sample Intention Statement

I AM ONE WITH THE ONE. My soul-full intention is to integrate all aspects of myself into a harmonious whole, where love, joy, peace and harmony abide. I desire to be completely at peace as a magick practicing Christian Witch and to be immensely fulfilled while doing so and to serve others from my **HIGHEST SELF. I KNOW WHO I AM. AMEN.**

Ritual of Light and Shadow

This chapter could easily be called ***This is Where You Take a Look at the Parts of You That Have Been Hiding, Wreaking Havoc and Being a General Monster***.'

Yep, Witchy Wonder, we've arrived at the juncture on this journey where we get to take a penetrating look at the parts of self we've been doing our best to avoid since childhood. The parts of self we've been blaming on other people. The parts of self that are so unacceptable, monstrous and horrifying that we cannot accept the fact that these are all part of our own psyche. These parts of self are so powerful that they can punk us in a heartbeat with one terrifying mental image (in waking or dream states).

These are the parts of self that have been wreaking havoc on you and your world, from deep in the cracks, crevices and caverns of the unconscious.

Every villain we perceive as scary is a representation of our shadow self seeking to be recognized, accepted and integrated. Think Count Dracula, or Silar from Heroes, or Lord Voldemort. Now consider how powerful you would be if you could clearly see ALL your inner villains, accept them, make peace with them, and get them on your side, or at least get to the point where they ceased opposing you and bringing havoc your way.

Wouldn't it make your magick that much better if you thoroughly plumbed the depths of your being to become aware of and master BOTH the light and shadow selves so that individuation occurs?

Ritual of Light & Shadow

To facilitate this process, there's an exercise we perform in the very first lesson of the 40 Foundations Lessons in the Covenant of Christian Witches Mystery School (CCW for short).

Here, we'll call it the Ritual of Light & Shadow. It's a conglomeration of a few processes I've read about and engaged in over the years, with a few extra touches added in.

It's a simple exercise, in which you'll create 2 lists and expound on each item on both lists. The first list you'll create will contain your 'light' qualities: what you love about yourself, your gifts, your talents, your divine attributes and any and all 'good' qualities you can call to mind about you. The second will be a list of your 'dark' aspects: what you don't love about yourself, what you see in yourself as dangerous or foreign, what you project on others, what you try to keep hidden, and what you generally think is 'bad' about you.

One Possible Objection

Before we go into the method, let's examine a possible objection. I've heard this objection from coaching clients, so let's address it here, just in case the same questions arise for you.

We understand the Law of Attraction and know that what we focus on expands. So why would we focus on what's ***not*** good in self? Isn't that antithetical to the idea of developing into one's best self?

Yes, it's true that what we focus on expands. However, we are not focusing on the shadow in this ritual. ***We are becoming aware of it.*** These are two wholly different ideas.

Why become aware of the shadow aspects of self? Because these aspects of self are **CREATIVE**. They're creating our life experience, from deep inside an inky well of the unconscious. We can either become aware of these energies and use them to our advantage by making them powerful allies, or we can allow them to unconsciously create pain, suffering and unfulfilled potential.

I choose the former.

I do not choose to focus on the aspect of me that would slit someone's throat in an alley and eat a chicken wing over the body while they bleed out. There's a cold-ass bitch inside of me. I know this bitch. I love her. I use her when needed. If I had never plumbed the depths of my being to become aware of her, she would still be running parts of my life, especially in intimate relationships, slashing people to bits.

At the same time, I don't sit around focusing energy and attention on her. I don't focus on any shadow aspect. I choose to become **AWARE OF EVERYTHING IN MY CONSCIOUSNESS THAT HAS CREATIVE POWER**. Doing shadow works cuts down on nasty surprises that seem to come 'out of left field.' Nothing EVER comes out of left field. The LAW states that every effect has a cause and every cause has effects. Everything came from somewhere. If the effects are in my life experience, the cause is somewhere in my own consciousness.

Is the Shadow Bad?

There's another consideration before we go into preparation for the ritual and the ritual itself.

Shadow does not mean bad, and light does not mean good. I see shadow and light as yin and yang, each with its own beautiful properties. Nor am I suggesting that you kill your shadow side. The dark aspects of self are vital for a whole being, and it's my personal belief that there's so much power in the dark that I wonder if it may be one of our most powerful allies. We simply seek to integrate shadow and light so that we have access to **BOTH** and become a **WHOLE BEING**.

This work can be easy for us because Witches have never been afraid of the dark. We relish it. Revel in it. Seek it. We know the dark holds secrets AND power.

Most people only have access to parts of self... ***the parts of self they like or deem acceptable***... or their angel self. The other parts of self — the parts they do not like or do not deem acceptable (the demon self) — are projected onto other people. This ends today. Today we choose to operate as **FULLY INTEGRATED, WHOLE BEINGS** of **INFINITE POWER.**

To that end, self-gnosis is a non-negotiable aspect of becoming an alchemical master. You won't be able to effectively change conditions, and keep them changed, if you can't change yourself.

Purpose of the Ritual

Before beginning, we must be clear about our purpose. From the purpose, we can craft a clear intention.

This ritual is for:

- **Self-awareness:** becoming aware of all the shadow energies that reside in consciousness. Awareness is 80% of transformation. We cannot change what we refuse to see.
- **Sovereign Power:** the more we know self, the more empowered we become. As Witches, power is our nature. We get to completely own our powerful nature. Great magick cannot be wrought without a visceral connection to power.
- **Peace:** with greater self-awareness comes peace.
- **Transformation:** perhaps we transform self, and perhaps we don't. It isn't always necessary to change self, nor is it necessary for every shadow aspect to leave. The purpose is to become **AWARE** of the shadow self, and **INTEGRATE** this energy for max **POWER.** Transformation will naturally occur the more we choose peace. If there's something about my darker aspects I'd like to transform, I have more information at my fingertips to make the change (more on this later).

Preparation for the Ritual

This ritual can be performed as often as desired and/or required. Once will likely not do the job. Make exploring yourself habitual. You can conduct this ritual each Full Moon for a year, in addition to your Full Moon Tarot Reading Ritual or other rituals you conduct. Allow 2-3 hours for this ritual, not including your ritual bath.

As always, when engaging in rituals or spiritual processes, prepare:

- **Yourself:** spiritually, mentally, emotionally, physically.
- **Your Environment:** set sacred space as you normally would. Select the best location for the ritual, where you will not be disturbed. Nature is best, or in your sacred space in your Temple.
- **Your Spirit Team:** invite in your spirit team of angels, spirit guides, enlightened ancestors, ascended masters, animal totems and/or whoever you work with in upper realms.
- **Your Materials:** to access the deepest parts of you.
- **Your Tools:** magickal implements to facilitate the ritual at hand.

This is somewhat of a 'black/white' ritual. Materials and tools you'll require:

- **2 New Grimoires (or magickal journals):** one will serve as the Book of Light and the other will serve as the Book of Shadow. When selecting grimoires, be sure color, size and style are sympathetic to the work you're doing.
- **5 Candles:** for the 4 elements, representing the 4 archangels in the 4 directions, plus a white candle for Higher Self. The elemental candles will be red for fire, green for earth, blue for water and yellow for air. These colors are not set in stone. Use corresponding colors that work best for you. Also present will be a white candle, for the center. You may 'dress' the candles if desired, though it's not required. (Dressing the candles is addressed in the chapter on "Candle Magick".)

- **Altar:** you'll construct an altar for this purpose.
- **Water:** a clear vessel of fresh, pure water. I use a glass or a vase. Fill the water all the way to the top, such that a bubble appears at the top of the vessel. This water will trap unkind energies.
- **Fire:** a fire pit is useful if you have access to one. I love fireside rituals. Otherwise, the candles will serve as representatives of the element of fire.
- **Air:** incense in Nag Champa (general spiritual work) or Indian Temple Incense (I LOVE this incense, it takes me right back to the temples of India) or any incense conducive to the working.
- **Flowers:** red roses are perfect for this kind of work, because they speak of love (this is a self-love ritual of sorts). Also good are any white flowers (for the light self) and deeper hued flowers (for the shadow self).
- **3 Large Crystals:** selenite and clear quartz are perfect for this kind of work, and for any work where I desire to see clearly and to pierce the veil. I also love purple amethyst for the crown chakra and contact with higher order beings. Pink quartz is also wonderful for this since it reflects the pure unconditional love of the heart. Make sure one of the 3 crystals is black — such as black obsidian or onyx — for the shadow self.
- **Tarot Cards:** The High Priestess (Key #2), The Sun (Key #19) or The Star (Key #17), and The Devil (Key #15). The High Priestess grants you access into realms of the unconscious. The Sun or The Star (whichever you choose to use based on intuition) represents the light. The Devil represents the shadow aspects of self. Bring to the ritual any other Tarot cards you're inspired to include.
- **Essential Oils and/or Herbs:** select your herbs and essential oils based on the nature of the ritual. Recommended for this ritual: Davana (really flowery and beautiful), Rose (who doesn't love rose for all things love), Melissa, Geranium and Ylang Ylang essential oils. These are selected due to their flowery and calming nature. Consciousness is ever unfolding, like a flower. The flowering of consciousness is represented

by the flowery aromas. Herbs can be used here as well, especially herbs used in spirituality and for opening the third eye such as Basil, Star Anise, Gotu Kola, Sage and/or Hibiscus. Use any herbs and essential oils you're intuitively led to integrate into this working.

- **Consecrated Anointing Oil:** the recipe for the oil you will anoint yourself with is in the chapter "Materia Magicka."
- **Pennies:** I LOVE LOVE LOVE penny magick and creating my magick circles with pennies on the floor of my sacred space. Some of the most potent magick I've done has been with pennies. I find pennies often, and when I do, I always feel like they're messages from angels. Whenever I see pennies, I pick them up. I keep receptacles of pennies (and coins of all kinds, including coins from countries I visit) in my magick space. In this ritual, a circle will be cast with pennies.
- **Beautiful purple pen:** for writing in a high vibration color. Crafting a beautiful pen yourself for your workings is a great idea if you're a DIY kind of Witch. Always search for ways to infuse sympathetic colors and elements into your spellcrafting, along with your creative energy at every step in a ritual where these can be appropriately added.
- **A Wand or Dagger:** choose what works best for you.
- **White Clothing:** if desired, to lovingly bring all aspects of self to the light. We're revealing what's hidden in the unconscious so that we become aware, assume innate sovereign power and become master of self. If white doesn't work for you, feel free to use any color that represents the work at hand. Skyclad (nude) is also a beautiful option for this ritual, as we're bringing everything hidden to the light.
- **Your Bible:** as this is a book of Christian Witchcraft, I'm making a wild guess here that you may have a Bible, or several Bibles. If not, I've quoted the Bible passages below for this ritual.

Be sure all items are cleansed, cleared, consecrated and blessed for the ritual.

Steps for the Ritual

Here are the steps for the Ritual of Light and Shadow. As always, trust your intuition and make any necessary adjustments, always implicitly following your Inner Knowing.

Ritual Bath

Take a ritual bath with the essential oils and/or herbs of your choice. Purity is essential. Ceremonial purity is required in some workings and I usually apply it to every ritual. I don't think there's such a thing as being too pure.

After exiting the bath, dry off and anoint your head, hands, feet and heart with consecrated anointing oil.

Don your magickal undergarments (if desired) and white robes or go nude.

Write out Your Intention Statement

You will write out your intention so that it can be stated in the ritual. Here's a sample intention statement for this working:

"It is my intention to experience **PEACE** and **POWER** as I lovingly explore my consciousness to uncover any shadow aspects of self that I may currently be unaware of, and that have been causing untoward effects/events in my life. I am ruthlessly committed to a life of **POWER** and **SELF-MASTERY. I AM THAT I AM.** I now engage this ritual knowing the results are perfectly returned to me, in perfect timing, by the unfailing **LOVE** and **LAW** of God. Amen."

Construct the Altar

Set up your altar, which will be in front of you to the north, outside of the magick circle. Arrange it beautifully. Take your time. Add to your altar:

- The clear vessel you've chosen filled with fresh, pure water in the manner described.
- Incense of your choice. Set it burning, so that the smell may waft through the air, preparing the space for angelic communication and deep spiritual work.
- Fresh flowers in a beautiful vase of water.
- Crystals of your choosing.
- Tarot Cards you've chosen.
- Any other items you feel led to add.

Create the Circle

You'll now create a circle of pennies on the floor or the ground (depending upon where you choose to perform this ritual). The purpose is to clearly outline sacred space, the parameters in which you'll perform your ritual. Create the circle to be 9 feet in diameter.

Before creating the penny circle, place the following items in the center so you have access to them once the circle is cast:

- Your 2 grimoires: one to be a Book of Light and one to be a Book of Shadow. Place the Book of Light on your right, with The Sun or The Star Tarot card atop it to fill it with light. Place the Book of Shadow on the left with The Devil card atop it to reveal the Shadow. Place the High Priestess in the center of the two books. She will grant you access to the deep well of the unconscious.
- The 5 candles: place each colored candle in the appropriate direction (east, south, west and north) and place the white candle in the center where you'll be sitting.

- Wand or dagger.
- Your Bible.
- Any other items you're led to have in the circle with you.
- Double check that you have everything you require with you inside the circle!

After you have placed all items at your disposal, place the pennies in a circle around you and your magick items. Take your time. I pray as I place my pennies.

Spirit Team Invocation

Stand in the center of your penny circle. Raise your attention, arms and hands heavenward. Call in the spirit team with the following invocations (a Spirit Team Invocation is also in the chapter "Your Spirit Team"). Speak the invocations with **VIGOR** and **POWER**! Speak the invocations over and over until you sense the presence of these Holy Helpers and Guardians. Your entire being is viscerally engaged in calling in the Spirit Team (this is NOT a head exercise).

- **Your Head Spirit/Holy Guardian Angel/Higher Self (looking UP):** "Higher Self I AM, I ask for your loving presence as I dive deep within the depths of my deepest, darkest interior so that I may know myself. I desire to understand what makes me tick, and what ticks me off. I desire to know and understand all aspects of my being and integrate these into a tapestry that is the whole and perfect, a mirror and holy reflection of my divine Self. THANK YOU. AMEN." As you acknowledge the presence of Higher Self, light the white candle.
- **Enlightened Ancestors (looking at your heart):** "To the enlightened ancestors who attend me, including (**NAME** your matrilineal and patrilineal ancestral line as far back as you know it), I ask for your power and presence to be with me now. I humbly ask for your wisdom and guidance to attend me in all my affairs and in this undertaking

so that I may fulfill the highest calling upon my life. **I COMMIT TO KNOW THYSELF AND MASTER THYSELF. THANK YOU.**"

- **4 Archangels Starting With Raphael (facing East)**: "To the divine keeper of the East and Holy Guardian of the element of AIR, the healing power of our God known as Raphael, the one who taught Tobias how to defeat the evil demon Asmodeus whom took to flight before you, I invoke thy presence now in my working, so that I may perceive aright and have a clear mind for the work before me and so that I may conquer and vanquish all that is opposed to the light. **THANK YOU!**" Light the yellow candle.
- **Michael**: "To the divine keeper of the South and Holy Guardian of the element of FIRE, the first of your kind created by our Mother/Father God, Ruler of the 4th Heaven, and instructor to Adam and Eve upon their exit from the Garden, holy Teacher to humankind, I beseech your presence now, to awaken in me the fire to passionately persist in all that is mine to do upon this earth plane, to discover the fire within my soul, and to bring the great fire and light of Ra to the bedarkened aspects of my consciousness. **THANK YOU!**" Light the red candle.
- **Gabriel**: "To the divine keeper of the West and Holy Guardian of the element of WATER, the holy one who visited upon our Blessed Mother Mary to announce the birth of the Christ, you whom visited upon Zechariah in the temple with the announcement "I'm Gabriel. I stand in God's presence." We now invite your holy and precious presence, knowing you bring forth the healing waters of the soul, purifying emotions, causing all divine goodness to flow through all like a river. **THANK YOU!**" Light the blue candle.
- **Uriel (facing North)**: "To the archangels of the divine presence of our Mother/Father God: to Uriel, keeper of the North and Holy Guardian of the element of EARTH, teacher to Esdras, I beseech your presence here now for this ritual of understanding the light in my soul and approaching the shadow within me so that I may be made new. **THANK YOU!**" Light the yellow candle.
- **Animal Totems:** "To the power animals who guide and protect me in

this incarnation, I call upon you for your strength, guidance, wisdom and power NOW, for this undertaking of self-gnosis. **THANK YOU!**"

- **Christ:** "Ascended Master and Way Shower Christ our Lord, I beseech your presence here, knowing you are the Keeper of the Age of Pisces, the Lord of Hosts and King of Kings. I ask that you attend me as I do as you did when after 40 days and 40 nights of fasting, you conquered your darkest self. I seek to meet and overcome the 3 great temptations of my darker self, so that I may rise above pride/hubris and lust for fame, lack/limitation and all symptoms of not enough in my consciousness, and the doubt that would have me tempt God. **THANK YOU!**"
- Call in any other members of your Spirit Team you desire.

Cast the Circle

After the spirit team is called in, face the east (land of the rising sun and spiritual enlightenment) holding your wand or dagger in both hands pointing away from you.

Cast the circle by drawing the circle (9 feet in diameter) around yourself moving clockwise. As you cast the circle, see a wall of light around you from the floor to the heavens. Continue all the way around to complete the circle. When complete, you are surrounded with a wall of celestial light. Know you are protected, guarded and guided.

Meditate

Be seated in the center of the circle for several moments in a meditative state. Meditate for 20 minutes or longer. When you feel ready, proceed to the next step. You're conducting this ritual from an altered state of consciousness. Don't rush.

Write

You'll now start with your Book of Light. Write all qualities about yourself that you love. Write your strengths, gifts, talents, skills, and your greatest accomplishments. POUR IT ON. GO FOR IT. It's not bragging. It's acknowledgement.

Take as long as required to fully write out all that you love about yourself and why. This is the love letter to yourself. Smile. Breathe. Be happy. Be thorough.

Next, bring forth your Book of Shadow and write out all you secretly hate or do not like about yourself, and dare not entertain, even in your deepest, darkest thoughts. Write out the things that make you angry and why. Write out all the aspects of self you wish you could change, as these represent hidden shards of self hatred. Write out all the mistakes you've made, and how you've messed up situations in your life. Write out all that grates on your nerves about you and your life as it currently is. Write out what you can't stand about other people, recognizing these as projections of undesirable or unknown aspects of self.

When writing in both grimoires, freely write as the stream of consciousness flows through your mind, with no editing. You may be surprised at what comes out on paper. Whatever it is, bless it, forgive it and keep going. No censorship. This is not a ritual based on logic.

Cool

After you've written all these out:

- Pause - be still.
- Breathe - take 10 long, slow, deep breaths.
- Still your mind. Your head may be swirling a bit from conjuring up all the things you don't like about yourself.
- Give thanks. Say a silent prayer of thanks for the insights.
- Allow anything else to come to you that you may have missed. Add

these as they come up. When complete, take these 'cooling' steps again.

Be patient with yourself. Love yourself through the ritual knowing that the process may not be sweet, but the results will be.

Completion

When you feel complete, take these steps:

- Pray a prayer of **THANKSGIVING**.
- Stand and stretch to allow yourself to return to waking consciousness. Move slowly. Be gentle with you.
- When you're ready, pick up your wand or dagger and open the circle pointing east and moving around the circle counterclockwise to release the white wall of light.
- Face the east and thank the archangel Raphael for his healing presence and bid him farewell. Snuff the yellow candle. Move on to the archangel Michael in the south, then to Gabriel in the west and finally to Uriel in the north, thanking each angel and bidding them farewell while snuffing each angel's candle.
- Remove the pennies in the opposite order in which you laid them down and place them back in the penny receptacle.
- Remove all items from the area you were working in and place on your altar.
- Clean and clear your Temple.
- Give **THANKS**.

What to do With the Information

You may have received a hefty does of self-reality. You may received visions, insights and/or revelations of exactly how your shadow has been working against you like a gang of inner villains.

Remember, we only see what Higher Self deems we can handle. We may want more. Rather than wanting more, let's work with what we have, yes?

What are we to do with all this information?

Nothing yet. We cannot assume that there's always something to DO after we discover deep, dark hidden tendencies and issues. Sometimes we need to be still.

TRUST.

We will receive next steps from Spirit. Expect answers and supernatural support. Healing modalities will flow to you that you will recognize as appropriate for you in the moment. It could be plant medicine, or acupuncture, or books or other healing modalities that will present themselves to you to address what was uncovered in consciousness and correct it all.

As you may intuit, this is an ongoing exercise. Once is not sufficient to address all the thugs and villains we carry around. Allow your intuition to guide you on how often to engage this ritual.

I pray you love this unfolding experience of self-gnosis as much as I do and experience **FREEDOM**.

Plant Medicine Ritual

This is how I turned a magic mushrooms experience into a magickal ritual.

First, I do NOT condone or recommend that you ingest illegal substances. Follow the laws of the land where you live. I do NOT recommend plant medicine. I don't know you, so recommending anything to you would be irresponsible. If you have mental health issues, ALWAYS seek help from a professional. If you are taking plant medicines, I recommend doing so under the care and auspices of an experienced shaman/healer/guide. BE CAREFUL.

Here's my experience.

Magic Mushrooms Virgin Experience

This was to be the first time I'd ever ingested mushrooms for the purposes of expanding consciousness, so I decided to do it in ceremonial fashion, just as a protection since I was alone. I figured that even if I didn't have people around to help me, the Spirit Team would be on top of things. I wasn't about to wander around in other dimensions without spiritual backup.

Acquire & Assemble Materials

These are the materials I used:

- Magic Mushrooms (not sure how many grams, but let's call it 3 even though Terence McKenna says 5 is the 'heroic dose')
- 4 Candles - to represent the 4 elements, directions and archangels: yellow for air in the east, red for fire in the south, blue for water in the west and green for earth in the north.
- Candle snuffer
- Crystals - one for each direction/element.

Preparation

In advance of the ritual:

- Determine the best day/date/time according to the cosmic weather best suited to your intention and desire.
- Intention: write out an intention. What's the ritual for? What's the goal/intention?
- Cleanse and clear sacred space.

Ritual Steps

My ritual steps were as follows:

- **Cleanse** - I thoroughly cleansed myself and wrapped in a white cloth until I was in the ritual, which I conducted sky clad.
- **Deep breathing** - I didn't know what to expect, and I desired to be as calm and centered as possible.
- **Pray** - As I entered my sacred space, I prayed.
- **Place the candles** - as I prayed, I placed the candles in the appropriate direction marking off where the circle would be drawn. After all

candles were placed, they were lit with an invocation prayer to the archangels for their presence. Invoke the appropriate archangel for the candle and direction.

- **Place the crystals** - I placed the corresponding crystal beside each candle.
- **Covering** - I placed a light blanket inside the space where the ritual circle would be drawn. I'm an Ayahuasca girl, and sometimes chills come with that plant medicine. I had a light covering just in case.
- **Materials** - any and all materials are to be placed inside the circle area (i.e. candle snuffer, wand, etc.)
- **Cast the circle** - with an index finger or wand. As I did, I saw a blazing, white glorious circle around me (the ritual was conducted at night).
- **Plant Medicine** - I laid down in the circle on the floor and chewed the magic shrooms (not delicious, but nowhere near as distasteful as Ayahuasca).
- **Relax** - and let the magick begin!

After the Ritual

When I came fully back to conscious awareness many hours later:

- Pray a prayer of thanksgiving.
- Snuff each candle while thanking the appropriate archangel and bidding it farewell with great gratitude.
- Open the circle - in the opposite direction of how it was cast.
- Remove all ritual items, cleanse and put away.
- Write out all insights, experiences, revelations and more in a grimoire. THIS IS CRITICAL.

I've only conducted this ritual once. It was so profound I still remember that night with awe and thanksgiving. I have a beautiful relationship and connection now with magic mushrooms. I'm thankful.

Confession Water Full Moon Ritual

This ritual came to me by inspiration while in Puerto Rico finishing up this book. The view out of the window of the 9th floor, beach-front condo I rented is spectacular. Hearing the ocean sing to me all day is exactly what I needed to complete this project.

Yemaya can be counted on, which is why she's pivotal to this ritual as be our formidable spiritual ally. There is no denying the power of our ocean mother. She could swallow us whole if she wanted to, yet she's let us hang around for millennia even though we may be the worst behaving species on planet earth. We've launched multiple attacks on the ocean and Yemaya's babies (all the ocean creatures) with our plastics and chemicals, yet she keeps teaching us like a wise and loving mother. Even still, she will resort to a pimp slap or two if need be.

This is a SIMPLE and POTENT ritual designed to **RELEASE** and **RID ONESELF** of **ALL** energies that in any way block, mitigate, limit, hinder, deny, repress, slow down or minimize the **CREATION** and **MANIFESTATION** of our **DIVINE GOOD, ACCOMPLISHMENT** of **DIVINE POTENTIAL**, and **COMPLETE** and **UTTER BLISSFUL FULFILLMENT**.

Let's begin.

Acquire & Assemble Materials

Materials required:

- A white or clear glass bowl or vessel with a capacity of about 8 ounces
- A white towel or mat to sit on in the center of your circle. White is easy to see on a dark beach.
- You: **READY TO RELEASE**

Preparation

Go to the beach on the Full Moon when it's dark and the moon is high in the sky, shining brightly. If there's cloud cover and the moon isn't visible, know that the work is still being done energetically.

Ritual Steps

- Pray: your own prayer or pray the 23rd Psalm or select a prayer of confession from the book *Magickal Prayers for the Christian Witch.*
- Select a space on the beach where you will conduct your ritual, out of sight of muggles (non-mages). Place your white towel and blanket where you will sit. Position yourself to face the ocean. (Marking your space with a white towel will help make it easier to see where you'll be sitting when you return from the ocean's edge with your water, especially if it's really dark.)
- Take your vessel to the edge of the ocean and collect 8 ounces or so of ocean water (it does not have to be exact) asking and thanking Yemaya for her help. As you approach the ocean, do so in reverence for our great ocean mother. When you've collected the water, carefully return to your designated place. Place the water in front of where you'll be sitting.
- Cast a circle with your finger, wand, athame or wooden stick IN THE SAND 9 feet in diameter around your sacred space. This is a barrier

between you and the outside world. You are entering ritual space and altered states of consciousness. After your circle is physically drawn in the sand, sit on your towel or mat.

- Close your eyes and turn your awareness and attention within. Raise a wall of light from your drawn circle in the sand to the heavens. You are fully encircled in light and love.
- Call the 4 directional/elemental archangels (the chapter "Your Spirit Team") one at a time starting with Raphael in the east. Move on to calling the next archangel only after you sense the presence of the archangel you just called.
- With your circle of light and love around you and the 4 archangels forming directional pillars for your ritual, lift your vessel of water and hold it close to your face, just under your mouth. Imagine that the bowl of water is catching all the confessions that pour out of your mouth.
- Begin confessing EVERYTHING that comes up for you, including EVERYTHING that's ever held you back, all issues that are keeping you from your attaining your greatest good in this life, all fears, worry, doubt, anxiety, confusion, distraction, procrastination, hurt, anger, rage, insecurity, spitefulness, revenge, disorder, littleness, shrinking, hiding, visibility issues, unwillingness to be vulnerable, comparison, pride, unworthiness, low self-esteem, blame, shame, guilt, judgment of self and others. POUR IT ALL OUT by SPEAKING IT INTO THE WATER. Don't think.
- When you feel complete, place the bowl on the sand in front of you and stand. Go to the edge of the circle that's closest to the ocean and create a doorway in your circle by moving the sand and seeing the wall of light open up enough for you to pass through.
- Go back to where you were sitting and CAREFULLY pick up the bowl, being SURE not to spill a drop of the confession water in your sacred circle. Walk out of your circle to the edge of the ocean.
- Ask the ocean mother to receive and transmute the energy of all you've released into the confession water. Ask for her mighty powers to turn

this confession water into beauty, thus freeing you of all burden.

- When you sense she's communicated with you, hurl the water into the ocean with **GUSTO** and **THANKS** that you are **FREE**! Give THANKS to Yemaya for her healing powers!
- Return to your circle and enter it. Close the circle by drawing the line in the sand and seeing the great wall of light close again, enveloping you inside.
- Return to your mat and offer a prayer of thanksgiving for your release! You can pray your own prayer, use Psalm 150 or select a thanksgiving prayer from the book *Magickal Prayers for the Christian Witch.*
- Thank the archangels for their healing and mighty power during your ritual and bid them FAREWELL.
- Take down the wall of light. Go to the edge of the circle and open it in the opposite direction of its construction by using your foot to smooth the sand so that the magick circle is no longer visible (VERY important to completely clear the circle).
- Walk away from the beach feeling lighter and almost high.

Thanking the Archangels

When the ritual is over, GIVE THANKS to the archangels as you BID THEM FAREWELL and GODSPEED on their return to the throne and presence of our Father.

Note: You can watch the video on my YouTube channel in which I conducted these steps on the beach in Puerto Rico (www.ValerieLoveTV.com).

Gospel Divination Ritual

This is a ritual I undertook many years ago that never fails to yield answers for the pressing questions in my life in the moment. It's a simple yet potent ritual that gives **RESULTS** in the form of **ANSWERS** and what to do next. This is a form of Bible Divination.

Disclaimer: as a reminder of what was stated earlier in this tome regarding the Bible: not one word in the Bible is literal. Those who take the Bible literally miss the entire point of the Bible as a book of metaphor, allegory, magick, mysticism and esoteric wisdom for life NOW, not thousands of years ago. Not one person in the Bible is a real person, as far as I can tell from the extensive research I love to engage in. I do not read the Bible literally, as this ritual will illumine.

Note: This ritual was originally published several years ago in my book ***Confessions of a Christian Witch: Expanded 2020 Version.*** There are only slight variations in the spell in that book and the ritual here. If you don't have that book, use this ritual. If you do have the book, compare both versions to employ the elements that best suit your requirements.

When to Conduct This Ritual

I've found this ritual to be most helpful when:

- You have major **LIFE ISSUES** before you that require your immediate attention and resolution, i.e. relationship issues, health issues, major issues with children, family care, housing/homes or any gnarly, pressing and/or urgent issue you have not been able to resolve otherwise that must be solved ASAP.
- You have major **QUESTIONS** concerning your destiny, life direction or other questions you have not been able to answer definitely.
- You have **OPPORTUNITIES** before you that appear to be compelling, yet you desire to be SURE you are moving in the right direction, perhaps because the stakes are high. There are no guarantees in life, and many opportunities carry inherent risk, yet we desire to make the highest and best decisions at any given juncture. We also know that if we take advantage of one opportunity, there will be less time, energy and attention for other endeavors, so there's also an inherent 'opportunity risk.' This can all be sorted with this ritual with a greater degree of overall clarity.

Acquire & Assemble Materials

- Your altar in your Temple.
- White altar cloth.
- The 4 Gospels of Matthew, Mark, Luke and John in any translation or version of the Bible that speaks most deeply to you. I use the Amplified Bible. My 2nd fave is the Good News Bible. (There are 89 chapters in all 4 Gospels in the Bible canon of 66 books.)
- 20 Minutes on the 'Opening Day'
- 20 Minutes per day for the next 44 Consecutive Days
- A brand new Gospel Grimoire.
- A beautiful purple pen.

- A white pillar candle on your altar.
- A clear glass of clean, fresh water replaced each day over the 45 days of the ritual.
- If you'll sit during the ritual reading of the Gospel chapters each day, have a meditation pillow or chair in your Temple.

Optional Materials:

- Essential oils for connecting the conscious mind with Higher Mind: Frankincense and Myrrh, Rosemary, Patchouli and/or others you're led to include.
- Essential oils for mental clarity: Vetiver, Spearmint, Peppermint, Orange, Clary Sage or others you're led to include.
- Incense in your most potent scents to induce altered states of awareness (i.e. Patchouli, Nag Champa, Indian Temple Incense and Dragon's Blood all work well for me; choose what works best for you).
- White flowers. I love fresh flowers on my altar, but please know this is completely optional and not required for best outcome.

Preparation

Check your moon cycle calendar for the most auspicious day to begin your 45 day ritual. This ritual will take place over more than one moon cycle so prepare accordingly.

Note: It's neither beneficial nor prudent to wait for several months to begin this ritual (to align with the perfect moon cycle) if an immediate answer is required. Begin on the most immediate, auspicious day.

Once you've selected the day and date the ritual will begin, choose a time most beneficial to the working. Early in the mornings is recommended, between 3 AM and 6 AM. (See the chapter on the mystical happenings in the Bible that all occurred during the 3 AM to 6 AM timeframe.)

Orient yourself so that you know the 4 directions from inside your Temple when you face your altar. If possible, position your altar in the east for this ritual.

Before engaging the 45 day ritual, prepare your altar in your Temple. If feasible, set up a brand new altar expressly for your stated intention (see below). You'll dress this altar with:

- white altar cloth
- white pillar candle
- fresh clean water changed daily during the ritual
- incense
- representations of all 4 elements
- incense burner
- essential oils diffuser

Prepare your mind, heart and body by reading your intention and FEELING it below your neck as ALREADY DONE. You must be an ENERGETIC MATCH for your DESIRE, more than you are with your current state. This requires acute awareness.

Ritual Steps

This ritual is engaged daily for 20 minutes per day.

Note: you may or may not draw a circle in which to conduct the ritual. I didn't, but that doesn't mean it shouldn't be done. Also, this ritual may be conducted sky clad (nude) or with ceremonial robes or any other magickal gear you desire. Do what best works for you and your magick.

Here are the ritual steps for each day (amend for your requirements as led by Higher Self):

- Cleanse your body and crown thoroughly. For the first day, a sacred bath or herbal bath is in order. On the next 44 days, a shower is sufficient.
- Anoint your crown, feet and heart with anointing oil of your choice, or make your own anointing oil following the steps in the chapter on

___________)

- Enter your Temple and stand or sit before your altar.
- Breathe deeply 10 times. Bring all awareness to the heart. Meditate for at least 20 minutes or until your conscious mind recedes and you are clear and lucid in mind. Fill yourself with golden light. (Mind chatter must be turned off before proceeding.)
- Pray for inner peace so that the Voice of Higher Self may be heard and deciphered with perfect clarity.
- Call in your Spirit Team (see the chapter on Your Spirit Team).
- Fill the clear glass on your altar with clean water. Pray the 23rd Psalm over the water as you fill the vessel and place it on your altar.
- Dress the white candle with the essential oils/anointing oil you've selected as follows: apply 1 drop of oil to your left index finger. With the candle in front of you on the altar, draw a line from the bottom of the candle to the center of the candle at four places on the candle that correspond to the 4 directions, starting with east, then south, west and north. There will be 4 half lines on the candle after this step (reapply a drop of oil to your right index finger as you go if required). Apply a drop of oil to the right index finger and draw a line from the top of the candle to the middle point of the candle in all 4 places to meet the line you've drawn from bottom to top, starting in the east and moving in the same direction as earlier. The idea here is to draw up earth energy and draw down heaven energy to meet in the center at your heart.
- Open your Bible. On the Opening day, read your Intention Statement aloud. Then read Matthew chapter 1 aloud in a resounding voice as if Spirit were speaking to you.
- On each of the next 44 consecutive days, read 2 chapters in the Gospels in order in the same fashion.
- Notice ANY and ALL inspirations, insights, revelations, intuitive nudges and divine ideas that come to you as you read. Notice any practical magickal components that you can apply to your Spellcrafting. **WRITE THESE OUT IN YOUR GRIMOIRE EACH DAY** with your purple pen.

- When you're complete with reading and writing for the day, **GIVE THANKS** with a prayer of thanksgiving for all that's been received. This is an important step and sets you up to receive more and more insight each day on your issue. (If you'd like specific prayers of thanksgiving, see the book ***Magickal Prayers for Christian Witches***.)
- Give thanks to your Spirit Team and bid them farewell.
- Extinguish the candle with a snuffer (I never blow out candles).

Repeat the exact same ritual each day. At the end of the 89 days, you may notice the following benefits:

- you've received multiple possible answers, solutions, ideas, revelations, insights and ideas with regard to your pressing issue or opportunity
- you've received many ways of looking at the situation, rather than looking at it one-dimensionally (as we humans tend to do)
- you understand Christ Consciousness on a whole new level
- you now have a grimoire full of notes that can be used in the future as a potent and personal Gospel divinatory tool

Note: this ritual can be employed with any set of books from the Bible. For example, one could read the prophets and create a prophetic divinatory tool. Use your imagination!

Sample Intention Statement

It is my intention to access wisdom of Divine Mind for the BEST answers, solutions and resolutions to all that concerns me, peacefully, joyfully and in grace. I know. I understand. I intuit. I am open, receptive and accepting of the BEST solutions and resolutions for me, my destiny, my health, my family, my homes, my relationships, my work, my finances, my wealth and all that pertains to me in this 3rd dimension and in all dimensions. MY SOUL RISES and I ASCEND in this life as if on wings of angels. AMEN

Life Partner Spell

As I write this, there's a spell cooking on my altar. I call it the 'Life Partner' spell, because this is exactly what I'm spelling for, a life partner.

I'm not spelling for the perfect lover. That's a different energy entirely. I've spelled for the perfect lover before and it worked out swimmingly. Me and that man went to heaven every time we came near each other physically. Literally, his kisses were electric. The love making was on another level. Though he said he loved me (and the feeling was mutual), I knew he was a lover and not a life partner. That's what I'd spelled for, and that's what I received. (See the video How to Manifest Your Perfect Lover on my YouTube channel.)

This spell is completely different.

Note: be careful what you ask for. I've noticed in myself and the people I work with a tendency to be muddled in the relationship area, which manifests muddled results.

I was crystal clear when I called forth the perfect lover, which is an added reason that the spell manifested so quickly and sublimely delicious.

Now I'm crystal clear on the Life Partner desire and intention, and its vast distinctions from the perfect lover spell. The design of this spell is not to manifesting quickly; it's to manifest PERFECTLY. This means that I am simply aligning myself, my energy, my thoughts, my feelings, my words, my actions, my environment with the PERFECT divine manifestation, at the perfect time, with the perfect person who is looking for me as I'm looking for him.

DIVINE PERFECTION. It's another way of saying that I'm aligning myself with cosmic forces that are already in motion for this to occur. How do I know this? Because the desire bubbled up in my heart. From where? I don't know precisely, I'd be lying if I said I did. Let's say it's an inner inspiration from the place where inspirations come. I follow this wholeheartedly. It's the right thing for me now, from KNOWING THYSELF. For others, there's no inspiration, or calling, to go in this direction. If that's you, skip this spell or give it to someone who could benefit from it. If you already have a delicious life partner, skip this chapter since you've clearly mastered this.

Before proceeding, we remind ourselves that we are Master Alchemists, which means we get to be crystal clear on desires (Step 1), intentions (Step 2) and sorting it all out within (Step 3). (See the full Spellcrafting formula in the chapter titled *Formula for Crafting a Spell or Ritual.*)

Acquire & Assemble Materials

For this spell, you'll require:

- 2 chalices (the fancier, the better)
- 2 white candles
- 2 crystals - one feminine, one masculine
- A chest or vessel
- 2 bird feathers
- Your Favorite Lovers Tarot Card

Let's examine the specifics of each requirement above, as well as alternatives.

2 Chalices

I'm using 2 chalices in this spell to represent water in both feminine and masculine energies. The chalices on my altar are reminiscent of those found on the 2 of Cups Tarot card.

To me, chalices (or goblets or wine glasses) stand for mutuality, communality, shared ideas and concepts. I wouldn't break bread or have a glass of wine with just anyone. The ones I do so with are ones I care about and respect.

The 2 chalices also stand for the concept of being 'with oneself' while being 'with another.' My desire in this spell is to cause the perfect unfoldment of a completely harmonious relationship in which we both are our own unique person, able to stand entirely as a Self, while simultaneously being in deep, rich, intimate relationship. This is not an easy task. We tend to either lose ourselves in other people or put up guards to love. Neither is desirable or acceptable in my intimate life partnership.

Thus, the 2 chalices play a pivotal role in this spell:

- to **MANIFEST** the perfect intimate partnership, in which each of us is fully oneself, while fully be with another
- to **ELIMINATE** codependent patterns (I know within myself that I've engaged in codependent patterns in the past and will have no parts of it. Therefore, I use spell work and other means to rule these out.) INEQUALITIES or INEQUITIES breed codependence. Equanimity is the answer: these two beings are matched, or a pair. Two turtledoves are a pair. The Bible gives an analogy here of being unevenly yoked. We do not yoke a bull with a rabbit. EQUANIMITY serves us well. While we will not be perfectly equal in everything (there's no need to be) we will be RIGHTLY MATCHED. Standing toe-to-toe with an equal calls the best forward in each partner.

You could say that perfect spell work MANIFESTS the desired intention, while simultaneously ELIMINATING unwanted tendencies and/o possibilities.

A master surgeon cuts away at what is not desired, while leaving vital organs in tact. The body is made better. A master chef cuts away fat and unwanted, distasteful parts of beef, to yield only the best tasting dish.

As a Master Alchemist, you cut away elements you DO NOT desire as you manifest your perfect results. This eliminates all mis-fired magick (I could do a whole book on that lol).

For this part of the spell, chalices are not required. They represent for me these important elements. You can use anything that represents these elements for yourself, as this is sympathetic magick and everyone has different sympathies.

Honor yourself.

2 White Candles

I use 2 white candles in the same way the unity candle is lit in a wedding ceremony. Each party comes together with a candle of one's own, and they light a UNITY candle, symbolizing their commitment to union and no longer doing life with solely one's own pursuits and ideals at the forefront. They are each committing to considering another person's pursuits and ideals along with their own. They are inviting and making space for another perspective, other than their own. They are making the ultimate leap in expanding awareness.

For me, the white candles represent purity and innocence. We both come from a pure place within with no false fronts and artificial personalities. We've built up these masks and fronts as protection from untoward experiences we've endured. These must go for a true, authentic, real, intimate life partnership.

For these elements, use appropriate candle colors for your desire and intention.

2 Crystals

Crystals are an energetic part of my magick and life, so I wouldn't think of doing any spell work or ritual without them. In this spell, I've selected:

- Lapis Lazuli for masculine energy
- Pink Quartz for feminine energy

These spoke to me and do the job well. The crystals are approximately the same size (once again to rule out any tendencies toward codependence).

Of course, you are to select any 2 crystals that speak deeply to you of your desire and intention. Use the healing work of the crystals to address issues in the relationship BEFORE THEY ARISE.

My mama taught me that an ounce of prevention is worth a pound of cure. If I have myself and my intimate partner on the altar represented by crystals, these crystals are 'working' on us all the time.

A Chest or Vessel

The chest is used as a representation of the relationship itself. It's said that the word relationship is indicative of what's happening energetically: we are in a ship with someone we're related to.

For me, I am choosing to experience an intimate partnership in which the two of us are entering a sacred space together; a shared connection that only the two of us experience.

The chest I'm using is orange in color, a perfect match for the sensuality and sacred creativity of the womb emanating from the Sacral Chakra.

Select for yourself a representation of the relationship itself. It may even be a mini model of an actual ship that the 2 of you are on and in, going on a journey that the 2 of you will share, creating experiences that soar both souls.

2 Bird Feathers

As I write this, I'm in New Orleans. I'm not sure if it's me, or if it's a naturally occurring phenomenon here: every time I go outside for a walk, I come across multiple, perfectly in tact bird feathers lying on the ground in front of me. I've been picking them up like crazy. My bird feather collection has grown exponentially in a short period of time. I only pick up and use in spell work bird feathers that are in pristine condition. (I don't like choppy looking feathers that have gaps and such. Just my preference.)

Love and partnership spells are the perfect opportunity to employ bird feathers, as birds mate for life. I'm bringing that energy into the spell, once again, by means of sympathetic magick.

Note: please ONLY use feathers that are released by the bird naturally. Be sure you know where your feathers were sourced so that no birds are harmed in your acquisition of any feathers! There are feather farms that hurt animals. **This is not to be tolerated or encouraged. Again, if you buy feathers for any purpose, be sure no animals were hurt.**

What I love about birds mating for life is that they're not 'stuck together' for life, whether they're happy or not (a strange and scary experience I've witnessed in humans and have no desire to engage). As far as I can tell, birds want to be together for life. They're peaceful in their union. They work together to build nests, acquire food and feed their young. They grow families together. They soar together. They're together forever and the union is harmonious.

Now's a good time to address the idea of being harmonious, which does not mean agreement, nor does it mean both parties are the same, nor does it mean that there aren't challenges, upsets and/or disagreements in the relationship. Robust and healthy disagreement is a good thing for people who are in it together. Standing on one's own two feet and stating what's true for self, whether others agree or not, can be done harmoniously. We may not have learned that skill yet. We can learn it. We can be harmonious within self, with others, and with the cosmos.

That's beautiful. That's what I'm spelling for.

Your Favorite Lovers Tarot Card

I tend not to use divination decks other than Tarot, with a few notable exceptions. Tarot does it for me, whether I like the messages or not. You get to choose what most deeply speaks to your soul.

I've chosen the Lovers card from the Morgan Greer Tarot deck, one of my all-time fave decks in the world, likely because I was influenced by my first ever Tarot teacher, Geraldine Amaral. She loves Morgan Greer. At the time, we were being trained in the classical Rider Waite Smith. Morgan Greer has become a 2nd classic for me.

The Lovers card in the Morgan Greer deck is evocative with imagery that speaks deeply to my subconscious mind with regard to the desire and intention.

Note: Your favorite Lovers card may not be from your favorite deck. Gaze at the Lovers card in each deck you have to select the most evocative, emotionally stirring, divinely perfect card for your desire and intention in this spell.

Place the Spell

All that's required is to place the spell in a place on your altar where it can 'cook.' These are the items I placed:

- The orange chest
- 2 chalices on top of the chest
- 2 candles before the chalices in front of the chest
- 2 crystals on the chest, right between the chalices
- 2 bird feathers on top of the chalices, lying together
- The Lovers Tarot card in the center standing upright before the chalices
- Light the candles
- Speak the intention with fervor
- Give thanks that it is ALREADY DONE

Leave the spell on the altar until it's fulfilled. Pay no attention to it in the meantime. You may even want to put it in a place where you won't see it every time you look at your altar.

Sample Intention Statement

Hear me oh Universe, it is now my intention to attract the divinely perfect life partner. This relationship is **HARMONIOUS, PEACEFUL, FULFILLING** and **JOY-FILLED**. We take on challenges with enthusiasm and grow through them together. We laugh. We cry. We make passionate love in perfectly aligned timing and deepest connectivity and intimacy. We communicate in a flow of divine love, truth, authenticity and grace. We see each other's perspective while staying true to self. When disagreements arise, we address these with love while **ETERNALLY HONORING SELF AND ONE ANOTHER**. There are no secrets here, for we know we are only as sick as our secrets. We understand honesty and commit to practice it all times from a courageous heart. Finally, we are at home with each other. We are thankful to have this union wrought by Higher Self, where the egoic little mind finds no space and the Divine as each of us is forever in charge. Amen.

Home Wards Spell

Many years ago I was buying a brand new home. Though I'd purchased real estate previous to this experience, I'd never bought a brand new home and gone through the construction process. It was a 'spec' home (many of the options were already selected by the builder) which made it easier, yet for me, it was still a daunting process.

The first time I saw the home and walked the land it sat on, an inspiration came to me to put up wards or a spirit boundary around the home.

I had no magickal tools or implements with me, so I got to work with what I always have: myself and access to heaven realms.

I began to pray. I prayed and walked the perimeter of the home in a circle. I don't remember which direction I was walking in, only that I circled the home. As I circled I prayed and asked the angels to encamp around the house with their love, presence and power. I asked that they stay and ONLY allow those with the best intentions to enter the home, and to only allow love to enter.

I felt confident within myself that the entire home was surrounded by angels and a huge circle of white light. Nothing that was untoward could enter. It would just be burned off by the ring of light, or the angels would transmute the energy before anyone could enter, or the person simply would not be able to enter.

I didn't really care how the angels handled my request. I left it somewhat open to how each situation would be dealt with, as there are multiple people who could come to our home and each one requires a personal touch. I couldn't spell for every possible variant, so I did a blanket 'take care of this' to the angels.

Please note that this spell was specific enough to state exactly what I desired:

- Peace in this home
- Only love can enter
- No untoward energies can enter

Yet, it was open enough to have it handled by the universe in the highest and best fashion for me, my kids and everyone who would possibly come to the home, including delivery people, which led to some very interesting experiences.

To name one instance, I remember a delivery person came to the door. We had an outside storm door that was clear in front of the front door. Sometimes we'd leave the front door open, for light to come in (a common practice during the day in the neighborhood) or if I went out for a walk. On this particular day, the front door was wide open and I could see — through the clear glass storm door — a delivery person approaching with a package. He could see me as well. I motioned to him to come on in, as the clear glass door was unlocked. He literally couldn't enter the home. It was a split second that I noticed his foot wasn't crossing threshold. I looked again. He seemed to be trying to come in, but it wasn't working. Something energetically was holding him at the front door, unable to enter.

I know this may sound like a strange story, but trust me, my life is full of strange stories that I'd be hard pressed to explain or understand. Since you're reading a book on magick, I trust you know exactly what I'm talking about.

All I can say is, this spell worked. I did it once, and though I reinforced it many times in my mind over the years I was in that home, I never did the spell again.

Why I Cast This Spell

The reason I cast this spell and why it was MISSION CRITICAL that my new home be peaceful and full of love, was that I was coming out of a tumultuous relationship in a household that was abusive.

I take 100% responsibility. There were many things for me to learn in that relationship, none of which have anything to do with anyone save myself.

Here were a few of my hard won lessons (I state them here as they relevance to the spell):

- Worth and value: I had to learn the very painful lessons of what happens when I do not know, own and honor my worth and value. For me, unworthiness played out in my finances and intimate relationships. Self-worth and self-value leave ZERO energetic space for anything other than the reflections of the same. If there's anyone in my world who I think isn't honoring me as worthy of the best and valuable as the one of a kind creation I am, it's because I'm not valuing me and this person showed up as a holy herald from heaven to show me this very fact. I cannot stop my world from being a mirror of my consciousness. **THIS IS LAW**.
- Self-appreciation: I didn't appreciate myself in all the wonderful ways that I am uniquely me. I didn't appreciate my accomplishments to the depth and breadth I could have. I was always on to the next accomplishment, without fully basking in self-appreciation for the amazing person I am and for what I'd just done. Striving over self-appreciation may be a hallmark of type-a personalities, but it's not rewarding or fulfilling to be continuously striving without appreciating or being **THANKFUL**.
- Intuition: listen to the Inner Voice. The Inner Voice clearly conveyed a message to my conscious mind 9 years before I concluded the relationship. It simply said "BE OUT.' It didn't give an explanation. It didn't say anything else. There was just this overwhelming knowing

that I was to LEAVE. I didn't. I paid dearly. And I'm thankful. I can say I needed those 9 years to come fully to my senses. Now, I trust my intuition over EVERYTHING else.

The bottom line, I was leaving a relationship that I allowed myself to create and stay in, even though it was far below what I desired and deserved. I no longer do that. Thank you Spirit.

The catalyst to this was a fight that broke out in the home, yet again, involving my husband and my teenage daughter. I was done. I had had enough of fighting. I had had enough of walking on eggshells in my own home.

We always know when we get to the ENOUGH point, because we make a DECISION.

I made a decision. The decision still holds to this day. The decision (which has nothing to do with anyone else) was to:

- HONOR MYSELF
- LOVE MYSELF
- APPRECIATE MYSELF
- TRUST MYSELF
- GIVE MYSELF WHAT I TRULY DESIRE & DESERVE
- TREAT MYSELF THE BEST I CAN IN EVERY MOMENT

Mind you, I couldn't just make the decision. **I HAD TO BACK IT UP BY BEING A DIFFERENT PERSON.**

If I wasn't willing to change my ENTIRE SELF to harmonize with my decision, I would have left the relationship and shortly thereafter met up with another painful, problematic situation that would only be mirroring my true inner state.

2 Reasons The Spell Worked

The spell worked marvelously. This home was the most beautiful, peaceful, luxurious, joy-filled, inspiring home I had ever lived in up to that point. Everything in it was brand new. It was as if I had climbed a ladder from hell to heaven. Every day that I walked in that beautiful home for the entire 4 years or so that I and my family was there, I breathed an exhale of love and THANKFULNESS that I was in such a place. It was an energetic graduation unlike anything I had EVER experienced. Though I had experienced not a few huge manifestations and graduations, this was on a whole new level. Thus the magick worked on a whole new level.

Why? Because:

1. I changed.
2. The energetic change was in alignment with what I spelled for.

That's it. There's no other reason this spell worked. I didn't use a certain tool, or wand, or hour of the day, or incense.

I used nothing but me and supernatural forces that I spoke to, envisioned and knew were there. And I did that from an energetic space in me that was DIFFERENT, and that was committed to that DIFFERENCE.

Why Spells Don't Work

This is as good a time as any to give a concrete example of how this spell could NOT have worked:

- If I was still angry moving into the house, I would have experienced anger in the home and thought the spell didn't work.
- If I was not ABSOLUTELY COMMITTED TO PEACE in every moment, and walking that out with my INNER STATES OF AWARENESS AND BEING, I would not have experienced the level of peace I did in that home (our home was super peaceful) and I would've thought

the spell didn't work.

- If I was not ABSOLUTELY COMMITTED to LOVE in ALL its forms and manifestations, loving myself, loving my children, filling my mind with loving thoughts and being in the vibration of LOVE, EXPANSION and INSPIRATION, there's no way the home would have taken on such a love quality (and I probably would've thought the spell didn't work).

The spell always works. The question is: do you? Are you BEING what you spelled for, rather than just saying it? Are you BEING the ritual, rather than just performing it?

Food for thought.

Steps for This Ritual

Considering the foregoing, you can intuit that the steps outlined for this ritual will be extremely simple, yet EXTREMELY CHALLENGING.

1. Change yourself to love, peace, joy, self-worth, self-appreciation, worthy, deserving most of the time (you may not be there all the time, do the best you can). If I'm in this space 79% of the time, can I go to 85%? Then 90% Can I make these my default states of being? Please know we're not talking emotions here. Emotions are, by their very nature, all over the place. As humans, we have access to a wide spectrum of emotions in every moment. This is beyond emotion. This is referring to **INNER STATES OF BEING THAT EMIT FREQUENCIES**. A STATE of peace is practiced. Being blissful is a blisscipline. We can make joy a habit, even if we don't feel like it.
2. Declare a beautiful border of love and light around your home. Call in the angels if it suits you. I did, only because my consciousness is deeply steeped in angel lore. If that's not you, use whatever beings that are communicating with your consciousness as the emissaries of

this light. They will hold the light boundary at all times.

That's it. You can reinforce the light boundary in your mind if desired by envisioning it when:

- You enter or leave your home.
- When you awaken and when you fall asleep. You can fall asleep peaceful that your home is surrounded by the angels and a ring of light that only allows love in.
- Whenever the thought comes to you.

Spell Warning

Let's address the mind that thinks it is unsafe. This was the mind I had. I grew up in New York City and spent the first 30 years or so of my life in the 'concrete jungle.' I harbored a feeling deep inside of perpetually being unsafe, always looking over my shoulder for a possible mugger, always watching my back for a possible rapist, always locking and double checking doors to brace against a possible intrusion.

No wonder I was robbed at gunpoint on the streets of New York. Energetically, I was expecting it. A friend of mine, Dr. Jewa Lea, who's an energy master, says:

You always get to be right.

Such is the power of the mind. Your mind is so powerful that it will create its match all around you, confirming that what you deeply hold in consciousness is true for you. You get to be right.

While this is not a charge to throw all caution to the wind and not have common sense, there's little peace for the mind that thinks it's about to be attacked at any moment.

I was on edge for years after leaving New York. It took awhile to let my 'guard down.' Being on edge and being peaceful don't go together. I had to pick one and abandon the other.

The warning for this spell: no amount of magick spells or locks will cause a mind to feel safe if deep within a feeling of being unsafe is stronger.

According to Albert Einstein, a fundamental decision must be made. We must each and all answer the query: *do I live in a friendly universe?*

For those who make the decision that the universe is unfriendly, no spell will create safety. The underlying premise in consciousness is that the universe is inherently unfriendly, which means protection is warranted, and perhaps even an offensive assault or two. We can intuit that these states of mind lead to behaviors ruled by, or at least marked by, control, manipulation and dominance.

Conversely, if you've decided — as I have — that the universe is indeed friendly, there's a sense of peace, power and poise. Nothing is about to jump out of the bushes at me, so I don't need to brace myself for attack. And even if something did jump out of the bushes at me, I spent time out of peace anticipating it, and time out of peace experiencing it, which still equates to a no-win situation.

Peace is not possible in the presence of constant thoughts of potential attack or harm.

This is not to say that we will never have a fearful thought. It would be rather unhuman to go through life and never have a thought of fear.

However, each person's consciousness has an **OVERALL QUALITY**. Is the overall quality — or dominant energy — of your mind love or is it fear?

I've decided.

I live in a friendly universe.

Notice that I did NOT say that this is a friendly universe.

Our EXPERIENCE of the universe is being conjured in the mind.

I've decided in my MIND that the universe is friendly, and that's all that matters.

I look at it this way: if the universe wanted to kill me, it's had countless perfect opportunities to do so, and yet I'm still here, even against impossible odds.

The very act of conception is an improbably 1-in-a-trillion event, and yet, we were conceived. We were miraculously kept well in our mother's womb, nurtured, fed and warm. We survived birth. Whether we were in an always loving home life or not, we somehow managed to grow up. What we received during childhood was enough to keep us alive and moving forward. As adults, we've managed to keep somewhat healthy, create families, acquire homes, manifest abundance, sustain rewarding friendships and relationships, create wealth, fulfill dreams (on some level, or at least know that we can fulfill our dreams), be happy and grow as people and souls. Something must be working for us.

This is of course, a perspective. Everyone holds a different perspective, and only you can choose how you will see the world. Your seeing determines what shows up. Quantum physics has taught us that the observed changes according to the observer, a phenomenon science cannot fully explain, yet which has been clearly expounded upon in the ancient mysteries.

In short: ***you're making the whole thing up in your head.***

If we **ACCEPT OUR GOD-LIKE POWERS OF CREATION** and take **UTTER REPSONSIBILITY** for our entire world and everything in it, with a **COMMITMENT** to Law and principle while taking the requisite **INSPIRED ACTION** from **INNER DESIRED STATES**, we win, even when things aren't going our way.

This is what it means to be a Master Alchemist.

Dumb Supper Christian Witch Style

Many years ago I attended a meeting of the Black Hat Society (a group of Witches who get together on a monthly basis to discuss Witchcraft while wearing black Witch hats… it was a hoot) and heard about Dumb Supper, a ritual conducted by Witches on All Hallows Eve. I was amazed.

In this chapter we'll explore what a Dumb Supper is, how it's conducted and how I conduct mine, and how this beautiful ritual of communication with the dead can supercharge your magickal practice and life throughout the year.

First I'll offer the steps as I learned them from the Witches of the Black Hat Society. Then, I'll offer the way I conducted my rituals, followed by modifications that can be made for Christian Witchcraft.

Dumb Supper/Feast of the Dead

In short, a Dumb Supper is a meal eaten in complete silence (hence the term 'Dumb') on All Hallows Eve (October 31st) in which one's ancestors and other dead loved ones are invited to participate and offer messages in any form.

At its simplest, it's a seance with a meal. You're essentially opening the door to spirit realms and asking certain spirits to come through and have a meal with you.

The term 'dumb' is a derogatory term formerly used to refer to people who could not speak, or people who could not hear. I offer my apologies for these derogatory uses and choose to refer to this ritual instead as the 'Feast of the Dead.'

Though we understand our ancestors are not dead, we use this term to clearly denote to neophytes, spirit realms and our own subconscious mind what's going on.

Reasons for conducting a Feast of the Dead could be:

- **Establish new connection** with a recently crossed over relative (someone who may have crossed over during the year since the last Feast of the Dead).
- **Deepen and clarify communication** with ancestors and dead loved ones you're already connected to. This is a powerful way to ramp up the communication and make it more visceral, meaningful and clear. No more mixed or muddy messages from ancestors! This is your opportunity to get really clear with grandma.
- **Determine which ancestor to call on, and for what purpose**. My great grandmother birthed 12 children, of which 8 made it to adulthood. If I were having a period of extreme grief (as I did when my mom passed over) I could call on Great-grandma Pinky to ask how managed to stay in her right mind and be the strong woman she was after losing so many children. When you have this kind of connection with each of your Enlightened Ancestors, you're better able to determine which one to call for the issue or magickal operation at hand.
- **Make requests**. Ask your ancestors and dead loved ones for what you require. Get supernatural help. It's available to you, and your ancestors have a vested interest in your complete well-being and ascension.
- **Get rid of negative spirits.** Negative spirits may be hounding you, in the form of persistent fears or spirits of jealousy or spirits of contention in a household. Enlightened Ancestors are well equipped

and positioned to handle negative spirits.

- **Honor, thank and bless**. Honor your ancestors. Thank your forebears for all they're doing in spirit realms for you and the world. Bless them and their rising to God. Every candle we burn for our ancestors and every mention of their name keeps their light glowing bright throughout all dimensions and powers up their ashe.

You can make the ritual as elaborate or as simple as desired according to Inner Knowing and intention. It's ideal to conduct the ritual each year on All Hallows Eve.

I've found that there are certain ancestors who will almost always show up, such as the ones closest to you, whether you specifically invite them or not. These are the close relatives that when you open the door, don't need permission to come through, like my mom, who's always with me.

What to Expect

Please keep in mind that you are communicating with the spirit world. You are summoning spirits. Therefore, you can likely expect all manner of strange occurrences and spiritual phenomena. There's no way of knowing exactly how any particular ancestor or dead loved one will communicate with you — and others present — unless you speak with this ancestor all the time. But the nature of this ritual is that you're possibly establishing communication channels with ancestors and dead loves ones you've never contacted or interacted with before. This could make for interesting paranormal activity. Items could fall off shelves, technology in the home could flicker on and off, or completely not work at all. Change of temperature in the room may happen, which is common when dead folk start moving around on this plane. You may smell familiar fragrances from crossed over family members and the like.

Be ready for anything.

Set Your Intention

Who are you contacting and why? What questions do you have? Are there prickly issues you're dealing with that you'd love clear guidance on? Is there an unresolved issue with your grandmother or another passed over relative? Are you at peace and would love to thank them for their obvious help in your life?

There are a million reasons why someone would want to speak with Enlightened Ancestors and/or dead loved ones. Also include what you'd like the relationship to look like going forward.

WRITE OUT YOUR INTENTION in your grimoire.

Timing

Next, the ritual is held on October 31 because All Hallows Eve is the night when the veil between this world and the world of the dead is thinnest, making for easier communication.

We've discussed cosmic weather earlier in the book. This is yet another example of why we do what we do as Witches when we do it.

You can start preparations for the Feast of the Dead well in advance, since you know when it will be each year.

Who

The ritual can be conducted alone or with company. If conducting the ritual with company, as with all magickal operations: **NO MUGGLES ALLOWED** (non-magickal people). This is not a dinner party. This is a magickal ritual that involves a feast.

If conducting the ritual with other Witches, Wizards, Warlocks or Magickal Beings, send invites to coven mates or members of your magickal community far in advance, or at least discuss it with them.

If you choose to invite others, each person is contacting and receiving communication from their own ancestors.

I've conducted my Feast of the Dead rituals alone, receiving powerful responses from my ancestors (more on this later).

Where

Determine the location. If you have a magickal space where your coven gathers to do magick, this is perfect, as magick is already in the air and there are likely many spirits already present.

Space is required in the room where the feast will be held for:

- **Ancestral Altar** - large enough to contain the items and candles from each participant in the ritual.
- **Large Dining Table** - for place settings for each participant and one place setting to represent that person's ancestors (more on this below).

It may be easier to transport food from the kitchen to the table if the ritual is conducted in a dining room. However, if the space is not a space normally used for magick, you will have to create sacred space for the ritual (see the chapter "How to Create Sacred Space").

This is a magickal ritual in which you will be opening the portal to the other side and actively summoning spirit beings into your presence. As with all rituals, creating sacred space — including cleansing and clearing, calling in helper spirits such as angels, archangels and spirit guides — is CRITICAL. You don't want anything to 'pop off' so take all your magickal preparation steps as you would with any ritual involving spirit realms.

I remember attending the annual Samhain fire festival held by Wayne, an incredible Druid and Shaman, in which he would open the portal at the beginning of the ritual so that all of us had the opportunity to commune with our ancestors, receive messages and guidance. He was a master at making sure all the spirits were back on the other side, then closing the portal.

I'm not saying you have to be an accomplished Shaman to conduct this ritual. I'm saying you get to be acutely aware of what you're about to embark upon, and treat the entire process of preparation, conducting the ritual and completion with the utmost magickal regard, taking all appropriate steps to ensure right results.

Plan the Menu

Since the feast is held in the fall, foods of the season are best. Pumpkins, root vegetables, apples and all manner of fall produce are perfect.

You will prepare an entire meal, from soup to nuts. Think ***feast***. Like Thanksgiving. If you're conducting the ritual alone, you'll prepare all the food yourself, or you'll acquire it (if you're not a chef or cook or not in a position to chef it up) from a place you trust.

Make sure to include on the menu drinks and foods your ancestors and loved ones enjoyed while they were in this life. This is critical.

I'm mostly plant based in my eating, with the exception of fish. However, my mother and grandmother ate meat most of their lives. If you're a vegan and grandpa was a steak eating somebody, have steak for grandpa and a vegan meal for yourself. Even though grandpa will not be eating the steak (of course, spirits don't eat human food), he will see the representation of your love and the depth of your intention when he sees the steak. This is touching, just as it is if someone you love got all your favorite things and invited you over to dinner. For me, this is love.

If others are joining you, have each person bring a dish. This goes a long way to make the ritual communal.

As the food is being prepared, keep in mind that this is ritual food, and is to be accorded due respect as such. Everything is energy.

Construct the Ancestral Altar(s)

On the day of the feast, each person participating will bring items representing their ancestors and dead loved ones to place on the Ancestral Altar, including pictures (if pictures can be obtained).

The Ancestral Altar can be set with sacred cloth in a color palette of fall colors, or deep hues (blacks and purples) or in white. Your choice. Candles are placed on the altar to light just before the feast. You can dress the candles with favorite oils from your ancestors (if they have particular favorites you're aware of), though it's not required. The colors of the candles are at your discretion, based upon Inner Knowing, your intention and the ancestors involved. Keep in mind that all the lights will be out when the candles are lit and while the ritual is being conducted.

Add to the Ancestral Altar items Inner Knowing brings to your conscious awareness that may seem strange, like a stuffed toy bunny rabbit or the like. This may be a favorite childhood toy of a crossed over ancestor. Pay particular attention to what arises within you about what to place on the altar, though it may make no logical sense.

We're Witches. We're accustomed to things that don't make sense, so this will likely be easy. Let it flow. NO THINKING ALLOWED. The surface egoic mind is NOT your friend in magick and ritual.

Set the Table

The table setting is one of the most crucial factors of the ritual, so pay very close attention to detail without being nitpicky.

When setting the table, it's important to set one place setting for each human person present, and one setting for the supernatural people who will be present. For instance, you will have a place setting for yourself, and you will also set a place for your ancestors directly across from you. It is of **GREAT IMPORTANCE** to position and set the ancestral place setting **OPPOSITE OF YOURS** as the spirit realm is a mirror image of the physical realm. If your fork is on your right, you'll place the ancestral place setting's fork so that it is on the Ancestor's left. ***When you look at the ancestral place setting, it is to be an exact mirror image of your place setting. As above, so below.***

An ancestral place setting does not need to be created for each ancestor you seek to commune with. Consider the ancestral place setting as a doorway and invitation to spirit realms. If you're seeking guidance from a particular ancestor, I would put that loved one's favorite food on the plate.

A variation I've made: when I conducted a Feast of the Dead for my mom and grandma specifically, I had 3 place settings. It wasn't hard to do, and each cup held what they wanted to drink: wine for mom (though not for grandma… she was a teetotaler) and coffee for grandma. I had Kombucha. This is a real meal with people you love.

If you're having a large gathering of your coven, it may not be possible to set a place setting for every Witch and every person each Witch would like to commune with, which is where a 'representational' ancestor place setting is useful.

When it's time to eat, you will put actual food on all the plates, yours as well as the ancestral plate. You will pour drink in your glass as well as in the ancestral glass.

As is true in many other cases in magick, it's important to go with your intuition. Exactly which drink you are to put into the ancestral cup/glass/mug will depend upon your intention and your ancestors. If they all loved coffee (like my people do) a coffee mug with fresh brewed hot coffee should do the job.

As an aside, if you google 'Dumb Supper' you'll see elaborate and beautiful Witchy tables that will knock your socks off. Some prepare for the table and places settings for this ritual as if preparing for a wedding. Indeed, we are welcoming honored guests.

Break Bread With the Ancestors

When all has been prepared, it's time to bring food to the table and eat with the ancestors and spirits.

Before sitting down to the feast, make sure everyone goes to the restroom. Treat the ritual as you would a magick circle: everyone stays put until the ritual is complete. We don't want unnecessary moving around in the room just as someone's ancestor is about to enter.

With everyone and the food ready, bring the food to the table.

Everyone can then be seated at their appropriate place setting at the table, opposite of their own ancestral place setting, as the host lights the candles on the Ancestral Altar, and then extinguishes all artificial light.

Turn off all electronics. If a television is in the room, throw a cloth over it. Television screens are portals, and we're not asking for any and all manner of stray spirits to wander in. Remember, All Hallows Eve is an active night for spirits, possibly the most active night of the entire year.

The items representing each ancestor you're calling are on the Ancestral Altar. The ancestral place setting acts as a portal directly in front of you for your people to come through with powerful messages, answers and solutions (and maybe even a joke or two, my people are funny and like to do funny things lol).

Eat the meal in **COMPLETE SILENCE**, keenly **AWARE** of everything going on in the room, especially sounds, smells, air movement, touches, impressions and more. Like I said, be ready for **ANYTHING**.

Completion of the Ritual

When everyone completes their meal, and you sense that everything is complete, close the ritual. It should have a natural conclusion. If things got lively, they've settled down. Everyone is likely to know when the ritual is over, since everyone present is magickal and is accustomed to dealing with spirits.

You or someone you appoint can offer thanksgiving to the ancestors and bid them depart in peace. We do not command ancestors in the way one might command belligerent spirits. These are our dearly departed and we treat them with utmost love, respect and honor. We thank them for their presence and we bid them fare thee well until next time. They know where their home is, so most will move along. If not, you can once again thank them and bid them farewell until all have returned to the other side.

When everyone is certain all spirit activity in the room has come to a natural completion, clear the table in silence.

DO NOT THROW AWAY THE FOOD ON THE ANCESTRAL PLATES. These are to be placed at the trunk of a tree, or in another place in nature, such as by a river or lake, if that's what your ancestors loved. I usually put ancestral plates at the base of a tree with great thanks.

You can return days later and retrieve the plate, as long as you know within yourself that the offering has been received and registered on the other side. At that point, if there was still food on the plate (the critters may have enjoyed it or the weather may have disposed of it) then I would put the food in the ground or in a body of water, such as a river and stream. I'm not advocating being a litterbug! I'm offering ways of respectfully releasing the food.

How I've Conducted My Rituals

I've conducted this ritual with profound results.

On one occasion my intention was to speak with my mom and grandma for guidance during an especially tough time I was going through. Because the mind latches on to ritual like few other things, I still remember the exact place I was sitting in the room when I conducted the ritual.

I happened to be living in a hotel that was paid for weekly (which gives you a glimpse into my financial situation at the time). There wasn't a kitchen to prepare food, so I acquired the meal from a store that sold high quality prepared foods (Whole Foods is an option).

I bought items from Michael's craft store to dress the table with, which by the way, was not a dining room table in the slightest, but a low coffee table that set before the couch in the living room area of the hotel room.

Yes, this was a low budget operation with no kitchen, which is exactly why I'm sharing my experience with you. It's not necessary to go over the top with cooking and other details, as the main point of the ritual is communication with our loved ones. They would come even if we didn't have food, so no need to go crazy. The food is a ritual offering representing our willingness and desire to have deeper, more meaningful and communicative relationships with them.

This low budget operation also illustrates that anyone can do magick, at any time, with any materials on hand, if a powerful intention exists. You'll make it happen.

Back to the ritual that night.

I created sacred space and carefully set 3 place settings: one for myself, one for mom and one for grandma. As stated, I had wine for ma and coffee for grandma. I carefully dished out the food for the meal on all three plates, just as I would have made their plates if they were in physical form.

I prayed, lit the candles, turned off the lights, and ate the meal in reverence and silence, waiting for them to answer, appear or do anything.

Needless to say, they both showed up, and had plenty to say. Yep, that's mom and my grandma. They didn't change as souls because they had new addresses in spirit realms. They were full of wisdom and wit, like usual, and the whole affair felt ***familiar***, like all the occasions when the 3 of us ate together on this side of the veil.

When it was over, it was simply a natural completion. We were all like, *well, this has been wonderful.* And it was over. Just like that.

I don't think magick is very different from life on the 3rd dimensional plane. There are correspondences (as above/so below).

I've honored All Hallows Eve many times with ancestors, and every time was so profound I can scarcely put words to it.

I pray you have profound moments with your spirit people.

Ancestors in the Motherland

If we were in Africa, a Feast of the Dead ritual may not be necessary as many of the ancestors are buried right on the land of the family. The ancestors are with them every day in every undertaking. When they leave the house, they nod at great grandma who may be buried in the front yard on the left. They're talking to great grandma. They're teaching the kids about great grandpa.

In a culture where there are no cemeteries and the presence of the ancestors is infused into daily life, having a Feast of the Dead may seem preposterous. Everyone's talking to the ancestors all the time.

However, for those of us in the west, who spend most of our time scrolling timelines, working and living in busy cities with ancestors buried in places we may not have visited in years (or since the burial), conducting an annual Feast of the Dead is almost necessary to strengthen and deepen the communication and the effect of the ancestors in this world.

Feast of the Dead Christian Witch Style

There are just a couple of modifications I would make to the foregoing for practicers of Christian Witchcraft:

- **Prayer** - I would open the ritual with prayers, either Our Father or the 23rd Psalm.
- **Bible** - I would place a Bible on the ancestral altar (unless your ancestors were of another faith walk that did not hold the Bible as their Holy Book, in which case you would use the Holy Book of your ancestors).
- **Christ** - I would ask Christ to be present with us and watching over us. He appeared to many after death, and we pray for the same.

I pray you have hair-raising and profound experiences (in a desirable way) with your Enlightened Ancestors.

RISE

Well Witchy Wonder, we made it! You and I together have been on a magickal journey of learning, growth and discovery. All I can say is **WOWEEKAZOWIE**!

This Christian Witch path is a blast in every imaginable way. From soaring heights to twists and turns, it's never boring.

There is one last word I desire to share with you: **RISE**.

RISE to your sublime potential as a Christian Witch.

RISE in consciousness so that you soar above all naysayers.

RISE to the occasion to walk this glorious path brazenly.

RISE to the call of your soul.

RISE Christian Witch, RISE.

I pray we're together again in the next book in this series. Peace be unto you!

Resources

THANK YOU for being here! Here are a few more resources for your magickal journey.

If you haven't picked up my other books in this series on Christian Witchcraft yet, you may find them helpful:

- ***Confessions of a Christian Witch***
- ***How to Be a Christian Witch***

Christian Witches Resources

This community is FULL of bad-a Christian Witches all over the globe who worship, spellcraft and ritualize in their own way. Here are a few links to our community gathering spots. Join in the conversation!

- Christian Witches Facebook Community - @ChristianWitches
- Christian Witches Instagram - @ChristianWitches
- Christian Witches YouTube Channel - https://www.youtube.com/c/ChristianWitches

Amazing Witches

There are more amazing Witches online than I could put onto a short list, so here are 6 to get you started. I've listed different resources in each of my books, so make sure to check out those as well.

- Mystic Dylan - Professional Witch
- Lilith Dorsey - Voodoo High Priestess & Author of ***Orishas, Goddesses & Voodoo Queens***
- Carolyn Elliott, PhD - All around incredible Witch I've loved from afar for years.
- Pam Grossman - I read her book *Waking the Witch* and can tell you it's a GEM.
- Lisa Lister - Author of the searing tome *Witch: Unleashed. Untamed. Unapologetic.*
- Craig Hostetler - Podcaster and Creator of the Black Sheep Experience

Magicians I LOVE

Here are a few magicians **I LOVE**. I pray you find these resources helpful in your magickal workings. FYI, I only recommend and mention magicians I know, have followed for quite awhile and have deeply studied their work, or whom I know from magickal circles. Each of these magicians is the **REAL DEAL**:

- Lon Milo Duquette is the author of 19 critically aclaimed books on Magick and the Occult, including one of my personal faves: ***Enochian Vision Magick***.
- Jason Miller of Strategic Sorcery and author of *Financial Sorcery* and *The Elements of Spellcrafting*. I especially love Jason's very common sense, down to earth, practical approach to practicing powerful magick and getting it right.
- Frater Ashen Chassan is a practicing occultist and grimoric tradition-

alist who has been involved in Western ceremonial magic since 1999. He's also a highly accomplished, master craftsman of magickal tools and implements and the author of ***Gateways Through Stone and Circle*** and ***Gateways Through Light and Shadow*** (a hefty tome which details his magickal workings over many years).

- Balthazar's Conjure: website and insightful YouTube channel.

Online Magick Stores

- Doc Solomon's Occult Curio: great store for procuring tools and supplies for traditional Solomonic magick as well as Hoodoo and general spellwork. Founded by Father Aaron Leitch. View a video of him consecrating holy water here to get a feel for the kind of work he does.
- Conjurings of a Witch - LOVE LOVE LOVE the Instagram.
- Wealth & Wellness Vortex - I acquire ALL my essential oils from a trusted supplier of pure, tested and high vibration oils sold exclusively through our online wellness shopping club (join the Wealth & Wellness Vortex Facebook Group to find out more). Text the word wellnessvortex (altogether, no spaces) to 47177 and you'll receive a text immediately with a link to enter the group.

May I Ask...

Witchy Wonder, I pray this work served you well.

May I ask a few minutes of your time to leave a review on Amazon or Goodreads for this book, or any of my other books? I'm most thankful for you and would love to hear your thoughts on how you're using this material in your magick as a practicing Christian Witch.

Also, we're seeking opportunities to connect with you, including speaking on podcasts and at relevant events. We're also planning a book tour to US cities soon. We'd love to meet you! If you have any speaking or media opportunities you'd like to share with Christian Witches, please go to Christian Witches and complete the form on Speaking & Media page. You'll also find a current Christian Witches media kit you can download.

THANK YOU IN ADVANCE FOR SHARING THIS WORK!

About the Author

Rev. Valerie Love (aka KAISI) is an ordained minister of spiritual consciousness, practicing Christian Witch and the author of 19 books on practical spirituality, magick and the occult. As a teacher of spiritual law, she leads retreats around the globe in exotic locations and energetically charged 'hot-spots' including Bali, Dubai, Peru, Sedona and Salem.

Her YouTube channel — where she teaches magick, money and metaphysics — enjoys millions of viewers from around the world and grows daily.

After 7 years as a financial advisor with American Express, Rev. Val sold her financial planning practice in 2004 to pursue her purpose and destiny of teaching via workshops, retreats and to finally **WRITE**, her true heart and soul's desire.

Rev. Val grew up in the cult of Jehovah's Witnesses, from age 4 to age 30. She made her exit in the midst of a dark night of the soul and deep depression. Since her exit almost 30 years ago, she's been committed to the path of truth and enlightenment.

You can connect with me on:

- https://www.christianwitches.com
- https://www.facebook.com/ChristianWitches
- https://www.instagram.com/christianwitches
- http://valerielovetv.com

Also by Valerie Love

Thank you for being here. I love and appreciate you for delving into this work, which is my heart and soul expression on the planet. If you enjoyed or received inspiration from this book, you may find these to be of benefit as you craft your magickal and spiritual practices as a Christian Witch. Hugzzzz!

How to Be a Christian Witch - Includes Initiation Instructions

As a beginner or experienced Christian Witch, you may have had critical questions along the way, as I did. Questions regarding celebrations/holy days, rituals, covens, magickal practices and initiation as a Christian Witch are very real on this path and beg soul-fulfilling answers. Because Christian Witches is a spiritual path and not a religion, there are no set protocols. The good news is: you get to create your own! That's where this book comes in. This cutting edge tome is packed with ideas, inspirations and experiences from my magickal journey. For me, being a Christian Witch is a spiritual path. On this path, our rituals, magickal practices and celebrations of sacred lunar and solar events sustain and grow us as practicing magicians. I pray this book feeds your soul, and inspires you to walk your path as a Christian Witch with your held high, sharing your gifts with the world, completely fulfilled in every imaginable way. I love you.

Confessions of a Christian Witch: How an Ex-Jehovah's Witness Lives Magickal & How You Can Too!

Because confession is good for the soul, if not for the reputation, I do hereby confess that I...Had no idea what a Christian Witch was, never heard the term, and would never have chosen to be one, had it not been for a burst of inspiration that literally spoke it through my mouth on October 22, 2011, the day I came out of the proverbial broom closet as a Christian Witch. Here's the whole weird and wonderful story, right from the beginning.Also included are reSources for aspiring Christian Witches, and comments, messages and emails from our beloved global community of Christian Witches, sharing straight from the heart. You will never pick up a book like this...

40 Money Mantras: 40 Days to Wealth Consciousness

ONLY if you're READY to ACTIVATE WEALTH CONSCIOUSNESS, dive in... Your intention created the experience of connecting with this book, these mantras, here and now. Each divinely inspired mantras on one side of the page (40 in all), with journal lined pages on the opposite side of each page, to journal your experiences with each of the 40 money mantras. Of extreme help and support in DISSECTING each mantra for maximum power is the 40-Video Playlist on YouTube in which the author, Rev. Valerie Love (aka KAISI) goes into detail for each mantra in a daily show she filmed live with her audience. Grab the book and head on over to YouTube for much more than you could have ever imagined at www.ValerieLoveTV.com Welcome to your new money world.

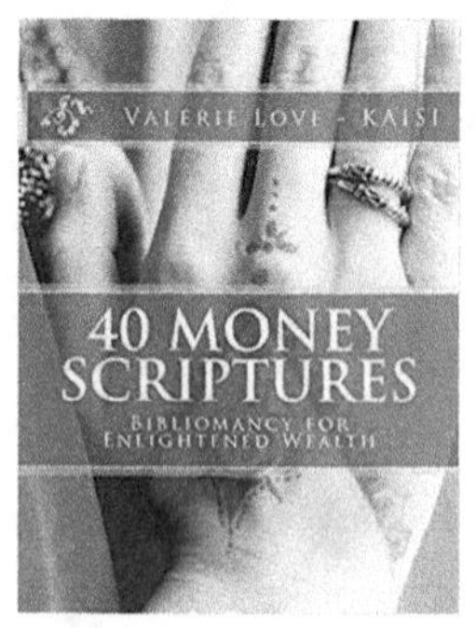

40 Money Scriptures: Bibliomancy for Enlightened Wealth

The Bible is a book of metaphysics, allegory, ritual, symbolism, astrology, magick, angelology, demonology, miracles and more, and is vastly misunderstood. This tome seeks to take the mystery out of using the Bible for enlightened wealth. Bibliomancy is a powerful means to source answers, revelations and insights on any situation and/or question and can be used for any and all aspects of the soul's evolutionary journey. If you're new to Bibliomancy, or using the Bible for Enlightened Wealth, you're invited to dive in and experience it for yourself. Only YOU are the true and final arbiter of what is right for you. Accompanying this book is a YouTube playlist where we'll have 40 videos to accompany each scripture here to be used daily. You'll find the playlist on YouTube by going to: www.ValerieLoveTV.com

40 Money Spells: 40 Days to Wealth Consciousness

This is a book of 40 short, powerful, practical, proven spells for WEALTH CREATION that WORK. Not included here is fluff, hype, gimmicks or platitudes, nor is anything here unnecessarily complicated, hard to understand or difficult to implement. The spells here are quite simply alchemy of the soul. As the introduction of the book states, these spells are not directed at outer effects. This magick is simple, born of necessity… my own burning desire to unleash myself from the shackles of lack and limitation that seemed to haunt me at every turn, even when I had money. In this 40-Day process, we only spell SELF. We do not spell outer conditions. There is no need to spell outer conditions. Outer conditions have no power. This magick acknowledges that all the power to effect change in your world is INSIDE YOU. This magick takes an 'inside-out' approach, rather than the forms of magick that cast spells on other people or on anything outside of self. When you change, all else changes. That's the heart and soul of this magick: SELF TRANSFORMATION as ALCHEMY OF THE SOUL. Also included are lined pages to journal your notes. BONUS: there's also a YouTube Playlist to accompany the book. The playlist can be found at www.ValerieLoveTV.com

Printed in the USA
CPSIA information can be obtained
at www.ICGtesting.com
LVHW010914011223
765057LV00072B/1460/J